Glass House Books

The Most Dangerous Man in Australia?

Barbara Winter was born in Western Australia in 1931 and graduated from the University of Western Australia with an Honours degree in modern languages. She won a scholarship that enabled her to study at the interpreters training centre attached to the University of Heidelberg, 1954-55, before she returned to teaching in Western Australia and Queensland. She gave up teaching in 1977 for domesticity, further study and a writing career.

While carrying out research for the degrees of Master of Arts and Doctor of Philosophy, she discovered in the records of the secret service organisations a lot of interesting and largely unknown material that did not fit into either thesis. What is included in this book is only a small part of that which exists.

Her previous book with Glass House Books is The Australia-First Movement.

Glass House Books
Brisbane

Glass House Books
an imprint of Interactive Publications
Treetop Studio • 9 Kuhler Court
Carindale, Queensland, Australia 4152
sales@ipoz.biz
ipoz.biz/GHB/GHB.htm

First published by Interactive Publications, 2010
© Barbara Winter and IP

All rights reserved. Without limiting the rights under copyright reserved above, no part of this publication may be reproduced, stored in or introduced into a retrieval system, or transmitted, in any form or by any means (electronic, mechanical, photocopying, recording or otherwise), without the prior written permission of the copyright owner and the publisher of this book.

Printed in 11 pt Book Antiqua on 16/18 pt Myriad Pro.

National Library of Australia
Cataloguing-in-Publication entry:

Author:	Winter, Barbara.
Title:	The most dangerous man in Australia? / Barbara Winter.
ISBN:	9781921479847 (pbk.)
Notes:	Includes bibliographical references and index.
Subjects:	Men--Australia--Biography.
	Crime--Australia--History.
	Espionage--Australia--History.
	Australia--Politics and government--History.
Dewey Number:	920.710994

The Most Dangerous Man in Australia?

Barbara Winter

Glass House Books
Brisbane

Acknowledgments

I am grateful to the staff of the National Archives of Australia in Brisbane, Canberra, Sydney, Melbourne and Perth. Over the years, there have been too many for me to name, and in some cases I have not known their names. Particular note must be made, however, of some who consistently went out of their way to be especially helpful: Cheryl McNamara, Carolyn Connor, Mara Seaton and Edmund Rutlidge.

Thanks are also due to the staffs of the State Libraries of South Australia and New South Wales and the National Library of Australia in Canberra for permission to reproduce photographs. The performances of the SLSA and NLA in getting material to me by internet within 48 hours of my sending an email request were especially brilliant.

Books by the same author:

Atlantis is Missing

HMAS Sydney: Fact, Fantasy and Fraud
    (German edition: Duell vor Australien)

Stalag Australia

The Intrigue Master

The Australia-First Movement: Dreaming of a National Socialist Australia

The Most Dangerous Man in Australia?

Contents

Introduction		viii
Chapter 1:	*The Vindictive Metallurgist*	1
Chapter 2:	*The Fake Alien*	12
Chapter 3:	*The Card-Carrying Spy*	24
Chapter 4:	*The Neurotic Chameleon*	36
Chapter 5:	*The Attorney-General*	45
Chapter 6:	*The Hired Hack*	63
Chapter 7:	*The Amorous Vichyite*	79
Chapter 8:	*The Bigamous Abortionist*	89
Chapter 9:	*The Vodka Priest*	103
Chapter 10:	*The Shanghai Gang*	133
Sources and Endnotes:		148
Index:		168

Introduction

Between the wars, during the Second World War and in the years immediately following, several persons were labelled by the Australian Security Services as 'the most dangerous man in the Commonwealth'. While only one of them could have been 'the most dangerous', several were dangerous indeed in various ways, while others were baffling enigmas.

Some were also scoundrels in financial and personal relationships, involved in tax evasion, usury, perjury, pornography, corruption, drug running, bribery, assault – a whole catalogue of torts, crimes and sins. Others were fairly decent men unable to realise the harm they could have been causing. Several showed interesting psychiatric symptoms. Many were British citizens, if not Australian born. Some were aliens whose activities were either notorious or fascinatingly mysterious. They were possibly worthy citizens of their own countries, but these were countries with which Australia was – or was soon to be – at war. This book examines the activities and characters of a representative selection of these persons.

Most of these stories have not been examined adequately; some have not been noticed at all. Selection has necessarily been subjective. Dr J. H. Becker, the founder of the Nazi Party in Australia and its leader for four years, has not been included because, although he was organiser of the Gestapo information collection in Australia and dangerous to the relatives of Germans, he was too closely watched and had too many enemies to be a serious threat to the security of Australia. Several other notorious Nazis could well have been included, but they do not have the mysterious quality of those in this book, as they were too conspicuous. Inevitably, some names recur in several chapters, for those engaged in activities detrimental to Australia were to some extent interlinked, and those who were trying to protect Australia covered many cases.

The business of the Security organisations was and is to keep the Government informed concerning potential threats to national security. They did not have the power of arrest. If, in the course of their investigations and possibly using methods that would have been illegal in police work, they stumbled across evidence of drug running, prostitution rackets, bribery, blackmail or assault, it was not their business to inform the police.

There is a wealth of dramatic, tragic and sometimes comical material in the repositories of National Archives Australia, particularly in the records of the Commonwealth Investigation Branch, the Commonwealth Security Service and the Australian Security Intelligence Organisation. It is baffling that authors, even academics, venture to write accounts of complicated and controversial history by talking to the children and grandchildren of

Introduction

the people involved without checking with original records. Or they look at a few files in a single series and think that these tell the whole story in a balanced form. The truth is elusive, but one approaches it more closely by reading a hundred files, with a healthy dose of scepticism, than by reading two or three, or even none.

In each file, names occur that could lead to other files, not yet transferred to Archives. An application may then be submitted through Archives to ASIO, stating the reason why a file might have been kept on such persons and the reason for the request. After several months, Archives will report that ASIO says that there never was such a file, or that they cannot locate it, or that it has been destroyed, or that it has been reclassified for public release and handed over to Archives. After several more months, Archives will give notice that it has been screened for privacy considerations and is available for perusal. The newly-released material may lead to another set of names, so the whole process starts again and may take another six months. After five or ten years, the researcher may have gained a fair idea of the facts. It is not a task for the impatient, superficial or faint-hearted.

Nothing that it is feasible to check should be left unchecked. People forget; people make mistakes; people tell lies, sometimes for no apparent reason. Dates and places of birth and marriage may be checked through Registry Office records on microfilm, microfiche or CD, sometimes online. The date of death may be harder to find. Then, depending on the locality, it may be possible to check naturalisation records, passenger lists, electoral rolls, old telephone books, Post Office Directories, old newspapers and various business records. Some of this information is readily available and just takes time and perseverance; some costs a lot of money and is only occasionally worth the time and money.

As this book is intended for general reading, endnotes have been kept to a minimum. For serious students who might wish to obtain further information, or verify what is written, a short bibliography and an indication of sources has been given for each chapter, although this is only a fraction of the material consulted. Some crucial ASIO dossiers were still being screened at the time of writing. Although many pages have been withheld, and others have tantalising expungements, there is a lifetime's work there for young academics with insightful and sceptical minds.

Chapter 1

The Vindictive Metallurgist

Not many persons designated at some time 'the most dangerous man in the Commonwealth' deserved this title, but it was particularly apt in the case of Louis Ignatius Burkard. He was one of the few whose activities could have damaged Australia's interests seriously, and he knew what he was doing – purposefully, maliciously and gleefully. For twenty years between the wars, he worked single-mindedly to help prepare Germany's armament industry to be in a position to win the next war. He did this by obtaining for the heavy industrial firm Krupp the tantalite and nickel needed to prolong the life of heavy artillery. His correspondence shows that he did not do this merely as a commercial proposition, but out of a deep bitterness, to avenge the defeat of 1918. Moreover, he did this after swearing allegiance to Australia when he became naturalised. However, while he was, from an Australian point of view, a cynical traitor, from his own viewpoint he was a loyal servant of the Fatherland, who would tell any lie, practise any deceit and make any sacrifice for his country.

Louis Ignatius Burkard (Karl Burggraf, *Die Deutschen in den Hauptstaedten von Australien*)

Born in Mannheim on 28 April 1879, Burkard had studied mining in Paris and Brussels before returning to Germany for compulsory military service. He wrote later: 'I had the honour to serve my Fatherland in the Regiment "Kaiser Wilhelm I" No. 110; Hindenburg was Corps Commander when I began my service in 1899.' He was discharged in 1901 as a lieutenant. His German army registration card from 1899 showed his name as 'Ludwig Ignatz', his 1921 British passport as 'Louis'; he used whichever best suited the circumstances.

German Businessman

Burkard arrived in Australia in December 1908 as an employee of Lohmann & Co., woolbuyers and agents for Norddeutscher Lloyd, and he claimed later that he was in partnership with Lohmann. This firm allowed its staff to be used by German naval espionage, but it is unclear how much Burkard knew about this aspect of its activities. Branching out into the mining business on his own account, he set up Burkard, Anderson Ltd, of which he was managing director. From about 1911, this firm ran the Whipstick Mines near Wyndham in Western Australia and they produced enough molybdenite and bismuth to make Australia self-sufficient. He also had an interest in the Cosmopolitan Mine, which produced gold and antimony. He exported large quantities of molybdenite to Germany, where it was turned into ferro-molybdenum, which prolongs life of guns three or four times. He wrote later to Consul-General Dr Asmis, 'Before the war, I was in close collaboration with the industry for heavy war weapons.'

In August 1911 Burkard married Adelaide-born Carola Elisabeth Lang, and they had a son, Carl, and possibly a second son, referred to in one letter as "Billy". It was not a happy marriage. Burkard wrote that Carola was very beautiful, but she had a cold heart.

Burkard claimed that he had applied for naturalisation in 1914 and had taken the oath of allegiance, but that a certificate had not been issued. Yet on 29 September 1914, eight weeks after the outbreak of war, he wrote to the United States to try to negotiate the sale of wolfram and molybdenite. It was suspected that these would be forwarded to Germany, and as such a sale could affect the course of the war, it had to be prevented. An Army Intelligence Report of 22 February 1915 said that he was resourceful and intelligent and had no equal in Australia in his specialty, but he had violently anti-English feelings and would not let a chance escape to harm British interests. Interned on 9 March 1915, Burkard unwisely claimed the privileges of an officer of the German Army Reserve.[1] It had been proposed that he be released, but his status as a reserve officer, and the fact that he had previously lied about this, changed the situation. A red Urgent Telegram of 17 March decreed that he remain interned, and a later claim that he was no longer liable for service was not believed.

Burkard caused trouble in Liverpool Camp, and Lieutenant Street (later Mr Justice Kenneth W. Street) noted in his dossier:

> Was president of the camp committee for a time. Implicated in a "Black Hand Gang" for which he was placed in No. 2 Compound for a few days and then removed to Trial Bay. Requires careful watching. Is very plausible.

Burkard deceived less perspicacious officers about his nature and sentiments. He was listed for deportation in August 1919 but, although his wife and son had been in Germany since before the war, he appealed to be allowed to stay in Australia, or to return to Germany at his own expense at a later date. Released on 3 March 1920 on a bond of £500, a *very* substantial sum at that time, he was warned to avoid attracting notice. Still listed for repatriation by *Main* on 5 June 1920, Burkard gathered references and testimonials from people who had known him in Wyndham, and from Trial Bay officers. The documents were so similarly worded that he had probably sent suggestions as to what he wanted them to say. They wrote of his 'open and frank character', calling him 'a desirable citizen', who was 'much attached to this country', 'a loyal Australian', not vindictive, aggressive or vengeful. When Burkard circulated petitions recommending that naturalisation be granted, he collected over a hundred signatures. One list was headed by (Sir) Earle Page, Country Party leader and briefly Prime Minister in 1939.

Australian Citizen

Naturalised in August 1921, Burkard obtained a British passport in October and headed overseas. His father had been born in Baden, his mother in Alsace, and he was consumed with hatred: of the French, who had seized Alsace; of the British, who had aided them; of Australians who had sold up his mining enterprises at an enormous loss. He planned to use his status as a British citizen to assist Germany to avenge her defeat. Burkard spent a year in New Zealand and two years in London, arranging export of frozen meat to Germany. Returning to Australia in 1925, he entered into partnership with Otto Silbernagel in Bondy & Co., taking it over completely in 1929. It operated a smelting concern in Australia.

On 23 August 1929, the *Deutsch-Australische Handelskammer* (German-Australian Chamber of Commerce) was founded in Sydney. The first election returned Ludwig Bersch as President, Hermann Erhard as Vice-President, and Commercial Attaché Dr F. E. Mueller as Secretary; Burkard was appointed Councillor and Karl Martin Burggraf, a fellow-internee from Trial Bay, was one of the committee members. The election of 23 July 1931 returned Burkard as President.

In October 1932 the new Consul-General, Dr Rudolf Asmis, arrived in Australia, and by the following May he had founded an organisation called the *Bund des Deutschtums* (League of Germanism). The Chamber of Commerce and the *Bund* jointly set up German-Australian Publications in November 1933 to support a weekly paper, *Die Brücke*. Chairman of the Board of Directors was Otto von Drehnen, formerly Austro-Hungarian Honorary Consul in South Australia, while Burkard represented the Chamber of Commerce. Both invested a substantial amount of money in the project. *Die Brücke* was never a commercially viable enterprise; the shareholders lost their money and the paper would have collapsed if it had not obtained a subsidy from Germany by about 1936. A police report in November 1939 said that Drehnen was 'one of the most dangerous men in Australia', but his actions, though possibly dangerous, were probably naïve rather than malicious.

A close relationship developed between Asmis and Burkard. When Burkard complained to newspapers that provocative and defamatory propaganda in the Australian press could damage Australia's trade, he was acting as a mouthpiece for the Consulate-General. At the request of Alfred Rosenberg's *Aussenpolitisches Amt* (Foreign Policy Bureau), he organised barter trading, and according to Asmis he succeeded in having the Country

Party included in the Government[2], and through them obtained customs reductions on imports of German industrial goods. Early in 1935, Burkard received a German medal for his services to commerce. Writing to Foreign Minister von Neurath on 18 July 1935, Burkard expressed pleasure at being honoured with an award: 'I have ever served my fatherland with joy and shall in the future.'[3] What he needed, however, was money, not medals.

In late 1933, former wartime pilot Colonel Baron Egloff von Freyberg-Eisenberg-Allmendingen arrived on a six-month tour of Australia and New Guinea; it is likely that, if he was not arranging espionage, he was trying to obtain supplies of tantalite and other metals. He wrote to Burkard on 15 June 1934 that he had been pleased to meet an old schoolfellow in Sydney, and it is a reasonable deduction that Burkard's subsequent activities with regard to obtaining non-ferrous metals were influenced by Freyberg's visit. As early as 1934, Asmis tried to obtain official support for Burkard, whom he described as a most deserving leader of a local internment camp during the war, Chairman of the Chamber of Commerce, a member of the *Deutsche Arbeitsfront* (German Labour Front), an undaunted champion of the New Reich and the 'soul and backbone of German Commercial life in Australia'. By pointing out in the right places that if the money was not advanced, Burkard's firm would collapse, German trade and resource interests would be 'tremendously damaged' and 'the Jew' would be pleased, Asmis secured a substantial loan for Burkard.

Burkard was obsessed with a passionate desire to supply as much ore as possible to Krupp: both Northern Territory tantalite and New Caledonia nickel. One of his suppliers of tantalite ore was the author Xavier Herbert, who took Burkard as his model for 'Felix Beaucoup' in *Poor Fellow My Country* although, as with many of Herbert's *persona*, this was a caricature rather than a portrait. Sadie, Herbert's Jewish wife, acted as a purchasing agent for Krupp. In August 1935, Burkard wrote to Asmis, then on leave in Germany, that he was doing a big deal with Krupp and would soon be going to New Caledonia where he would study the nickel mines and delivery facilities and arrange a supply of nickel. In November he wrote from Noumea: '[We] all love our Fatherland so much, that we all serve it and the proverb says quite clearly that we cannot serve two Gods!' In September 1935, between the dates of these two letters, SS officer Dr Friedrich Wilhelm Mohr, head of the *Ostasiatischer Verein* (East Asian Association), visited Australia. One of his tasks was to bring the Sydney Chamber of Commerce, which was already affiliated with this Association, firmly under Nazi control; Burkard remained nominally Chairman until July 1937, although by that time he resided mostly in Noumea.

Burkard was not only thoroughly German, whatever his passport said, but he was also thoroughly imbued with Nazi ideology. At the Memorial Day for war dead on 17 March 1935 he proclaimed: 'In greatest distress,

Chapter 1: The Vindictive Metallurgist

when the German nation seemed to be at the end of its existence, Divine Providence gave it Adolf Hitler.' As head of the Chamber of Commerce, he was consulted by Dr J. H. Becker, the first leader of the Nazi Party in Australia, on the appointment of a representative for the Economics Department of the NSDAP, for which position he recommended the Hamburg-America Line agent, Captain Robert Köhler, who knew Australian trade and shipping well.[4]

In order not to draw attention to the complicity of the Consul-General in the armament-related dealings with Krupp, Burkard sent information to Asmis secretly by ships' officers, and addressed many of his letters from Noumea to Köhler or Drehnen for transmission. Although Köhler was a German citizen, Drehnen was also naturalised, and neither could have been in any doubt as to his sentiments, of which the following are samples:

> We must hit, hit hard and into the battle - we cannot let our dear brave Hitler down... (To Köhler, 3 May 1936)

> [The French] must get afraid and then they'll stay quiet... Always underhand and malicious and now into the bargain, with all those Jews in France and they will attend to the war-mongering. (To Drehnen, 2 June 1936)

> You would not believe how much I value your letters in this sort of voluntary imprisonment into which I have put myself, because I love our dear Fatherland above all else and only want to see its greatness once again and we must have nickel for our army and that alone will regain for us regard, respect and right in the world. (To Drehnen, 20 December 1936)

> I know and so do you why we MUST have nickel... nickel is necessary: think of our dear soldiers, they alone can make us great again... we shall only recover our colonies with force and with nothing else. (To Drehnen. 14 June 1937)

> I, on the other hand, love our fatherland so much and know... how important and <u>urgently necessary</u> this nickel supply exactly is and so will just do <u>everything</u> to do my <u>part in the duty</u> in the great work of building up here too and for once also do something for our Fuehrer (To Asmis, 14 July 1937)[5]

Burkard loathed New Caledonia as much as the French detested him, but by persistence he managed to get certain restrictions on the export of nickel removed, and the first cargo was sent to Krupp in March 1937. His job was not made easier when Krupp, having sent to Sydney (in January 1936) a representative who spoke no English, sent to Noumea (in mid 1937) a mining expert who spoke 'no French and little English'. Nor did it help his commercial activities that he was expected to publicise propaganda articles sent by Asmis; if he could not get them into the press, he passed them around by hand. Burkard's activities were well known, for apart from the British Honorary Consul, Australia had informants from both the army and the naval reserve in Noumea. Among Burkard's Sydney employees was Jack Hilton, whose German maternal grandfather had asked Burkard to look after the lad when he died. Hilton had worked for Burkard since 1925, but he left under acrimonious circumstances in 1938. When questioned by authorities, he said that he had no knowledge of any subversive activities by Burkard, which was to be expected, as Burkard had warned other Germans to 'be careful that Hilton did not hear or see anything'.

When Asmis visited New Caledonia for several days in December 1937, he spent most of his time with Burkard. One outcome of their consultations seems to have been that Asmis agreed to try to have Burkard made Honorary Consul in Noumea, which might give him limited protection in a crisis. This took time and formalities had still not been finalised eighteen months later. On 24 July 1939, Burkard wrote to Asmis, who was again on leave in Germany, to thank him for what he had done in Berlin regarding the matter. His nomination as Consul had been confirmed in Germany, and he needed only his Exequatur, the consent of the French authorities, who did not look favourably on Burkard. Optimistically, he asked for advice on the size of the flag and the crest he should use. He wrote how much he would like to be home again, adding that he had to stay to 'help our good Führer'.

In the meantime, late in 1938, his lady friend, Lillian Bovell, had arrived in Noumea and was sharing his apartment. A nursing sister, whose father had been a parliamentarian in Western Australia, she had begun nursing Burkard several years earlier during a diabetes crisis, and the relationship had blossomed. He employed her to type his confidential correspondence and to help manage his diabetes. She had had control of his house in Vaucluse during his absences and had managed other business for him. She insisted that their association was only business and friendship, but they addressed each other as 'darling' and 'dearest', so the security services did not believe her.

By the time Hitler's armies marched into Prague, Burkard felt that war was imminent, and that his lonely efforts would not have been in vain. On 21 March, he wrote to his sister in Germany that 'this time the war will not be conducted with the Kaiser's "kid-gloves" but with a mailed fist'. He had planned a trip to Germany in 1940 to consult with Krupp. In October 1939, Censorship, intercepting a letter from Krupp, noted that he seemed to be in some trouble with the firm.

Internee

At the outbreak of war, the French withdrew Burkard's residence permit; he was arrested in the early morning of 2 September and held in Nouville Prison until he could be deported to Australia as a British citizen. They noted: 'His pretended [sic] British nationality however prevented the complete sequestration of his property for the benefit of the French state.' A few days later, he began a series of complaints to W. Johnston, the British Consul, regarding his treatment, and asked him to bring his case before Sir Henry Gullett, the Minister for External Affairs, whom he had known for years. He also tried to contact Drehnen secretly by enclosing a letter in a copy of *La France Australe* to get it past censorship. Possibly its main effect was to build up the case for Drehnen's internment in July 1940.

Burkard was put aboard *Cagou*, bound for Port Kembla. Lillian Bovell had delayed her own departure until she could go by the same ship. On arrival in Australia, he was re-arrested and sent to 'Malabar Internment Camp' – in actuality, Long Bay Gaol. He protested vehemently, claiming he was one hundred per cent loyal and had never said anything disloyal against Britain. However, six correspondence files had been found containing carbon copies of his letters to Asmis, Drehnen and Köhler, and to Captain Eugen Mathy, who had replaced him as Chairman of the Chamber of Commerce. Twenty-four letters out of hundreds were translated in full and their abuse of everything British was noted. A Military Police Intelligence report, 13 October, commented: 'Perusal of these translations will show that Burkard's claim that he was a loyal British Subject is utterly false… It will be seen that he is a man who might be termed "the power behind the throne" in German affairs in Australia… [He] is a definite menace to the well-being of this Country and totally unfitted to retain his naturalisation as a Subject of this Country.' A Notice of Intention to revoke naturalisation was served on Burkard, probably in 1940, but it was not implemented.

On 17 November, Lillian Bovell was called to Police Headquarters for an interview. The police did not doubt her personal loyalty, but they knew that she stalled and lied when it came to Burkard's activities. On leaving, she said that Burkard was 'her man', and any woman would lie to protect her man. She insisted that he was loyal, even though he had written to her: 'Even if we lose again, it is better but we take a few millions of the liars with us.'

With the increased powers provided by wartime regulations, the police and military could investigate Burkard more thoroughly. They found that he – allegedly – had two machine guns in a city bond store, and it is difficult to see that he had any legitimate use for machine guns. It is not on record whether these guns were recovered. It was found that Burkard possessed a non-commercial code that was used by Nazis in various parts of the world. When his house at 7 Olola Avenue, Vaucluse, was searched on 16 September, some unusual alterations to the cellar and lower floor were noted.

> There are a number of carefully built wall cabinets and a narrow passage running the full length of the study, behind the rear wall. In this wall there is a china cabinet which communicates directly with the passage behind it. From the passage a small door opens into the china cabinet, and when this door is opened any conversation in the study can be plainly heard. In the other rooms there are similar compartments.

One door opened into a cocktail cabinet. The cellar under the house had been subdivided, and a swastika flag was still hanging in the cellar. A naval officer who was a tenant in the house said that under the house there were several locked rooms to which he did not have a key. The police were of the opinion that somebody, perhaps one of Burkard's business associates, had removed documents from the house.

Because he was a British subject and insisted he was loyal, Burkard was sent to a non-Nazi camp, where there were people who knew his true sentiments. He was assaulted at least three times. He was a troublesome inmate, feuding with communists and Nazi sympathisers alike, even with his former ally, Dr Becker. He drew swastikas on each page of his diary, and he tried to evade censorship, for which offence his typewriter was confiscated until he complied with regulations. He would not co-operate with the doctors in the treatment of his diabetes, claiming he could not tolerate insulin. In short, he made as much trouble as he could.

Dr Asmis, who had been on leave in Germany on the outbreak of war, made a bizarre attempt to have Burkard released. On 25 March 1941, he wrote to the Foreign Office in Berlin, pointing out Burkard's services to Germany in arranging nickel supplies, but acknowledging that Burkard was an Australian citizen. Even more oddly, it was the German Embassy in Paris that replied in August that the (Vichy) French Government would find it difficult to intervene on behalf of an Australian citizen.[6]

However, they would instruct the French Consul in Sydney to try to intervene. If contact was ever made with the French Consul-General in Sydney (Charles Lancial), he had enough other problems already. On 15 January 1942, the Director of the Civil Cabinet of Marshal Pétain reported that it would be impossible to intervene, owing to inadequate communications, but perhaps the Protecting Power (the Swiss Consulate-General) could do something. The German Embassy in Paris reported this to Berlin on 6 February. Nothing came of any such endeavour. Perhaps it was never made, but in any case the Allies were reading the Vichy codes, and the Australian postal authorities were being obstructive regarding the delivery of communications to Vichy representatives.

Chapter 1: The Vindictive Metallurgist

When Germany lost the second war during his lifetime, Burkard was devastated and lost all restraint. He wrote to Lillian Bovell:

> Germany, which is and remains my Fatherland, but who settled in Australia nearly 40 years ago, employed hundreds of Australians and paid millions into the country and would have fought against yellows, negroes and any who attacked and to protect and to defend here my self elected home and hearth... Now that Germany has lost the war and lies bleeding and prostrate at the boots and heels of Victors ... They have now French niggers in occupation and American niggers of all dilutions... (12 May and 16 June 1945)

Ironic Aftermath

It can be seen from the above that Burggraf, who had known Burkard for thirty years, had some justification for calling him 'the most dangerous man in the Commonwealth', and urging that he be deported. A Security Service report commented with restraint that he had 'not honoured obligations as a British subject'. However, decisions as to whether internees would be allowed to stay in Australia were not made entirely on the basis of what they might have done or said in the past, but whether they might be a danger to Australia in the future, or whether their presence would cause an outcry from 'returned soldiers' or the communists. When cases of individual internees were reviewed in mid 1946, Burkard was in hospital, too ill to be heard. In view of his advanced age and poor health, he was released on leave on 16 July 1946, pending a decision on his future. In the same month, he entered hospital in Stanmore, New South Wales.

On 28 July 1946, the *Sunday Telegraph* featured on its front page an article entitled 'Secret files expose plots of Hitler agent against Australia'. Bearing the by-line of Ian Fitchett, it proclaimed that it told 'the story of a man who swore loyalty to Australia and betrayed his oath'. Fitchett wrote: 'I have been through a file of his letters written in the years 1935 to 1939...' One original letter, written to Asmis on 14 July 1937 and bearing Burkard's signature, was reproduced photographically. On the following Sunday, 4 August, a similar article featured three other former internees. Probably the articles would not do Burkard much harm; they were a nine days' wonder, and there would be new sensations next week and the week after. However, this material had obviously come from Commonwealth Security Service files, and nobody outside the CSS had a right to see it. It was worrying that such a secret document should fall into the hands of the press, and the leakage of information was causing concern to the Attorney-General, Dr Evatt.

Fitchett and the *Sunday Telegraph* editor, Cyril Pearl, were interviewed on 9 August to try to ascertain how they came to be in illegal possession of official documents. Pearl forbade Fitchett to comment; he claimed that it was he who had given Fitchett the material and refused to reveal his source. 'I am not concerned with any Crimes Act. This is a newspaper,' he said. 'All newspaper men deal only in facts. Their articles have to be authentic, otherwise they are not employed.' In view of the *Daily Telegraph*'s record for making errors or faking material, this was farcical. Fitchett claimed that Burkard had been a member of the Nazi Party, which he was not and could not have been, as he was not a German citizen. Even with Burkard's signature in front of him, he wrote about 'Burkhard'. And after writing that Burkard had been naturalised in 1921, he referred to a letter written in April 1938, 'nearly seven years after he had sworn allegiance as a naturalised Australian'.[7]

As the interviewers had no success with Pearl, an internal inquiry was conducted. It was determined that the material from which the article on Burkard had been written had come from summaries prepared between 20 June and 1 August 1944. Three copies had been made. One copy was in Canberra, one was kept in Burkard's dossier, and a reference copy had been retained by a Sergeant Hollis. Hollis had returned to the police force in May 1945, and it was his copy that was missing. All staff members who might have had access to his files were interviewed, with one exception: Constable First Class Hughes was on leave. Several weeks later, shortly after Hughes had returned, the missing file mysteriously turned up; it was decided that it had simply been mislaid, and had never been in the hands of the newspapers. As the newspaper had carried a photographic reproduction of material in the file, it sounds as though some CSS agent was very obtuse.

Thus the possible involvement of Alfred Thompson Hughes was not pursued. This was unfortunate, for Hughes had allegedly been a secret communist since 1932; he had been recruited by Walter Seddon Clayton as a Soviet spy, and Moscow Centre had given him the code name BEN. Failure to pursue this line of enquiry, and Pearl's recalcitrance, allowed the presence of a Soviet spy to go undetected until the defection of Vladimir Petrov in 1954. As a spy in the heart of the Security Service, Hughes was infinitely more dangerous than Burkard, until he was returned to the police force and transferred to the Vice Squad. His application to join the Australian Security Intelligence Organisation was rejected; he did not have the character or social standing to be Australia's Kim Philby.

Fortunately, on the other hand, neither Pearl nor Fitchett realised that the 'G.C.' in small handwriting at the head of the translations of some of Burkard's letters meant that the originals had been taken in 1942, in breach of international convention, from German Consulate-General records that should have been held in Swiss custody.

Inquiry Agent W. H. Barnwell reported on 4 September 1946 that Burkard seemed to be a broken man, a suicide risk rather than a security risk. He said he was just waiting to die. On 18 September, Bovell wrote that he was in a psychiatric clinic. Six days later, he was formally given permission to remain in Australia.

Considering the importance of Krupp cannon during the war, one may wonder why Burkard was not tried for treason. In Australian law at that time, the essence of treason was 'aiding His Majesty's enemies', and in peace time His Majesty's enemies are not clearly defined. Burkard's activities had ceased at the outbreak of war. Possibly the most that could have been done was to revoke his naturalisation and deport him, but when he was released at the end of the war he was fairly old and very ill. There was nothing in his dossier to indicate that his wife and son had survived the war, nor to indicate that they had perished, except that there was apparently no reunion of the family.[8] The Karl L. Burkard who died in a French prisoner of war camp in October 1945 might have been his son; this man was born in October 1912, but German war graves records do not show where. Burkard was allowed to stay in Australia and probably to draw an Old Age Pension. After all, he had been paying Income Tax in Australia for more than thirty years. He died on 6 June 1952, alone and embittered.

Chapter 2

The Fake Alien

The mysterious and unpleasant Lars Gustav Brundahl, whom his neighbours dubbed 'Ivan the Terrible', acted on behalf of the German Consul-General Dr Asmis in matters with which it was undesirable for the Consulate-General to be associated. In other words, he did some of the dirty work for them. A violent man, a liar and a thief, a bigamist and a thorough scoundrel, he hoodwinked the Germans and puzzled Australian authorities for many years. His shameless duplicity can be appreciated best if the truth about his origins is told at the beginning. The Security services knew at an early date that he was a brazen liar, but although they knew that what he said was false, they seem to have been unsure of his true identity until about May 1949, when the *Sunday Telegraph* printed a facsimile of his birth certificate, which their New Zealand correspondent had obtained. This identified him as Lars Agustoff Brundall, born in Westport on 28 December 1885, son of Peter Mathias Brundall, carpenter, born 'Sunsdille', Sweden, and Melinda Jane Scantlebury, born St Austell, Cornwall. They had been married in 1877 at Greymouth, New Zealand.[1]

Lars Gustav Brundahl (Karl Burggraf, *Die Deutschen in den Hauptstaedten von Australien*)

This was Melinda's second marriage, and Lars was the eighth of her nine children. He was not yet six years old when his father died, and it is probable that his childhood years were spent in poverty.

Beginning of a Charade

From 1914, 'Brundahl' created several identities for himself, and he associated closely with Germans, who often wrote his name as 'Bründahl'. A great deal about Brundahl was shady, and two basic questions interested Military Intelligence. What was his true identity? And how had he acquired the substantial amount of money and property that he owned? It might have come from criminal activity or from espionage, but it did not seem that it could have been earned honestly. Suspicions deepened in 1927 when Consul-General Büsing appointed him Commissioner for the Leipzig International Trade Fair. It was an unwise choice, for Brundahl was perhaps the most

Chapter 2: The Fake Alien

unsavoury character associated with the German community in Sydney. It was an unpaid position, and not many people could afford to do it. How could Brundahl afford it, and why did he want it?

Two people who had known Brundahl in his early years – one in New Zealand and one in Sydney – reported his history to authorities in October 1939, but the documents apparently lay unnoticed in a very large file, and the truth was not rediscovered for nearly ten years. In 1903-05 he had been a biograph operator in Auckland, where he was allegedly living with a Maori woman to whom he was not married,[2] and he drew his pay under the name Blundell, probably to evade taxation. (A biograph was an early type of film projector.) By 1907 he was in Sydney, possibly arriving as a crew member of *Sierra* on 7 March. On 26 June 1908, he married Ethel Mary Lazarus, giving his name correctly as Lars G. Brundall and his birthplace as Westport. Much was made later over the 'fact' that he lied on this marriage certificate, but it was almost the last time he told the truth about himself, except that he gave his birth year as 1886.

In Sydney he was employed at the Colonial Theatre, again as a biograph operator, after allegedly presenting American identification papers showing he was born in New Zealand. Here he was caught stealing from his employer, and while trying to destroy evidence he accidentally set fire to the theatre. He may have left Australia at this time to escape the consequences of these actions, travelling to the United States, then to Shanghai via Manila, where he was working with motion picture equipment. He was living with an American woman, Estelle Louise Mendelsohn, whom he claimed to have married in 1911, though he probably did not divorce Ethel until 1918. Their son, registered as Lars Virginian Brundall, was born in Shanghai on 26 October 1913. When Estelle died a few months later, he travelled to Australia with the boy and set up an agency for motion picture equipment sales. From then on, he re-invented himself constantly.

Central registration of births, deaths and marriages did not begin in the USA until around 1900, the date varying from state to state. Thus it could be quite difficult to verify a claim as to a person's identity. The issue of passports was rather haphazard, and statements made by applicants were not checked rigorously. Although conscription was not introduced in Australia during the 1914-18 war, Brundahl could not know that in advance. On 26 October 1916, just two days before the first conscription referendum, he registered himself as an alien, a neutral American, as conscription in Australia would presumably have applied to New Zealanders as well. When registering as an alien in 1916, Brundahl gave his birthplace as New York.

In the early years of World War I, the United States looked after German interests, and Brundahl, who was registered as an American, acted as Welfare Officer for an internment camp. This was how his long-term association with Germans began. By now he was claiming that his mother had been born German, but had been the widow of a Canadian when she married his father.³ He was subjected to cursory checks in 1917, but there were few misgivings when he failed to produce documents to prove his identity.

In April 1919 Brundahl married Elsie Emily Baldock. The only mention in Brundahl's dossier of his son's presence in Australia is that he was sent to his mother's relatives in America because he did not get along with his stepmother, but no date is given. Brundahl now owned a poultry farm where he put immigrants to work so that they could say they had a job, and a 1927 Investigation Branch report referred to him as a wealthy, retired American who assisted Germans who could not be helped directly by the Consulate. Lutheran Pastor Schenk in Sydney knew he could send to Brundahl German migrants and seamen who were in difficulties, but he may not have known *how* Brundahl 'helped' them. He apparently had them work on his property at slave rates, and Arnold von Skerst, one of the key men in Nazi activities in Sydney, said later that ships' deserters were 'in financial bondage to Brundahl'. A registered money lender from 1921 to 1928, he later lived off property investments. In 1933, Colonel E. E. Longfield Lloyd of the Investigation Branch, copying from an old report, wrote misguidedly that Brundahl, who had been under observation since 1916, was 'a man of pleasant disposition... liked by all who knew him'.

German Connection

When the German Consulate-General re-opened in Melbourne in 1924, Brundahl became acquainted with the Consul-General, Dr Büsing. In view of Brundahl's aid to German internees during the war and his financial independence, Büsing appointed him Commissioner for the Leipzig International Trade Fair. The position carried with it some status, and in 1931 Brundahl received a certificate from President Hindenburg in recognition of his contribution to migrant welfare.

Brundahl's imagination now worked overtime. Not only did he tell different stories about himself to different people, but he also told different stories to the same person. He was born, he claimed, in October or December of 1885, 1886 or 1888, in New Zealand or New York or San Jose or at sea off California. It was convenient to claim he had been born in California and that the records had been destroyed in the earthquake of 1906, and even more convenient to claim San Jose, for county records there had been lost in a fire in 1931. His mother's first name was Melinda or Linda Jane or Lynda Melinde, and her birth name had been Scandborg or Scantlebury or Scantelberg or Schonberg or Boleyn or Bullen or Wilhelmi.⁴

His father, Peter, had been a master mariner and owner of a vessel called *North Star*. He also claimed that he had studied medicine at Berkeley University, but had given up the course; and that as a member of the US militia, 1905-08 he had taken part in action against looters during the San Francisco earthquake in April 1906. He had arrived in Australia in 1907 or 1909 or 1913 or 1914 aboard *Sierra* or *Eastern* or *St Albans*.[5]

At least once, he claimed he had deserted from the American fleet in 1910, but the great American 'White Fleet' had visited Australia in August 1908, while Brundahl was in Sydney. The German Consulate-General did not have the ability to check these statements, and the Australian authorities did not establish the truth until much later. After Brundahl and Elsie were divorced about 1931, he married Bessie Whitmore Rogers on 18 March 1932. She put up with him for more than twenty years.

At the beginning of October 1932, the new Consul-General arrived: Dr Rudolf Asmis. He saw fairly quickly that Brundahl could be a handy tool for certain underhand jobs that had to be officially 'deniable'. The first consideration was that Asmis held Brundahl's fate in his hands; one complaint to Germany and Brundahl would lose his position as Trade Commissioner. While it was an unpaid position, it could be profitable in the hands of an unscrupulous man, for it was in his power to distribute certain agencies and trade favours. Although Brundahl's registration as a public money lender probably lapsed about 1929, he still lent money privately, and Asmis used this discreetly to gain control of key people. On request, Brundahl did a few other jobs for Asmis. The unholy alliance was mutually beneficial: profit for Brundahl, power for Asmis. He also became an important figure in the German-Australian Chamber of Commerce and was deeply involved in Nazi manipulation of barter trade.

In 1933, Asmis prodded the Chamber of Commerce and the German *Bund* to sponsor jointly the publication of a weekly magazine, *Die Brücke*. Brundahl was one of the major shareholders, taking out two £25 shares, and he was a provisional director of the magazine, which issued its first number in February 1934. Clerical staff was shared; the typists for the Chamber of Commerce and *Die Brücke* now also did Brundahl's Trade Fair work.

The most important loan made on behalf of Asmis was to Walter Ladendorff, who became the Nazi leader for Sydney in 1936 and for Australia in 1937. Asmis had had a lot of trouble with the previous leader, Dr Becker, who sent untruthful denunciations of many people, including of Asmis himself, to the Gestapo. This was a common situation around the world, and in many places there was constant friction between representatives of the Party and the Foreign Office. It took Asmis over three years to depose Becker from his position and to see that Ladendorff was appointed. He then ensured that a similar situation did not arise again by arranging for Brundahl to lend Ladendorff money that he would not find easy to repay. Having been in a difficult financial situation, Ladendorff was grateful. He also realised that he could not afford to attack or offend Asmis. While it sometimes seemed to Australians as though Ladendorff took precedence over Asmis – which he did at Party functions, but not at consular ones – nobody who knew of Brundahl's role doubted who held the reins of power.

In 1936, Brundahl was rewarded for ten years of service to the Trade Fair with a commemorative plaque and a sponsored trip to Europe to attend the spring session in Leipzig. By now, passport controls had tightened everywhere. Brundahl never claimed to be Australian, nor did he claim Swedish citizenship, and America would not recognise him as an American citizen by birth or naturalisation, as he could prove neither. Thus he had to travel on documents of identity. He and Bessie spent about twelve days in London and two weeks in Leipzig, and they visited Bremen, Hamburg, Lübeck, Hanover and Berlin, mainly on business. Then they went to Brundahl's father's birthplace in the north of Sweden. They returned via the United States, so that Brundahl could show his wife his alleged birthplace in San Jose, arriving back in Sydney by *Mariposa* in June 1936.

Thus far, things had gone well enough for Brundahl, but now they began to unravel. In New Zealand, the Wellington branch of G. Hardt & Co. represented the Trade Fair. Herbert Engelbert Hardt, a former SS man who had arrived in Australia in June 1935, tried to pressure Brundahl into putting certain barter deals through Hardt & Co. This was dangerous, for Hardt had connections with Himmler through the Reich Minister for Food Production, Walter Darré.[6]

Nevertheless, Brundahl refused. In 1937, Hardt began to take action against him, complaining that the Trade Fair position should be held by a German. This was not necessarily pure spite, as the Chamber of Commerce and the Trade Fair were expected to provide cover for activities that should not become known to anybody who was not under the control of the Nazi Party, or at least of the German Government. As Brundahl was more useful to Asmis than Hardt could be, Asmis warned Brundahl that Hardt was trying to have him removed.

In August, Brundahl began his counter-attack. He wrote to Dr Hellenthal, who had recently moved from Sydney to become Consul-General in New Zealand; Hellenthal had no particular connection to the Trade Fair, but he was a solid Party man and a long-standing friend of *Reichsmarschall* Göring. He wrote also to Dr Raimund Köhler, President of the Trade Fair Office, complaining that a person who had demanded unsuccessfully that all barter transactions negotiated by the Sydney office be passed through his firm was trying to remove him using the excuse that he was not a 'full-blooded' German and not a Party member. When Dr Köhler replied that they had complete confidence in him, and asked the

Chapter 2: The Fake Alien

name of the firm concerned, Brundahl reported that it was Hardt. The rest of the correspondence is not on file, but it is likely that Hardt wanted the position for himself or a crony, so that his own firm could obtain the best deals that passed through the office.

It suited Asmis to have certain jobs done by somebody who was known not to be a Party member, and Brundahl became his mouthpiece. When anti-Nazi films were shown, or anti-Nazi articles appeared in the papers, Asmis sometimes complained officially, but there were too many such articles, and some of them were too trivial to justify official notice. Then Brundahl was sent into action. After the *Sunday Sun* published one of Eric Baume's articles attacking Hitler, Brundahl called on Baume and said he would be sorry for Baume's wife and family if these did not cease. (Baume was Jewish.) On another occasion, he called on another Jewish writer and told him it was a pity there were no concentration camps in Australia to which his sort could be sent. After an incident on Anzac Day 1939, when a mob attacked the Consulate-General until the swastika flag was removed from the building, Brundahl again represented German interests, this time not at the instigation of Asmis, who was on leave in Germany, but for the Acting Consul-General, Dr Oscar Seger.

Not all Brundahl's nefarious activities were on behalf of official German interests. In January 1939, the *Daily News* ran an article on him in connection with the shooting of a neighbour's dog. He had been convicted and fined, and although the conviction was quashed on appeal, he was known in Rose Bay as 'Ivan the Terrible'. He was already showing signs of mental deterioration before an accident on 21 August 1939, in which he suffered a head injury.

Internment

On 4 September 1939, Brundahl was arrested for internment but released the next day when it was discovered that he was not German. He was arrested again on 10 September, for he had been terrorising the neighbours with threats of what would happen to them when the Germans arrived. The police were not short of complaints about him.

When Dr Seger reached Batavia by a repatriation ship in October 1939, he reported immediately to the Foreign Office in Berlin on internments in Australia and on his talks with the Swiss Consul-General, Hans Hedinger. He wrote that Bründahl – to whose name he accorded an unwarranted German spelling – was a controversial character, with a Swedish father and a German mother, but American citizenship. He asked whether the American authorities could help to have him released. Berlin replied on 21 December that they could not imagine that the Americans would allow one of their citizens to be interned, so it was presumed that he had been released. However, the Americans, knowing that Brundahl had never been an American citizen, had no interest in him.

Brundahl's appeal against internment was heard over three days in November 1939. Here, on oath, he had to repeat and clarify his contradictory claims about his origins and activities and defend them in the face of evidence that they were mostly untrue. His claim to the Appeals Tribunal was that he had been born on 28 December 1888 in San Jose, son of Peter Matthias Brundahl and Linda Wilhelmi. This date did not sit well with his claims that he had joined the militia in 1903 or that he had studied at Berkeley University. Brundahl tried to account for the fact that there was no record of his birth in California by relying on the convenient 'destroyed in the earthquake' story. He claimed he had travelled from America to Asia on an American passport, but he could not produce the passport or account for the American statements that he had never been issued with an American passport or recognised as an American citizen.

He was confronted with contradictory statements that he had made regarding his arrival in Australia. When he applied for a travel permit in 1931, he said he arrived in December 1913 from China, aboard *St Albans*. When he applied for a permit in 1933, it was September 1915, from Shanghai, aboard *Eastern*. On the statement of personal particulars filled out when he was interned, he said 1914, *St Albans*. Whatever date or ship of entry he claimed for 1913-14, research showed that he was not on the passenger list; lists of crew discharged were less reliable, and there was some evidence that he had worked his passage. He claimed he had been engaged on ships plying between America and Australia for many years, and had spent eight years in the Far East, in China, Japan and Siberia. How he fitted this in between 1908, when he married Ethel Lazarus in Sydney, and 1914, which is the latest date at which he could have arrived in Australia to settle, is a subject for mathematical wonderment, but that did not seem to bother him.

Between 1914 and 1920, he had earned £10 to £15 a week, a good income for those times, but not enough to account for properties he had bought, to the value of £15,000, between 1920 and 1939. He said that he had brought £2,700 from China, but there was no bank record to confirm this. Then he said that in 1908 his mother had distributed to her children $15,000 from the estate of his father, who had died in 1892. With some of this, he had made a trip from San Francisco to Honolulu, Pago Pago and Auckland, arriving in Sydney about 1909. He denied that he had been in New Zealand 1903-05. Faced with the certificate of his marriage to Ethel Lazarus, he denied that he was the person named. When it was shown that this claim was ridiculous, and that there was no trace of any such money, and that he was not on any feasible passenger list, he admitted that the legacy and the trip were fabrications. As the statements had been made under oath, this amounted to perjury. When he realised he could not sustain his fantasies, he broke down and wept. The subsequent report stated that 'he did not account to the Committee for his present wealth', and he was entirely discredited with regard to evidence concerning his life between 1906 and 1914.

Soon after the Appeal hearing, he was sent to the Reception House, Sydney, for a month for investigation into his mental condition. The report said that he was perfectly sane. The military reported that he was an 'unmitigated and unscrupulous liar and one of the cleverest malingerers in Australia'. However, although he might not have fitted any of the standard patterns of mental illness, he was clearly unbalanced, to judge from his previous and subsequent behaviour and reports by fellow internees, who had to live with him, that he would sit in a corner for hours, just rocking.

In camp he produced more stories; he had already claimed that his son was studying medicine in Chicago; *and* that the son was a cadet at a Naval Academy. Then he progressed to claiming that his son was a Surgeon-Commander in the United States Navy. He was a difficult inmate. One of the entries on his record card shows that he was sentenced to seven days in detention for assaulting an officer and trying to take his pistol. This mild punishment for such a serious offence is perhaps an indication that his sanity was in question, no matter what the army doctors said. A recently released internee said in January 1943 that Brundahl was definitely insane. Every day he would pick on a different victim and subject him to a barrage of accusations so devoid of reason that they indicated an unbalanced mind. An officer endorsed this: 'Brundahl unbalanced for many years.' But where lay the distinction between unbalanced and insane? At the end of the war, there was no justification for continuing to detain him on the grounds of National Security. He was released on 14 August 1945, possibly temporarily to another mental institution. Expungement from records of material relating to mental conditions makes it impossible to determine where he was sent or how long he remained there.

After the War

When he returned to his home in Rose Bay, authorities investigated the possibility of deporting him. He could not be deported to Germany; his father was not German; he had not been born in Germany; and even if his mother had been German, that would not have conferred German citizenship on her son. The American authorities would not recognise him and would not have him. External Affairs wrote to the Royal Swedish Legation to check on Brundahl's ancestry. The Foreign Office replied that there was no record of the birth of a Peter Mathias Brundall at any time or place that fitted even approximately the claims made; and even if there had been, his Swedish citizenship would have been lost after he had lived abroad for ten years without registering with a Consulate, and so it could not have been transmitted to his son. Sweden would not have him. The Department of Immigration conceded that Brundahl had lived in Australia for thirty-four years, and as no country had an obligation to take him back, he could not be deported.

In November 1947, Brundahl attracted attention again. Dr Becker, leader of the Nazi Party in Australia 1932-36, had been released on parole pending deportation. Having disappeared from Tanunda and then flown to Sydney under the name 'John Henry', he turned up with his luggage at Brundahl's Rose Bay apartment. Bessie Brundahl slammed the door in his face, but Brundahl came out and let him in. He took charge of the luggage, and Becker left again.

The police had already discovered that Becker was intending to make contact with Brundahl. Military Intelligence knew the identity of his friends in Tanunda; they paid some visits, did some searching, found some documents, and finally by leaning heavily on Max Riedel they found that he had re-addressed a letter to Becker care of Brundahl. Brundahl owned the block of flats in which he lived, and the police called on one of his tenants and asked her to inform them if Becker turned up. Thus, soon after Becker left, the police called on Brundahl and found Becker's luggage there. They did not find Becker, who had gone to the docks to try to get a passage to South America. When the captain of an American tanker, *Cedar Breaks*, allegedly refused his alleged offer of £1,000 for a passage, he stowed away, intending to make his way to Venezuela. Discovered and arrested aboard the ship on the evening of Wednesday, 26 November, he was flown to Perth to join *General Heintzelmann*, the repatriation ship bound for Europe. Guessing that his tenant, Mrs Florence Wawn, was implicated, Brundahl began to make life hell for her. This potential for violent vengeance was the reason why internees were not given the chance to question people who had informed against them, or even to know their identities.

Several small items of information, mentioned briefly in different places that were perhaps never read by anyone who could collate them, raise interesting questions. A Sydney *Telegraph* article claimed that Becker said he had friends in the German-Argentinean Cultural League, and if he could get to Argentina he would take charge of this League. A Security file mentioned another connection between Becker and South America. When filling out a form concerning his choice of destination when he was to be deported, he had given Venezuela as his first choice, Bolivia as the second; that much is documented. Brundahl had applied for permission to transfer to South America funds that would not normally have been allowed out of the country under the existing currency controls. There was a persistent rumour that secret funds of the Nazi Party and the Consulate-General

Chapter 2: The Fake Alien

had been transferred to Brundahl's control. Allegedly, neither Brundahl nor his wife had bank accounts in their own names, but what did they do with the money they collected from their rental properties? And why did Becker go to Brundahl? Where did he obtain the money he allegedly offered the American captain? It looked as though Becker knew or believed that Brundahl had Nazi Party or consular funds in a bank account under a false name, and wanted to make sure that some of this money would be available to him if he could reach South America. If an answer was ever found to this monkey puzzle, it is not in an accessible file.

That left just the matter of Brundahl's revenge against Mrs Wawn unresolved. He terrorised and persecuted many of his tenants and neighbours, but he concentrated on Florence Wawn. He interfered with bread and milk delivered to the doorstep; he rattled door handles and entered tenants' flats while they were out, using duplicate keys; he spat at them, swore at them, turned a hose on them, lit smoky fires when they hung out their washing. He was truly the Landlord from Hell. He threw water over Mrs Wawn from an upstairs window. Since he believed (correctly) that she had informed on him regarding Becker's visit, his annoyance with her was understandable, but a small boy who had been hosed while riding a tricycle along the footpath had done him no harm. The police received many depositions from his victims, and desperate complaints, especially from Mrs Wawn. They said they could do nothing unless there were witnesses to an assault serious enough to warrant a prosecution. That was to come.

Military Intelligence, still watching him, reported in June 1948 that Brundahl was 'a most obnoxious individual and almost certifiable under the Lunacy Act'. In August he was charged with assault on Mrs Wawn and put on a good behaviour bond. He sought further revenge, and on 3 September four men attacked Herbert and Amy Dell, and Florence Wawn and her son Anthony. Brundahl was not present during the attack, but one of the assailants was recognised. Through him, the others were traced, and they confessed that Brundahl had hired them. This was reported in the *Sun* on 6 September. The next day, he was mentioned in Parliament. Herbert Dell and Anthony Wawn were returned soldiers and members of the Returned Servicemen's League, and the RSL did not stay silent when their members were assaulted by people with Brundahl's character and history.

The Minister for Immigration, Arthur Calwell, said in September that Brundahl's contempt for the law was notorious. In mid October, he was fined £10 for failing to register as an alien. The irony of this was that, having been born in New Zealand, he was *not* an alien and did not need to register, but he had been posing as an American too long for him to recant then.

The Wawn case went to court in late April 1949, when Brundahl and his hired thugs were charged with assault. This case attracted enough attention for the *Sunday Telegraph* to investigate, and on 15 May it published the story of Brundahl's true origin and status. The assault case and civil claims by the victims dragged on until 1950, and by the time it was finished Brundahl have been ordered to pay over £5,000 in damages and sentenced to four years in prison on a charge of conspiracy to assault.

The question of deporting Brundahl arose again. There were questions in Parliament and demonstrations in the street demanding that he be thrown out of the country. On 31 October 1951, Harold Holt, the new Minister for Immigration, rebuked Calwell, for he of all people should have known that the Commonwealth had no legal power to deport Brundahl to New Zealand, owing to a quirk of the legal arrangements between Australia and New Zealand.

The RSL Legal Adviser reported that Brundahl should be indicted for perjury for his false registration of nationality in 1916 and his evidence at his trial.[7] RSL members participated in the public demonstrations demanding deportation. RSL members tend to rush in with emotional opinions when they are not in possession of the necessary facts. Their service makes them deserving of consideration, but it does not confer on them supreme wisdom or infallibility, and it does not reveal to them the contents of secret dossiers.

Prison did not teach Brundahl anything. In October 1955, he was in court again, charged with assaulting a neighbour with a broomstick. By then he was nearly seventy years old.

There was a belated postscript to Brundahl's story. On 21 May 1961, a geologist from Colorado arrived at Mascot airport (Sydney) bound for Brisbane. His name was Lawrence Brundall. He declared that he had been born on 25 October 1913 in Shanghai, son of Lars Gustaff Brundall and Estelle Louise Mendelsohn, and that he had last been in Australia in 1933. He stated in 1961 that he had one relative in Australia, a Paul Mendelsohn, who lived in Double Bay, Sydney. However, Lars Brundahl was still living in Sydney; he did not die until 1963. Did his son not know he was alive, or did he think it unwise to acknowledge a relationship? Lawrence Brundall made several trips between Australia and the United States, and in 1963 his wife and children accompanied him; they stayed in Brisbane for two years. It can be taken for granted that he was telling the truth, and his details tie in with Brundahl's story in a few places, but it is unlikely that he was ever a Surgeon-Commander in the US Navy.

Were any secret Consular or Nazi funds left with Brundahl? The trustees might well have thought that the war would be over in a few months and they would be able to retrieve any such money, but things turned out differently. Dr Seger, the last Acting Consul-General, would have been the man who knew about secret Consular funds; he was caught by the

Russians in 1945 and disappeared into one of their camps. The last Nazi Party leader in Australia, SS *Bannführer* Alfred Henschel, would have dealt with Party funds; he was last reported alive in Shanghai in 1943, and after the war news from American sources in Germany indicated he had been killed. If the money existed, there was nobody to claim it. In addition, the Nazi Party was so short of funds that Henschel had to borrow money from the Labour Front when he wanted to travel to Perth on Party business in August 1939. If any money belonging to the German Foreign Office passed secretly through Brundahl's hands, it most likely stuck to his fingers.

Chapter 3

The Card-Carrying Spy

Germans cannot be reproached for having acted in the interests of Germany, nor can Australia be reproached for having acted to ensure, as far as possible, that the damage they might have caused in wartime was minimised. Most efforts of German agents in Australia in the 1930s were directed towards persuading ethnic Germans to maintain their links with the land of their ancestors and influencing Australian politicians and journalists to promote the use of German imports and to develop such friendly feelings for Germany that Australia would stay out of the next war, which had long been planned. Of necessity, their activities were fairly public and attracted attention.

Spies, on the other hand, avoid attention, and the few genuine German spies in Australia have been almost entirely overlooked by historians. The Consulate-General and the Nazi Party made a potential spy out of every German citizen, but some were more involved and more professional than others. Some were resident in Australia while some were transients, but there was a thread connecting the pre-1914 espionage system and the system between the wars, and it involved mainly the representatives of the shipping company Norddeutscher Lloyd (NDL) and the Hardt family business. These were not scoundrels but solid, respectable merchants who had access to sensitive commercial and shipping information and contacts with the policy-makers and financiers who controlled Australia's destiny.

World War I

A doctoral thesis by Peter Overlack at the University of Queensland devotes a chapter to the establishment of the *Etappendienst* (Supply Service) of the *Marinenachrichtendienst* (Naval Intelligence Service) in Sydney prior to 1914. He identifies Walter de Haas as the Consular head of the *Etappe*, while Oscar Plate, agent for Lohmann & Co. and North German Lloyd, was the naval expert and operative head, with Otto Bauer as sub-agent. The *Etappe* was formalised in 1911 when instructions were issued regarding arrangements for outposts.[1]

Michael McKernan wrote in 1980 about Oscar Plate, whom he described as a harmless, innocent, German businessman, who was interned simply because his house at Elizabeth Bay overlooked the Garden Island Naval Dockyard and Sydney Harbour: interned even though his wife was British and had four brothers in the army.[2]

A dossier gives her maiden name as Davies, and it claims that she was born in Queensland. That is untrue; she was the daughter of Sir Edwyn Sandys Dawes, KCMG, and their only connection with Australia was that he had been director of the London branch of the Bank of Queensland. Overseas postal censorship extracted from the mail a letter from Seattle, dated 21 October 1914, asking Plate for information about the movements of Australian troops heading overseas. While the firm appeared to be American, its headquarters were in Germany, and the ANZAC troops were due to leave Australia in November. The writer knew whom to contact, for Plate was a spy.

In addition, every Honorary Consul was supposed to furnish reports that found their way to the navy. These consisted mainly of compilations of shipping statistics, the volume of trade through various ports at different times of the year, their destinations, and comments on their cargoes. This information was available publicly, but it had to be organised and submitted, and the Consuls did this. Some of these reports, particularly those compiled in Brisbane 1907-13, mainly by Dr Eugen Hirschfeld, are available for perusal. The material concerned mainly routine statistics, and it might seem stretching a point to call the men who supplied it 'spies', but the information was exactly what a navy needed to run a blockade effectively, which was what the German navy planned to do along the east coast of Australia. These plans were thwarted through lack of suitable ships, and only *Emden* operated in the Indian Ocean.

Naval Espionage Resumed

The *Etappe* in Australia was re-established early in 1933, probably during the visit of the cruiser *Köln*. These agents probably did no significant damage, but their activities could have had detrimental effects if the war had taken a different course, or if the Commonwealth Investigation Branch and Military Police Intelligence had not taken prompt action to disrupt any sabotage or espionage networks by interning all suspects. Not surprisingly, the first choice as head of the new *Etappe* was the current NDL agent in Sydney, Captain Emil Mertgen, who was given the cover name 'John Anderson'. The Consul-General, Dr Asmis, must have been involved in this work, for by regulation the codes, ciphers and secret instructions had to be stored for security on the premises of a Consulate-General or an Embassy, and issued only on command when there was danger of war (*Spannungsbefehl*). It is possible that Mertgen did not receive such material, for he was killed in November 1933. Very early on a Sunday morning, while travelling home from a Saturday evening function, he took a corner too fast and crashed his car into the war memorial at Hunter's Hill.

Given the cover name 'Kent Howard', a Fremantle import agent, Josef Janssen, was appointed representative in Western Australia. As there was only an Honorary Consular Agent in Perth, Janssen had no secure repository for secret material, and it might never have been issued to him. Janssen had arrived in Australia in September 1926 at the age of twenty. He set up business in Fremantle (Mercantile Traders); then in 1935 he sold this business, moved to Melbourne and set up an import and indent business covering Adelaide, Sydney and Brisbane. Before becoming naturalised in July 1935, he had consulted the Consul-General about the possibility of retaining German nationality as well, or regaining it later, stressing that he wanted naturalisation only for business purposes. Janssen travelled a lot within Australia as well as abroad, and he was in an excellent position to obtain and forward information on harbour facilities and shipping around Australia, but no record has been found of any reports he might have provided.

Although an informant claimed that Janssen had boasted at Bondi (Sydney) that he was a follower of Hitler, who would beat Great Britain and rule the world, he does not seem to have had close contact with local Nazis. When he had a trade problem in 1937, he was refused consular help because he was naturalised. He had a trading relationship with a firm run by Czech Jews, and he was not allowed to engage in barter trading.

Mertgen was replaced in March 1934 by Captain Eugen Mathy, who inherited Mertgen's cover name and the designation of *Leitender Berichterstatter* (Leading Reporting Agent). His wife and two children followed in May. Mathy had been Third Officer aboard the NDL vessel *Thüringen* in 1914; captured in Fremantle harbour in August, he was interned on Rottnest Island (Western Australia) and at Trial Bay (New South Wales). Some records say he was interned in September 1914 at Liverpool, but he was definitely still on Rottnest in May 1915, and he was in close personal contact with H. B. Albert, a bookseller in Perth with a shop in Forrest Place opposite the Commonwealth Bank, and with Albert's daughter, Violet. He was also definitely at Trial Bay, as he won an essay contest run by *Die Brücke* with his story of a disastrous attempt by internees to boil down blubber from a dead whale washed up on the beach.

In one of his letters home, he had written that he intended to join the navy after the war and to be on active duty some day. Part of this letter was translated to read that he intended to 'don the Emperor's frock coat'; if the translator knew that the phrase 'des Kaisers Rock anziehen' was the equivalent of 'to put on the king's uniform', he did not make this clear. Mathy's internment record made nonsense of a later report that he had been a Zeppelin commander during the war. He was repatriated in May 1919 aboard *Kursk*, and by the time he reached home he was twenty-eight, and too old to begin naval cadet training.

Chapter 3: The Card-Carrying Spy

The Mathys, like Burkard, were part of the small German Catholic community in Sydney, and they were closely associated with the Nazis. Eugen's NSDAP membership dated from 1 July 1936 and he was one of the Party's auditors; he was also a member of the Labour Front, while his wife, Maria, was a member of the *Frauenschaft*, the Nazi women's organisation.

The next *Etappe* agent, who arrived in Sydney in February 1935, was Herbert Engelbert Hardt, woolbuyer, son of Gustav Hardt, who had founded the Australian branch of G. Hardt & Co., a family firm that had existed since 1760. He was born in Charlottenburg (Berlin) in January 1911, and his Argentinean-born mother, Emma Plate, seems to have been related to the earlier spy, Oscar Plate; she was possibly his niece, but some of the information needed to verify this is lacking. A secret report compiled about November 1945, and based on information obtained from captured German Archives, said that Hardt had been sworn in and initiated, and had been issued with the 1930 and 1936 editions of the *Wörterbuch für Scheintelegramme* (Dictionary for Bogus Telegrams) and the *Vertrauensmännerschlüssel* (Agents' code), which had been lodged with the Consulate-General. Mathy, however, although initiated, had not been sworn in, and he had only the 1930 Dictionary. Nevertheless, Mathy, with his naval experience, remained in charge of the naval side of operations, while Hardt became the *Wirtschaftsleiter*, the commercial reporter for the overseas branch of the Nazi Party.

Hardt had extremely good Nazi connections; he was a member of the NSDAP, and on his registration with the Consulate-General he declared that he had been a member of the SS until he left Germany and was still a *Förderndes Mitglied* (supporting or auxiliary member) of the SS, which meant little more than that he paid a fee and received an SS publication. No SS card for Hardt has been found in the Berlin-Lichterfelde Archives, but records are not complete. However, Herbert's grandfather, Engelbert, had been associated in Argentina with the father of Walter Darré, Minister for Food Production in the Nazi Government and a close friend of Himmler, so the SS story was probably true, and people were wary of Hardt. As a representative of the family firm, he travelled a lot, going to Europe nearly every year and to New Zealand several times a year, so he had good opportunities to act as a courier. On the orders of Consul-General Asmis, Mathy and Hardt were 'elected' Chairman and Deputy Chairman of the German-Australian Chamber of Commerce on 29 July 1937. In these positions, they were excellently placed to collect commercial information useful for military purposes, for they

Herbert Engelbert Hardt (Courtesy of National Archives, Australia: SP1714/1, N18365: Herbert E. Hardt)

could legitimately ask questions of Australian authorities, and they could demand answers from German businessmen.

Military Police Intelligence suspected that others were involved. Otto Woelke, leader of the Brisbane branch of the Nazi Party for a time, had spent twelve years in the German navy, and he allegedly travelled extensively along the Queensland coast. In 1938, Woelke returned to Germany; his sons had already returned to do their military service, and his wife and daughter followed later. On his arrival, he was employed again by the navy. After the war, the Woelke family returned to Queensland, the Australian immigration officer in Germany being very impressed by the 'quality' of the Woelke grandchildren. It is not clear whether authorities realised what he had been doing before the war; in any case, the family belonged to the category of migrants who would make excellent citizens as long as Germany and Australia were not at war, and Woelke's activities, whether as Nazi leader or possible spy, had not attracted public hostility.

In Melbourne, attention was drawn to Hans Renz, a ship's provedore, who was leader of the Nazi Party Harbour Service (*Hafendienst*). This entailed collecting propaganda material from visiting German ships and reporting to the Party on the conduct of ship's crews, these reports being forwarded to the Gestapo. He also came under notice when he gave a lecture on 'The Foreign Intelligence Service and its workings' to a Labour Front meeting in May 1939. It sounded as though he had been a spy in the 1914-18 war, but he had merely been a naval wireless telegraphist who had seen something of how the system worked.[3]

Another man whose activities were questionable was Willi Heiler. He was Party leader in Melbourne for a time; he organised some of the *Arbeitsfront* activities, and through Dr Becker in Adelaide he reported to the Gestapo. A former naval telegraphist, he left for Sydney when Asmis wanted somebody who could take down the Morse news broadcasts from Germany. He left when his wife died suddenly in Europe; then he returned to Australia briefly, perhaps just to wind up his affairs, but his behaviour suggested a more earnest purpose. He travelled from Australia to Noumea before returning to Germany. His trip has the feel of somebody setting up a sort of clandestine system, but there is no evidence as to what it was.[4]

While both Woelke and Renz reported to Germany, they were collecting mainly political information rather than naval information, and what Heiler was doing in the way of espionage – if anything – is unknown. None of them appears on lists of *Etappe* agents compiled after the war.

The *Etappe* was tested in 1938 during the Sudetenland crisis; a crisis warning ordering preparation for action (*Spannungsbefehl*) was issued on 28 September, and withdrawn on 30 September. It appears that the Australian agents did not receive this order, but Asmis wrote to Dr Seger, the Consul in Adelaide, that during this time, without waiting for an order, he had burnt part of the 'most secret' material, which probably included the *Etappe* codes.[5]

As Mathy's legitimate business also covered New Zealand, he made a trip there early each year, possibly also on some sort of courier errand as well, the last one in January 1939. On 17 February, Mathy and his family left for a vacation in Germany and he was due to return in October, although it was probably intended that his children should stay in Germany, for both were of an age to be inducted into the Labour Service. Mathy had always said that, after having spent five years in internment in Australia during one war, he was not going to be caught in an enemy country if there was another war. Word later reached Australia that he had died in Germany in July 1943, possibly a bombing casualty.

The *Etappe* in England was dissolved in March 1939, and the unit in Australia was probably closed about the same time. Hardt left by air on 25 June, leaving behind certain material and documents; this suggests that he probably genuinely intended to return in September. Of course, he did not return. By early in 1940, he was operating again as an *Etappe* agent: in Holland in 1940 and in Spain about 1943. After the war, he claimed his right to settle in Argentina by virtue of his mother's birth in that country, but he set up new business links with Australia through Heinrich Krawinkel, son-in-law of Hermann Homburg.[6] Military Intelligence did its utmost to ensure that he never again set foot in Australia.

Josef Janssen visited Germany to see his family and returned by air shortly after Easter 1939, at a time when the more important undercover agents and political leaders were leaving Australia. His activities had gone almost unnoticed, but he was interned from 1940 to 1943. When his status as a Naval Intelligence agent was discovered after the war, steps were initiated to revoke his naturalisation, but the decision was probably not implemented.

Although the Naval Intelligence Service in Australia never operated as intended, its structure and the identity and activities of its agents are fairly clear compared with other mysterious and murky characters who engaged in secret activities for other agencies. Since it is one of the necessities of their trade, spies strive not to draw attention to themselves, so some come and go unnoticed. Count Felix von Luckner, who visited Australia in 1938, was not a spy; he was far too flamboyant and controversial to have the necessary privacy to carry out spying assignments. He was simply a propaganda agent, under the direction of Propaganda Minister Goebbels rather than the armed forces.

Günther Dorn

One man, however, was certainly a spy of some sort, although there is doubt as to the organisation to which he was attached. In his book *Boots and All*, Austin Laughlin tells the story of a man who allegedly boasted that he was 'the spy who will never be caught'. Laughlin claims that in August 1939 Military Intelligence lost sight of him until there came 'a faint tally-ho' from Western Australian, where he had been taken off the Trans-Australia train in Perth. While Laughlin's book is very unreliable, there is just enough truth in this story to identify the man as Günther Gustav Theodor Dorn, but MI had not lost sight of him, for shipping and travel agents were notifying them of bookings made by Germans, and it was noted that Dorn was to leave Melbourne by *Manunda*, with an onward booking to the Netherlands East Indies.

Günther Gustav Dorn (Courtesy of National Archives, Australia: A367, C67579: Gunther G.T. Dorn; Internment and Deportation)

Dorn was born in Wiesbaden on 16 July 1914. His family allegedly owned a hotel in Hamburg, but not much is known for certain about his background. One of the files on him alleges that he had been a 'Nerotherführer', but it was not discovered what this meant. The *Nerother* were members of one of the branches of the *Wandervögel* movement; they might be compared to heavy-duty Boy Scouts, engaging in hiking and camping and outdoor activities, but with a greater political and nationalistic component. The *Nerotherbund* was dissolved in 1933; some of the younger members transferred to the Hitler Youth – some with genuine Nazi inclinations, others with the intention of disrupting it. Some of the older members joined the *Jung-Stahlhelm*, a nationalist and militarist organisation open mainly to sons of soldiers. A membership book found among his documents showed that in 1933-35 Dorn had been a member of the *Jung-Stahlhelm* for 13 months. It was not originally a Nazi organisation, but in June 1933 it was taken over by the SA.[7] Once again, members went different ways. Some joined the SA, others the SS, while some simply left the organisation.

One interesting thing about Dorn is that he had documents of which no other copy was found in Australia, and connections in Germany that were unknown in Australia. He hung a swastika flag in his room in the Chevron Hotel in St Kilda Road and was obviously a Nazi, but he was not a Party member. He told Intelligence officers that the membership rolls for the Party had closed in 1934 or 1935, while he was still too young to join.[8] The only Nazi-associated organisation of which he was definitely a member was the *Deutsche Arbeitsfront* (DAF = German Labour Front), a

Chapter 3: The Card-Carrying Spy

group to which all employees and employers had to belong, unless their trade or profession was covered by some specialist group. He joined this in Germany on 1 June 1937 and remained a member in Australia, renewing his membership on 19 August 1939. The various Security and Intelligence organisations in Australia were composed of people of widely varying levels of experience and common sense, and one of them decided that DAF stood for *Reichsarbeitsdienst* (Labour Service). Labour service was something that one did, not something of which one was 'a member'.

Another error made by a local Security organisation – or rather by a translator employed by it – was the comment that a friend had written to him urging him to join the VDJ – *Verein Deutscher Jugend*, and the translator had commented that 'AKOTECH' appeared to be a department of this. Error within error. One is that Dorn was probably too old for the VDJ, though the upper age limit is not clear. The important one is that Akotech had nothing to do with the VDJ; it was associated with the VDI (*Verein Deutscher Ingenieure* = Association of German Engineers). At that time, many Germans habitually typed 'J' instead of 'I', and occasionally some still do. Dorn was allegedly an electrical engineer, although he was not carrying with him any documents that looked like an engineering degree or diploma, either originals or certified copies. If they had understood it, 'Akotech' would have sent cold shivers up and down the spines of any Intelligence agents who encountered it, for it stood for *Arbeitsgemeinschaft für Auslands- und Kolonialtechnik* (Study group or syndicate for foreign and colonial technology). Dorn was poking his nose into things out of which Australia wanted to keep foreign noses, especially if there was even a hint of interest being shown in the Mandated Territory of New Guinea.

A document in his Melbourne dossier gives his *Wehrdienstverhältnis* (Military service status), showing that he was 'Beurlaubt nach Australien, 3/6/38' (On leave to Australia, 3 June 1938). Unless medically unfit, Dorn should have done military service about 1936-37, but it is not entirely clear whether he did. The statement could have meant either that he had been serving and was granted leave, or that he was granted a deferment, which was usually for a period of two years. If he was a serving member of the army 'on leave', this would explain why he was not a Party member, for regulations prohibited servicemen from joining the Party.

Dorn had arrived in Sydney on 5 August 1938 aboard *Nieuw Holland*. This vessel had come from Singapore via the Netherlands East Indies and Brisbane, which was the first indication that there was something suspicious about this 'businessman'. He had spent over two weeks in Singapore in July, unusual behaviour for a new business arrival in Australia. He had allegedly submitted a report on Singapore and taken photos of 'vital points'. Although the identity of the recipient of this report is not stated, it was apparently the *Zeitungsdienst Graf Reischach*,[9] which is mentioned elsewhere in his documents, and it had little to do with his alleged business as a representative of Allgemeine Electricitäts-Aktiengesellschaft (AEG; General Electric). A passenger who travelled with him in *Nieuw Holland* reported that he had worn a Nazi badge on his lapel aboard ship, but it might not have been a Party badge.

A letter written to the Intelligence Section General Staff, about two months after Dorn arrived in Melbourne, mentions information received via an RAAF ex-serviceman reporting to Naval Intelligence that a Melbourne chemist (Maxwell Porteous) had been developing films for a German, and that they were all of industrial undertakings, bridges and wharves, never of scenery. It is mentioned in the same letter that Dorn was 'worthy of attention'.

In 1939 a branch of the Chamber of Commerce was founded in Melbourne. Arnold von Skerst, the business manager for the Sydney Chamber, was instructed to have Dorn appointed as its Melbourne representative. There can be no doubt that these instructions came from Germany, probably through the Consulate-General. When Skerst reported later that some so-called economic investigators or foreign trade experts lacked entirely any business experience, he might well have had Dorn in mind; he was not a credible representative. The recently arrived Dr Franz Joseph Haslinger, Export Manager of Auto-Union and a genuine businessman, was appointed as head of the Melbourne branch, with Dorn as his nominal deputy.

Dorn was paid directly from Germany, partly by AEG, and partly by Dychem, an Australian subsidiary of IG Farben, for which he was allegedly Melbourne representative. This alone was suspicious, for it was one of the characteristics of both German and Japanese spies that they were subsidised by or paid through two or more business firms. A diary entry for February 1939 was also suspicious: 'It's a pity I can't have a typist or stenographer but owing to the secret nature of some of my correspondence I suppose it can't be helped.'

Since the Nazi Party and the Consulates managed to find confidential typists, one must wonder in what way his correspondence was so much more secret that he could not use a typist. Later, a folder with cables and telegrams in code, together with coding and decoding of actual messages, was found among his possessions, but neither the nature of the code nor the content of the messages is on record. The identity of any organisation from which he might have been taking orders is unclear as well. It was unlikely to have been the navy, and probably not the Party, as they had other effective agents. The army or the *Abwehr* is a possibility, but there could have been a more complex arrangement. It was known that the journalists of the Graf Reischach organisation were engaged in espionage tasks, and in August 1937 several of them had been expelled from Britain for 'improper activities'. So the Reischach agency was providing cover for spies; but now the Reischach journalists themselves needed a cover story. In the case of Dorn, it seems to have been provided by AEG, through a 'Department X'. Dorn's diary for 1938 showed that he had sent Telegram No. 1 to X on 8 August and Telegram No. 3 on 21 November. What links this to AEG is a letter that Th. E. van Staveren in Batavia wrote on 19 September 1939 informing Dorn that he had written to 'Department X' of AEG. Three separate dossiers on Dorn, containing different material, were held in different locations, and nobody had a chance to join the dots and see the whole picture.

In Melbourne, Dorn took a room at the Chevron Hotel on St Kilda Road, and he became very friendly with a woman who was also staying there, a well-known Melbourne socialite, Mary Ida Kelly, known as 'Keenza'. In letters that he sent to her when they were apart, he addressed her in affectionate terms that a married man of honour would not have used to another man's fiancée. He told her he could speak Spanish and had visited South America with his wife, but his *Abmeldungsschein* – a document recording that a person left one police district for another – filled out in Berlin only a few days before he left Germany showed him as unmarried, and his passport, issued in 1936 when he was 22 years old, showed no such visit. The generally believed story was that he had married just a few weeks before leaving Germany, but a truly suspicious mind would find room for doubt whether he was married at all, or whether his alleged wife, Doris, was only a cover address for espionage information. However, there was a marriage certificate among his documents, so why did he lie on an official document, the *Abmeldungsschein*?

It is also suspicious that Dorn apparently received warning to leave Australia earlier than did more senior representatives of Dychem, or he acted upon it more promptly, but even Dorn left his escape too late. The Government Gazette of 25 August promulgated a regulation that resident aliens had to apply for an exit permit fourteen days in advance. Shipping and airline companies were to notify authorities of aliens making bookings. On 23 August 1939, a shipping company reported that Dorn was leaving Melbourne on 25 August aboard *Manunda*; he planned to join *Charon* for the Netherlands East Indies at Fremantle on 8 September.[10]

Correspondence intercepted en route from the Melbourne Consulate to the *Auslands-Organisation* (AO) in Berlin notified them that Dorn, 'a German liable for military duty', was leaving for Batavia for an indefinite period. The AO was the body controlling Nazi Party members and activities overseas, and if the Consulate notified it of Dorn's movements, it might be assumed that Dorn was a Party member, even though no registration card for him can be found. However, reports to the Gestapo on all Germans returning home were routinely channelled through the AO.[11]

Thus at the outbreak of war Dorn was trapped aboard a British ship headed for a British port. *Manunda* arrived in Albany on 4 September, but he was not arrested then, as no warrant had arrived. When he was in trouble, Dorn turned not to Dychem but to AEG. From Albany he cabled 'Eleksyd', asking for £150 to be sent to him urgently. That was the telegraphic address of AEG Sydney representative, Waldemar Weber, leader of the Sydney Nazi Party branch. Dorn received no answer, for Weber had been arrested a few hours earlier.

By the time the ship reached Fremantle the next day, a warrant was available and Dorn was taken from the ship to Roe Street lockup, then to Fremantle Prison. Dorn was a troublesome prisoner. He agitated to be removed from prison to a private hospital at his own expense, and he possibly faked illness to support his demand. There was blood and pus in his urine, except when a properly supervised sample was taken by a doctor. He might have had kidney stones, but an X-ray did not show any. He later wrote a letter to a friend outlining how he had pricked his finger to fake a kidney disease. Knowledge of how to fake illness indicates an experienced army malingerer or a trained espionage agent. Dorn was one of the very few internees who refused to state on his internment registration form when, where or whether he had done any military service. Again, the dots were not joined, for on his A42 form, a declaration made by aliens at a ship's first port of call in Australia, he had answered 'yes' to the question as to whether he had done any military service. (Brisbane, 2 August 1938)

The Kelly family was wealthy and influential; on 12 October Keenza arrived in Perth to 'look after his interests' and had permission to visit him. On 18 October, having received no answer from Weber, Dorn cabled to AEG in Batavia, but his communication was not sent because it contained a code word (QKNS) which Dorn claimed was to authenticate his request for money. Staveren sent the requested £200 without the authenticator; it arrived on 19 November. Dorn was placed aboard *Katoomba* in a comfortable cabin paid for by Kelly; she travelled by the same ship to Melbourne and was allowed to visit him twice a day, a situation that authorities vowed would not happen again.

Some of Dorn's luggage had been transferred automatically from *Manunda* to *Charon* and carried on to Soerabaya. When the cases were returned, they were searched, and an 'automatic revolver' was found in one.[12] German businessmen in Australia usually did not carry concealable weapons, licensed or not, but senior Party functionaries did. Also found was the code material mentioned, plus a book not seen in Australia before: *Spione, Verräter, Saboteure* (Spies, Traitors, Saboteurs). The book was annotated and passages had been underlined, including the sentence: 'Every German can be a carrier of secrets.' (*Geheimnisträger*) It was decided that the markings had been made when Dorn was preparing a lecture for the DAF in Melbourne, and that led to the discovery that he had been trained in a Propaganda Ministry school for political speakers.

Dorn's activities in camp were a source of annoyance. He allegedly tried to control the camp clandestinely by using threats of violence to arrange the election of his chosen nominee as Camp Leader, and once he went on a hunger strike. However, he was only a small frog in a small pond, and in the long run neither the camp authorities nor his fellow internees were impressed by his antics. When his case was reviewed on 23 January 1946, Mr Justice Simpson reported that Dorn was 'a particularly dangerous German who should not be readmitted to Australia'. He was deported on 30 November 1947 by *General Stuart Heintzelmann* and does not reappear in Australian records.

A lot of things connected with Dorn are suspicious. Although none individually is incontrovertibly incriminating, the totality looks bad, but perhaps still not quite bad enough to claim that he was definitely a spy, if it had not been for Laughlin's identification of him as such. Laughlin had been an Intelligence officer during the war. Although his book is full of untruths and deliberately misleading half-truths in detail, his overall picture is valid, and he had no doubt that Dorn was a spy. Although the CIB and MPI had made some mistakes, and there was much that they did not understand, they took the correct action. He was interned, and any information that he might have been carrying in his memory was not available to the enemy.

Louis de Jong wrote: 'In 1937, the central office of the AO was extended with a liaison section of the *Abwehr*, headed by Heinz Cohrs, so that use might be made of the many ramifications of the AO for the collection of military espionage data.'[13]

That might have been the section to which Dorn was reporting. However, the Nazi system made spies of all Party members, and to a lesser extent of all Germans abroad; they were expected to report on their work colleagues and employers, as well as on commercial and military matters. Those mentioned here went somewhat beyond this duty.

Chapter 4

The Neurotic Chameleon

One of the strangest characters in Australia between the wars was a man who arrived at Port Adelaide aboard *Essen* on 9 October 1926 with a passport giving his name as Richard Rudolf Johannes Bohn.[1] During the next fourteen years, he used at least five names, gave two different dates and places of birth, and two different dates and vessels of entry. He claimed that he:

- had worked for the German, Spanish, Soviet and Chinese Intelligence Services;

- had known Hitler personally when Hitler was associating with Munich communists;

- had been a cadet at a military academy in Stuttgart when Rommel was instructor there;

- was a cousin of the Count Anton von Arco-Valley who had assassinated Kurt Eisner, the Socialist Premier of Bavaria, in 1919;

- had been an officer of the Spanish Foreign Legion under Franco in Morocco; and

- was a school friend of Count Claus Schenk von Stauffenberg, who planted the bomb meant to assassinate Hitler on 20 July 1944.

The Commonwealth Investigation Branch and Military Police Intelligence could not work out which of his stories to believe, if any: whether he had lived an adventurous life and was dangerous, or whether he was a pathetic, delusional liar. Paranoid or otherwise, he slept with a gun under his pillow, for he was genuinely afraid.

Mysterious Background

In front of every statement that Bohn made, a mental 'alleged' or 'allegedly' or 'claimed' must be inserted, unless there is documentary evidence. From a national security point of view, he first attracted 'unfavourable attention' from authorities in June 1938 while in Mount Isa, but it is perhaps a little less confusing to follow his story – or stories – chronologically. He had grown up in Stuttgart believing that he had been born in Neu-Ulm, Bavaria, on 13 May 1903. His father, who was connected with the police force in Stuttgart, was Julius August Bohn, or Julian Maximilian von Bohn. His mother, according to a statement made in 1940, was Sophie Anne Marie von Stauffenberg, which would seem like another of his fantasies

Chapter 4: The Neurotic Chameleon

linking himself with the famous and infamous, except that he gave this name *before* Count Claus Schenk von Stauffenberg planted a bomb under Hitler's table, and at that time it had no particular significance.

On his eighteenth birthday, so he stated, he had been approached by Count Anton Phillip von Arco-Valley, who claimed him as his son, Alexander Nicolai von Arco-Valley, born in Smolensk in Russia on 18 May 1903. He claimed that the von Arco-Valley family would not recognise Anton's secret marriage in Vienna to Mathilde von Bohn and had it annulled; she had then been sent to the family of a friend on the Russian Military Information Staff in Smolensk, where Alexander was born. She had died when he was young, and he had been entrusted to the Bohns to take the place of their son, who had died in infancy. His age when this allegedly happened is not indicated, but there is an indication that he could speak some Russian, so he may not have been still an infant. Nothing else about his childhood is mentioned. Anton von Arco-Valley had allegedly served in Asia Minor under General Liman von Sanders and commanded a Turkish division during the war.[2]

Richard Rudolf Bohn (Courtesy of National Archives, Australia: A659, 1939/1/15127: Von Arco-Bohn, R – Naturalisation)

Either Bohn was an amazing fantasist with a passion for intrigue and a taste for name-dropping, or he really was a member of the Arco-Valley family, in which case much of what he claimed would have been possible. He allegedly entered the army in May 1920 or January 1921, and at various times was at a Military Academy in Munich, with the 18th 'Light Horse' in Stuttgart where, according to his claims, Erwin Rommel had been one of his instructors, at the same time studying geology at some University.[3]

He claimed that in 1924 he was sent to Lithuania and/or Leningrad on a trial espionage mission; it is true that German Intelligence was operating in Lithuania at that time in connection with Memelland, but Bohn's involvement cannot be checked. He then trained with 'Special Branch' Berlin in preparation for Staff College, followed by nine months Special Police training in Karlsruhe. In 1925, he was a lieutenant with a German advisory group attached to the Spanish Foreign Legion (*Tercio de Extranjeros*), as adjutant to one of Colonel Francisco Franco's staff officers. He crossed several times through the lines as an envoy to contact the Riff leader, Abdul Karim (Abd el Krim), while at the same time carrying out certain unspecified German plans. This could be dismissed as another of his fantasies, but the bullet wound in his right knee was genuine.

When he was interned in 1940, he stated on one form that he had served in the army 1921-1926, on another form that he had no military service at all. At another time, Bohn claimed he had joined the Nazi Party in 1921 and had been an instructor with the Hitler Youth; however, by 1921 he was also allegedly in the army, and serving members of the armed forces were forbidden to join political parties, while the Hitler Youth was not formed until 1926, by which time he was allegedly in Morocco.

He claimed that he was very much attached to England, and when ordered to carry out a secret mission against England in May 1926 he refused, caught a ship back to Spain, thence went to Germany and reported to his headquarters, where he was placed under arrest awaiting trial on a charge of high treason. On the day of his trial, he was left alone in an empty room. His father (Arco-Valley, not Bohn) had died, but an uncle had influential friends, and a man appeared with a false passport and instructions to leave immediately via Belgium for Australia, picking up certain materials in Aachen on the way. The court allegedly sentenced him in absentia to ten years' imprisonment.[4]

A fraction of this can be proven, for a passport, issued in Stuttgart on 16 July 1926 for Richard Rudolf Johannes Bohn, merchant, bears a Belgian entry stamp dated 11 August, Aix-la-Chapelle (Aachen).

In Antwerp, Captain Orgel of *Essen* arranged for him to be smuggled aboard and hidden until the ship sailed. His passport shows that he did sail from Antwerp aboard *Essen* in 1926. Bohn arrived in Adelaide on 9 October 1926, possibly as a crew member. He claimed that Orgel knew his story and had taken him aboard because they were both members of an organisation known as *Kreuz und Adler* (Cross and Eagle), which he said aimed at separating Catholic Bavaria from Protestant Prussia and uniting it with Catholic Austria under a Habsburg monarch. He alleged that both Hitler and Göring had been members of this organisation in 1921, but had betrayed it.[5]

Here again we seem to be in fantasyland, for the only *Kreuz und Adler* to which reference can be found is the one that was founded by Franz von Papen in April 1933 and dissolved in October the same year. Its aim was to unite Catholic laymen against communism, but reports of its stance towards Nazism are contradictory. It did not exist in 1926, much less in 1921. He also claimed to be a member of a secret organisation known as RR (Revenge Röhm). Obviously, since Röhm was killed in June 1934, this organisation also could not have existed in 1926. However, he could have had in mind a desire to avenge not Röhm but Otto Ballerstedt, leader of the *Bayernbund* (Bavarian League, also known as the *Bayerischer Heimat- und Königsbund*).

Chapter 4: The Neurotic Chameleon

Australian Exploits

Bohn settled in Adelaide, and in May 1928 he married seventeen-year-old Jean Walton, under the name Count Richard Rudolf Johann von Bohn-Boham. Their daughter, Olga Jean Agnes, was born in September. His father's brother insisted that he return to Germany, a pardon having been arranged, but first his marriage would have to be annulled; this he refused to allow. These communications came through the family's representative in Australia, 'Dr Kirchner', who travelled from Sydney to Adelaide to interview Bohn. There were a number of persons named Kirchner in Sydney, and the precise identity of the alleged go-between – if he existed – cannot be established.

In 1931, he was allegedly contacted by a former colleague, Maximilian Stolle, who had been working for German Intelligence at the same time as Bohn, then after 1926 or 1929 for Soviet Intelligence. At that time, there were many German officers in the Soviet Union, owing to arrangements for secret military training, in particular of the Luftwaffe. But the only Stolle on lists of alien passengers entering Australia, 1927-1939, was an Erich Stolle, passenger in *Orsova*, who landed at Melbourne on 23 September 1929. However, the A42 index of returns of alien passengers is not complete, and an Intelligence agent could well have been issued with a passport in a false name.[6]

Bohn certainly had more than a casual interest in the Soviet Union. He spoke some Russian and was apparently in contact with a Sophie Olga Bohn in Leningrad. Although his itinerant life-style meant that he travelled light and had few possessions, the authorities found later that he had kept press clippings relating to the trial and execution in June 1937 of senior Soviet army officers for alleged treason.

Bohn deserted his wife and child and headed for Alice Springs in August or September 1932, having stolen and sold his father-in-law's horse. This attracted the attention of the police, but not the Commonwealth Investigation Branch, as it had no security implications. In the Northern Territory, he worked at various mining sites, including at a tantalite mine, and it could have been in connection with Krupp's search for sources of tantalite for the armaments industry that Baron von Freyberg contacted him in early 1934.

Major Baron Egloff von Freyberg[7] arrived in Adelaide in late November 1933. A well-known pilot during the war, he was involved in building up the secret Luftwaffe, and it is hard to believe that he would spend months touring Australia indulging his interest in geology and natural history. Going north from Adelaide, he visited Hermannsburg Mission and allegedly spent six weeks on a cattle property in Central Australia. Bohn claimed later that Freyberg was Chief of German Army Intelligence Staff and had visited Australia to contact all German Army Intelligence men while playing the part of a tourist. Still, he would hardly have found many Intelligence agents on a cattle property in Central Australia, so another ulterior motive needs to be sought. The clue may be in his geological interests: the Northern Territory was one of the world's richest sources of tantalite, which was vital for military purposes. When Freyberg continued on to New Guinea, his presence in Rabaul was noted. He arrived in Sydney from Rabaul aboard *Malaita* on 11 May 1934, and left in *Magdeburg* on 22 May, and it is simply not known how much of his trip might have had a military purpose. It is hard to imagine that it would have had none.

On 28 March 1934 while still in Alice Springs, Bohn applied for naturalisation, almost immediately after Freyberg's visit. In his application he gave his name as Richard Rudolph Franz Nikolai von Arco-Bohn, of Russian nationality, born in Smolensk, and claimed that his father, named this time as Julius August Petrovich von Arco-Bohn, had been an officer in the Imperial household of Tsar Nicholas II and had perished with the Imperial family. In correspondence he alleged that the Hitler *Putsch* of November 1923 was intended to set up the Habsburg monarchy over Bavaria and Austria (although Hitler had in fact condemned this movement) and that Hitler betrayed the names of the members of the movement, as a result of which he and others were court-martialled. This does not make sense, nor does it tie in with his other claims, especially the claim of service in Morocco. Naturalisation was refused in October.

Bohn left Alice Springs for Tennant Creek about February 1936, and claimed he left the latter in September 1937. However, on 16 November 1937 he sent the German Consul-General a telegram (using the Bentley commercial code) saying that he had discovered the outline of a plot to kill Hitler, and that he would reveal this if Asmis sent him the fare (£47) to Sydney, and this telegram was lodged at Tennant Creek. Dr Asmis, suspicious of the claim, wired him to send more information. Bohn wired back that this was not possible, as he had to leave for China.[8]

Asmis refused the money but referred the claim to the Foreign Office in Berlin. The CIB also became interested in Bohn, for the local Postmaster reported the telegram to them immediately, adding: 'Well known in Tennant Creek, been there for 18 months. Was in the Post Office 15 minutes ago and appeared quite normal – no obvious mental instability.'

Bohn must have left Tennant Creek soon after this, for he was in Mount Isa in February 1938 when Stolle, allegedly on a second visit to Australia, allegedly asked Bohn to find out the name of a German Intelligence agent working in Mount Isa Mines. Bohn did not say whether he attempted to do this, but it was known that now – with or without cause – he became frightened and slept with a pistol under his pillow. However, while claiming to be afraid of being murdered on account of his previous

Chapter 4: The Neurotic Chameleon

activities, he made no attempt to hide these, recounting them to many people he met. He claimed that Stolle also told him that Kenichiro Yoneda, Sydney representative of Yamashita Kisen Kaisha (Steamship Company) was operative head of Japanese espionage in Australia. Stolle, who was allegedly attached to the staff of General Brusilov [Brussiloff], one of the generals who were executed by Stalin in 1937 and 1938, had (again allegedly) been sent to Australia to gather information about Japanese intentions in the South Pacific. Again, Stolle's presence cannot be verified, but some of the story makes sense, and a Combined Operational Intelligence Centre Appreciation in January 1941 also reported that Yoneda, whose secret name was 'The Tiger', was controller of Japanese espionage in Australia. It is a mystery how Bohn could have known this unless he had connections with some Secret Service.

In June 1938, Bohn left Mount Isa and worked along the North Queensland coast. He went first to Herberton, then in December to a tantalite mine at Forsyth, thirty miles west of Cairns. He claimed that he had gone aboard the yacht *Seeteufel* in August to visit Count von Luckner, whom he had met in Stuttgart in 1921, and who related to the Arco-Valley family, and that he had seen that some of the charts used by Luckner had Japanese annotations. At about this time, he offered his services and his knowledge of Japanese Intelligence in Australia to the Chinese Consul-General, Dr Pao, and when he had been drinking too much, he boasted that he was in contact with the Chinese Secret Service. On another occasion he claimed he was investigating Russian and Japanese activities in New Guinea of behalf of British Intelligence. He also said that Stolle had offered him a post with Soviet Military Intelligence and he was to leave Australia in December 1938. In fact, at that time he was trying to obtain a mining job in Fiji.

In Innisfail in October 1938, after an alcohol-fuelled row with another German, Hans Peukert, he was denounced as an illegal immigrant. At the time, he was using the name Alexander Erickson (or Eriksen), and he now claimed that he had left Austria when Hitler marched into the country (untrue); that he had recently returned from Russia where he had been working as a mining engineer (untrue); that he had landed illegally in Sydney from SS *Liverpool* in mid 1938 (untrue), and that he would be returning to Russia to join the Secret Police to raise support for another attempt on Hitler's life. He also told Peukert that his cousin had tried to assassinate Hitler in 1934. Peukert, a seaman deserter, was a Nazi Party member, and he claimed 'Erickson' owed him money, but there was a woman of doubtful character involved somehow in their altercation. Clandestinely searching Bohn's belongings in his hotel, Peukert found the hand-delivered letter, allegedly written from Leningrad by Sophie Olga von Bohn and addressed not to Richard Bohn but to Alexander von

Arco-Valley. This would seem to prove that he was indeed Arco-Valley, but as the letter had no post-mark he could have written it to himself. It contained material written in code, and on 15 December Peukert reported the situation to Asmis. He did not mind if his own status as an illegal immigrant was discovered, for he planned to leave in January anyway. Peukert's own activities were of a dubious nature, for there seemed to have been no valid reason for him to have been given a deferment of military service just to jump ship and work in Australia for a year or so. Under the influence of alcohol, Peukert would boast that he belonged to the SA and had been a member of Göring's bodyguard, but that is a different story.

In July 1939, Bohn was in Brisbane; then he went to work in the mines at Drake in New South Wales. During his stay there, the mines were visited by Yoneda. He applied again for naturalisation in October 1939, but this was refused, and the CIB reported: 'It is questionable if he is maliciously dangerous but may possibly become a nuisance on account of his intense stupidity.' Registered as an alien under the name Alexander Erickson, he had had so little contact with German social circles, and moved around so much in isolated areas, that he was not interned until 6 June 1940, when it was noticed that in May he had gone from Drake to Sydney without the necessary permit, and had tried to enlist is the army as Alexander Arco (or Arko).

Internment and Aftermath

Bohn was sent to Loveday internment camp in South Australia and a 1941 report from there said: 'We believe that he is an unblushing liar... He seems to have a passion for intrigue, real or imaginary, and in our opinion is a most dangerous man. He professes anti-Nazi sentiments, but his assertions are worthless.' In order to obtain the allowance that the German Government allotted to internees (*Reichsgeld*), he signed a declaration that he was loyal to the *Reich* and would take the first opportunity to return to Germany. An Intelligence report in August 1943 said that his correspondence gave the impression that he was 'a very dubious customer' and might have been 'a German agent of a very unpleasant kind', but it was reported in May 1944 that Bohn had 'burnt his boats' and sent a letter to the Swiss Consul, for transmission to the German Government, that they were 'a gang of mental derelicts', that nobody under the protection of the British flag need fear them, and his greatest regret was that he had not been able to do anything to hasten their downfall. His allowance was stopped.

The most complete, consistent and possibly truthful account of his life is in an eight-page statement he wrote on 20 August 1945, a few days after the end of the war in the Pacific; it endorses the changeling-child story. In it he mentions that the Count who made tried to assassinate Hitler in July 1944 had been a school friend of his. As Count Claus Schenk von

Chapter 4: The Neurotic Chameleon

Stauffenberg was four years younger than Bohn, this is unlikely, but his brothers Berthold and Alexander were about the same age as Bohn, and the papers had not given Stauffenberg's Christian name. Besides, Bohn's (foster?) mother was apparently a member of the Stauffenberg family. He was allowed to remain in Australia, as it was considered that he was not intelligent enough to do much harm of his own accord and was too indiscreet for any foreign Intelligence Service to think of employing him. Released on 7 February 1946, Bohn return to Drake for a while; then he went to Cobar, then on to Captain's Flat. His qualifications in geology at least appear to have been genuine.

For several years after the war, Bohn's sister or foster-sister, Mrs Olga Schmalzried, tried to establish contact with him. On 13 October 1947, she wrote from Lorch in Westphalia to Australia House in London, giving information that might help to identify and trace him. Their last contact, she wrote, had been a letter written in May 1940 (before he left Drake) and forwarded through Russia. She gave his particulars as Dr Richard August Heinrich Bohn, mining engineer, who had arrived in Australia in 1933 (wrong, 1926) and married Jean Walton in the same year (wrong, 1928). He had, she wrote, visited Germany with his wife and daughter Olga in 1934, 1937 and 1939. Wrong; his location in Australia at those times was on record; he had not seen his wife and daughter since 1932, and his wife had instituted divorce proceedings in 1937.[9]

As so much of this is wrong, and the writer was probably not deliberately lying, one explanation that seems to make sense is that they did not meet on these alleged visits, but he wrote to her giving this information, possibly having somebody post letters in Germany on his behalf.

A further inquiry from Olga Schmalzried on 4 February 1949 was referred to the Commonwealth Investigation Service, and there was yet another inquiry via the Swiss Consul on 19 October 1950. They identified him, under a slightly different name, but he had not been registered as an alien since July 1947, when he was at Captain's Flat. They found that he had left there in April 1949, and there was no further trace of him. There was no naturalisation record under any of the names he was known to have used; no record was found of his departure from Australia. They found no further trace of him, for apparently he died in Sydney in 1949. The only other record found that is in any way linked to him is an application for a passport for Sophie Agnes Jean Olga von Bohn Boham in 1947, with a request for a visa to transit Italy en route to Trieste. That was clearly his daughter, who was then aged eighteen. It was not a good time for a young girl to travel alone to that area. Had she made some contact with the Bohn family?

The Most Dangerous Man in Australia?

A question mark remained over his true identity, and whether he was a spy, and if so, for whom. It is impossible to determine how many of his fantasies were true. He was probably not a danger to Australia, except that the time wasted in trying to figure out who or what he was could have been utilised better. There is a saying that a liar needs a good memory. Bohn or Arco, or whatever his name was, seemed quite unabashed about telling different stories to the same person. Those who attack Australia's internment policy during the war might ponder how they would have handled a case like that of Richard Bohn – or Nikolai von Arco – or Alexander Eriksen. Pity the Security Service personnel who tried to make sense of him!

Chapter 5

The Attorney-General

In books and articles, writers have told heart-rending tales of the injustice done to Hermann Homburg, his forced resignation from the position of Attorney-General of South Australia during the First World War and his internment in the Second. Poor loyal misunderstood Homburg, who was persecuted unjustly by the military authorities, although he had been born in Australia, and who was forced to resign simply because he had a German name! The sympathy is somewhat misplaced. There were others with German names in South Australian public life. The authorities did not just put their names in a hat and happen to pull out 'Homburg'. There were reasons why Hermann Homburg was singled out. He was an egotistical hypocrite, a perjurer, a solicitor and politician skilled in misleading people with half-truths and emotional obfuscation. A fairly tall man and built to match, he could be physically intimidating. He was arrogant, a bully to his family, overweeningly ambitious. This may seem an unduly harsh judgment; but the facts set out here largely confirm it.

Hermann Homburg (Courtesy of the State Library of South Australia, SLSA: B4614 – Executive Council, inc. Hermann Homburg, 1927. [Section of photo only.])

Let it be said at the outset: Homburg was not a spy. He did not consider himself to be a Nazi, although he was strongly anti-Semitic. He might not have thought that his support for Germany's commercial and political interests could be detrimental to Australia. However, a man who had so much power, who relished using it and wanted more, who was strongly attached to German ways, and who considered himself too important to need to comply with even elementary wartime regulations, had to be curbed.

Family Background

Because of the important part that their family and national background played in their attitudes, actions and fates, it is instructive to consider this in some detail. (If genealogy bores you, skip the next few paragraphs.) Hermann's grandfather, Friedrich Wilhelm Adolph Homburg from Brunswick, allegedly left Germany in 1853 and arrived in Melbourne in 1854.[1]

Some sources assume that his wife and children arrived at the same time; others claim that they followed about a year later, when Hermann's father, Robert, was about six years old.

According to most reports, the family left the Victorian goldfields for Tanunda in South Australia in 1856.[2] Robert's father died in May 1860 aged only forty-four. They did not belong to the pious rural folk who had left Prussia for the sake of their faith; nor did they fit exactly into the pattern of the turbulent, revolutionary '48ers. On 30 April 1873, Robert married seventeen-year-old Emilie Margarethe Marie Peters, who had been born in South Australia in June 1855 to German parents who had arrived in September 1849 aboard *Ocean*, the ship famous for having evaded the Danish blockade under the guise of a Russian ship, *Wolga*. Hermann Robert Homburg, their first child, was born on 17 March 1874. They had two more children, Robert in 1876 and Thusnelda in 1878, before Emilie died on 17 May 1882 of tuberculosis, when Hermann was just eight years old.[3]

On 16 October 1882, Robert married Johanna (Johanne) Elisabeth Fischer, born in Australia in 1856 to German parents.[4] There were five children of this second marriage: John (1886), Fritz (2 September 1887) and three girls: Hansie, Gerta and Gretchen.[5]

The eldest of eight children, Hermann ruled the roost. It is a matter of perspective whether he took care of his siblings or bullied them. It was not until November 1883, when he was considering a political career after 27 years in South Australia, that Robert applied for naturalisation. (This was granted in December; his father was apparently never naturalised.) The family prospered in the late nineteenth and early twentieth centuries and enjoyed a good reputation and high status. Robert was State Attorney-General from 1890 to 1893 and again from 1904 until 1905, when he was appointed Justice of the Supreme Court. He died in 1912. He lived long enough to see at least four of his children married and settled with children of their own.

Hermann Homburg followed his father into law and politics. In 1897, Hermann joined his father's legal firm, which became Homburg, Melrose & Homburg, and on 29 November he married Emma Lydia Louise (Louisa) Herring. Her mother, Catherine Hicks Campbell, was of Scottish ancestry, and her father Frederick was the son of John Morris Herring and Louisa Balls. Hermann and Emma had three children: Reta (1899), Renolf (1906) and Marsi (1910). Hermann entered Parliament in 1906 as member for Murray and became Attorney-General in 1909. Life had been kind to them and their world looked good – until 1914.

World War I

Early in the war, Major John Leslie Hardie – later a major-general – called on Homburg in his office and a probably hostile interview ensued.[7] There are several myths circulating concerning this occurrence. It was not the case that 'two military officers entered his office with fixed bayonets', as Harmstorf writes and Everard Leske repeats (without attribution). If Harmstorf or Leske had had any military experience, they should have known that officers do not carry rifles with fixed bayonets. He may have been accompanied by one or more soldiers, with or without rifles and bayonets, but that would not really have been necessary. Homburg was not 'arrested in his own office', as Al Grassby (former Minister for Immigration) writes in his introduction to Harmstorf's book; in fact, Homburg was neither arrested nor interned in the First World War. Imaginations have run wild here. Unfortunately, if a written record of this visit exists, it is not available.

One result of this visit, and of other circumstances, was that Hermann Homburg resigned from the position of Attorney-General in January 1915 and did not stand in the election of 27 March. His brother Robert, who had been a member of the Adelaide City Council in 1911 and Member of the House of Assembly for Burra Burra since 1912, also resigned. Another myth is that Hermann resigned as a result of the hostility aroused when casualty lists from Gallipoli began to appear. As he resigned in January and the first Gallipoli landing was on 25 April, this too is obviously ridiculous. They resigned because they had attracted so much hostility that it would have damaged their party if they had stood for election in March. In the *Australian Dictionary of Biography*, Harmstorf writes of 'gross slanders' about Robert, so what were the accusations against the Homburgs, and what were the sources?

In many cases, there is a problem obtaining information relating to World War I dossiers; in Homburg's case, the problem is worse. One would expect that there would be a voluminous dossier on him running into five or six archival boxes, but the Adelaide file bearing his name is quite meagre. This situation gives the impression that Homburg may have used his not inconsiderable personal power to have his main dossier destroyed or severely culled. However, his power did not extend to his files in Melbourne and Canberra, or to having somebody trawl through other files to remove any mention of him. His Canberra dossier runs to over 700 pages. Owing to the bureaucracy's practice of making multiple copies of reports, there is a lot of material scattered around, but there is an impression that important information relating to the Homburgs and World War I has been lost permanently: for example, the originals or full transcripts of letters of which there are only partial transcripts in other people's files. There would normally be reports from both the police and the army on file. His parliamentary colleagues and possibly legal associates would have been asked for information. As it is, there is a copy of only one contemporary letter, a very important one, and some comments collected years later about the Homburg family in the First World War.

The most telling denunciation was written in 1916 to the Minister for Defence, Sir George Pearce, by Reginald Arnold Fraser, husband of Hermann's sister Thusnelda. Fraser wrote that he gave the information reluctantly, as any action taken against the Homburgs would reflect upon him and his own family, but that he felt that his action was necessary. He reported that John was loyal, but Fritz was not; Robert was the 'arch-traitor', but Hermann was shrewder. This is strange, for he made no specific charges against Robert, but he wrote that, when heavy Australian casualty lists were coming through, Hermann had said that 'it would be a good thing for a few thousand Australians to be shot off as they were mostly loafers', and Fritz had agreed with him. Fritz expressed regret that he could not fight for Germany and said that, if conscription came, he would do something to get himself interned rather than fight for Australia. Unmarried and aged twenty-six at the outbreak of war, Fritz would have been conscripted if the 1916 referendum had been passed. Regarding Hermann, Fraser put it bluntly:

> I disbelieved many of the statements reported of him, simply because it surpassed my comprehension that any man Australian born, who had lived under the freedom of our rule, and of British rule, who had been elected, irrespective of his lineage, to a Parliament in a British possession… could be such a bastard as to be in the slightest degree disloyal to the country that had given him his all.

According to Fraser, another brother-in-law, H. J. Brewster-Jones, had stopped visiting rather than listen to the disloyal utterances. His wife Gerta, however, had allegedly said at a dinner party in November 1914 that the Kaiser was *her* King. The police reported in September 1916 that there were 'disturbing rumours' about Fritz Homburg. A later report commented that the best that could be said of Hermann Homburg's actions was that they 'lacked enthusiasm for the British cause'. No specific complaints about Robert are on record, and none at all about John, who had moved to Murray Bridge, away from the influence of his brothers. Like Robert, he had not married a woman of German descent, and they did not run their household along German lines. No overt action was taken as a result of Fraser's letter, but it was filed for reference.

Between the Wars

After the war, the Homburgs recovered their social position fairly quickly. Hermann was re-elected to the House of Assembly for Murray in 1927 and was appointed Attorney-General again; he lost his seat in 1930, but was elected to the Legislative Council in 1933. Robert returned to the Adelaide City Council in 1934 and was for a time Acting Lord Mayor. John was a councillor at Murray Bridge for fifteen years, and Fritz was a councillor at Tanunda for twenty years, being Chairman for much of this time. It could be considered that the Homburg brothers served their communities diligently and took their civic responsibilities seriously. Another interpretation was that the Homburg brothers were too big for their boots: that they were ambitious, power-hungry and dangerous, especially in the case of Hermann.

In 1920, Hermann's elder daughter, Reta, married Heinrich Krawinkel, who had arrived in Australia in October 1912 (per *Seydlitz*). According to her aunt (Emma Homburg's younger sister, Maud Prisk née Herring), Reta had said that she would never marry an Englishman or an Australian, but Hermann had given his consent only on condition that Krawinkel become naturalised, and that he should always reside in South Australia. Reta was twenty-one, and legally she did not need her father's consent, but it was difficult for any of Homburg's family to escape his domination. Homburg tried unsuccessfully to hasten the naturalisation process so that his daughter would not become an alien when she married. 'The idea is most distasteful to me,' he wrote. They married on 27 October 1920, and Krawinkel was naturalised on 11 January 1921. When he was obeyed, Hermann could be generous; he set Krawinkel up in business and was probably behind his appointment as Honorary German Consul in 1927, a position from which he had to resign on 28 November 1930 when his firm went bankrupt.

Krawinkel claimed that his great-grandfather had fought at Waterloo in 1815, and being of Hanoverian descent he preferred to live under British rule. In 1922-23, the Krawinkels visited Germany with their baby daughter (Marie), Reta's mother and her young sister, Marsi. One of Heinrich's brothers had been killed during the war, and he wanted to arrange for his parents and his remaining brother, Karl, to join him in Australia. His parents did not, but Karl arrived in August 1924; largely for business reasons, Karl joined the Nazi Party in 1936, which gave their combined business enterprises access to German trading contracts and barter trading permits, but it made things difficult for them both when war broke out.

Hermann and Renolf also made a trip to Europe, leaving on 15 November 1928 by *Otranto*; Hermann attended to some government business while in London. One of the false claims made against the Homburgs was that

Renolf had spent some time in the German army while away. As they had spent only about two weeks in Germany, and the German army was still under severe restrictions at the time, this was ridiculous. Equally ridiculous is the claim that they were out of Australia for only two weeks; there were no airline services at the time, and two weeks would not have been sufficient for a round trip by ship from Adelaide to Singapore. They returned to Adelaide by *Ormonde*, having arrived in Fremantle on 25 June 1929. Krawinkel had obviously accompanied them during part of this trip, for he returned on this same voyage.

It was not until after Hitler came to power in January 1933 that the Homburg-Krawinkel family embarked on a course that would bring trouble upon them. When the Consul-General, Dr Rudolf Asmis, paid an official visit to South Australia, it was natural that he should meet Homburg, one of Adelaide's most prominent citizens of German descent, and Krawinkel, the former Honorary Consul. As Homburg was determined that Krawinkel should regain this position when his business was back on a sound footing, they were very cordial to Asmis. Late in 1933, Asmis approached Germans of good financial standing to invest in shares in the weekly magazine to be published by the German *Bund*; in December Homburg wrote to Asmis saying that this would place him, as a Member of Parliament, in an embarrassing position. It would indeed, if it became known that Homburg had given financial support to what was obviously going to become the official Australian mouthpiece of the Nazi Party. He referred Asmis to Krawinkel, who donated money ostensibly to support the foundation of a German Secondary School in Melbourne. Asmis diverted all the money raised for the German school to the Nazi magazine, and it was all lost.

In June 1934, the *Queensländer Herald* published an infamous and untruthful attack by Dr Becker, the Nazi Party leader for Australia, on the influence of Jews in the German clubs. As a result, the South Australian German Club passed an ill-considered motion banning members of any political party from becoming active (voting) members; this was refined in September to exclude only members of 'foreign or international political parties'. While this excluded Nazis and communists, its specific target was Becker. Krawinkel made a deal with Becker: if Krawinkel could have the ruling overturned, Becker would support his efforts to regain the position of Honorary Consul. In March 1935, Krawinkel succeeded. Becker did not attempt to join the Club, but in the next few months enough new members were admitted, both Party members and sympathisers, for the Nazi Party to take control of the committee. Krawinkel carried out his part of the bargain, but Becker did not, for the Party could only recommend; the Foreign Office made appointments, and Becker had too many enemies there.

Chapter 5: The Attorney General

The grubby, underhand deal was obvious to Club members. In November 1935, Krawinkel wrote ruefully to Dr Hellenthal, Acting Consul-General during the absence of Asmis, that the Club was on the verge of splitting and he could not prevent it: 'As I have always spoken in favour of Dr Becker and the Party, I am marked as a "Hitlerite in disguise"...' He was marked not only by Club members, but by the Commonwealth Investigation Branch and Military Police Intelligence, which followed his other activities closely.

On 7 February 1935 the German-Australian Centennial Committee had already been formed with Krawinkel as Chairman. The association worked to restore the original names of Hahndorf, Lobethal and Klemzig, which had been changed during World War I. It was only a token gesture, for many other German names had been lost at the same time. While Krawinkel was the public front for the endeavour, Homburg worked behind the scenes on his political colleagues. They also planned to raise money to refurbish Klemzig pioneer cemetery and erect a memorial, and to put up a monument to Carl Linger, a South Australian composer of German descent, who had written the music to *Song of Australia*.[8]

Later, Becker confirmed that Homburg had been behind the movement to restore the place names, but had used his son-in-law's name. In 1937, when the Centenary celebrations were over, it was decided to keep the group together as the South Australian German Historical Society. Krawinkel remained as Chairman.

In 1937, Mrs Emma Homburg and Marsi paid a lengthy visit to Europe. *Die Brücke* reported that the South Australian Historical Society (Krawinkel) had asked Miss Homburg (his sister-in-law) to establish personal contacts with Pastor Grollmus of Klemzig, who had been contacted previously with regard to the Centennial celebrations. Klemzig had been the home of the earliest German settlers in South Australia, but *not* of the Homburgs, nor apparently of the women whom they had married. Emma and Marsi attended the Coronation of George VI on 12 May, and in early July they spent four days in Klemzig. On 4 July, they attended a service in the old wooden church where Pastor Kavel, leader of the early migrants, had preached, and Marsi gave a talk in German at the pastor's house. Homburg later tried to play down the Nazi connections of their trip by emphasising these aspects, but the women spent much of August and September going from one Nazi event to another, and Marsi had spoken of this so widely that his deceit merely helped discredit anything he said.

They attended the Congress of the *Ausland-Institut*, which by then was thoroughly under Nazi control. They were treated as official representatives of Australian *Deutschtum*, being escorted around Stuttgart by the local leader of the *Frauenschaft*, the Nazi women's organisation. Marsi was interviewed by the press, and the *National Socialist Courier* of 5 August 1937 ran a report headed: 'They want to see the Fuehrer. Halfway across the World to the Homeland'. When asked how she liked the New Germany, Marsi answered, 'Oh, immensely. It has become quite different from when we were here last time in 1923.' She said that they would be going to the Nuremberg *Reichsparteitag*, adding:

> We want to see the Fuehrer! ... The sensible people, especially those who have known Germany before are full of admiration and respect for the Fuehrer and what he has done. My father ... is always working for folk-German interests.

The paper reported that they would be 'champions of the New Reich in their distant home'. Marsi returned as a publicist for *Deutschtum* and Nazism. Shortly after her return, she was crowned Queen of a carnival at Hahndorf, and speaking in German she gave a message from 'our people'. She also allegedly began wearing a Nazi badge in public. It could not have been a Party membership badge, although some people thought it was.

On the recommendation of Dr Becker and Dr Hellenthal, Acting Consul-General, the *Ausland-Institut* in Stuttgart awarded Krawinkel a bronze plaque by for services to Germanism. In return, Homburg tried to use his legal and political influence to get Becker a permit to practise medicine in South Australia.

Homburg tried to make his son, Renolf, a clone of himself, but he had bullied the lad so much that he was rather spineless. Renolf was taken into the legal firm, which became Homburg, Melrose, Homburg & Homburg, and Security authorities reported, probably erroneously, that Hermann forced him to stand for parliament in a seat that he had no chance of winning.[9] He took to drinking and driving. One of the secretaries in the legal office reported in 1945 that Renolf had appeared before the court several times for disorderly driving and drinking in his car, but Hermann had always managed to keep this out of the papers. Nowadays there would be quite a fuss made if it became known that a parliamentarian tried to do this, but those were different times.

In January 1938, the Homburgs and Krawinkels went on holiday at Glenelg. Several years later, a fellow guest stated that Marie Krawinkel, then sixteen years old, had asked her mother: 'If there was a war, who would Uncle Rene fight for?'

Reta had replied, 'Sh, Marie, we don't talk about that.'

By 1938 a career Consul, Dr Oscar Seger, had been appointed to Adelaide, and Krawinkel had little more to gain by being friendly to the Nazis. Seger reported to the Foreign Office that Krawinkel was now opposed to the 'New Germany', and Ilma Bohlmann, a regular informant, had written the same to the *Ausland-Institut* in a report that would automatically have been forwarded to the Gestapo. As a result of Hermann Homburg's pressure and manipulation, Krawinkel was in trouble with everyone.

Fritz Homburg operated in a different milieu. Chairman of the Tanunda District Council, auctioneer, real estate agent, director of E. Schrapel & Son (one of Tanunda's main stores), co-owner with Charles Goers of the Tanunda-based *Barossa News*, and conductor of the Tanunda *Liedertafel* (the German choir), he was the most powerful man in Tanunda, and he helped keep it a German town. In December 1920, he married Viola Mathilde Agnes Nettelbeck.

Fritz was associated closely with Dr Becker. It was alleged – but not definitely established – that he had been a member of the Friends of the Hitler Movement, but it was proven that he had associated publicly with its replacement, the *Fortbildungsverein* (Association for Further Education). He was probably also a member of the German *Bund*, possibly unwittingly, as every subscriber to the Nazi paper, *Die Brücke*, was automatically listed as a member. Nevertheless, Paul Beckmann, who had been Secretary in the Adelaide Consulate and leader of the Nazi Party group in Adelaide since March 1938, wrote to Asmis in November 1938 re Fritz Homburg: 'He regrets any connection with the Third Reich and everything connected with National Socialism.' Still, he did not regret sponsorship of everything German, and when war broke out he reverted to German nationalism.

World War II

The Homburgs and their close associates were bound to be in trouble when war broke out. Their legal business probably did not suffer greatly, because many of their clients were German, and there was plenty of work for them to do handling internees' cases, some of which they handled without fee. Robert had attracted no adverse attention between the wars. Although he was still in partnership with Hermann, it was said that they were no longer on very good terms. Robert lost his seat on the Adelaide City Council in July 1940, but that is one of the hazards of politics and not necessarily a result of the war.

The outbreak of war caused fury in the household of Hermann Homburg.

'Damn the bloody English!' exclaimed Emma Homburg.

'England must always stick her sticky beak in,' said Marsi.

Hermann's contribution was: 'England always starts wars.'

This, of course, followed precisely the Nazi line, and the report is a clear indication that there was still an informant close to or within the Homburg family. It could no longer have been Reginald Fraser, for he had taken his wife and son to England.

Something must have happened in September or early October 1939. Perhaps Hermann had been touting for business among relatives of internees, for on 6 October at least three internees at Keswick Barracks wrote to warn their wives to beware of Hermann Homburg, to show him the door, to put him off the premises if he turned up at their home.

Military Intelligence, Special Branch and the Commonwealth Investigation Branch made inquiries about the Homburgs and Krawinkel, and letters of denunciation and statutory declarations came in spontaneously. Paradoxically, one of Hermann's nephews, Robert Brewster-Jones, Gerta's son, was under surveillance as a secret member of the Communist Party; he went under the (communist) cover name of 'Bob Lambert', while his wife's secret name was 'Dot Dunne'.

Reports came from Members of Parliament, including from his own party, that Hermann Homburg had shown disloyalty by never attending the opening of Parliament or being present during the Governor's address. It could be taken that he felt he had more important things to do in connection with his business than to attend such ceremonies, but he was being paid to fulfil certain parliamentary duties, and he was not doing so. Monitoring of overseas mail showed that Marsi was maintaining contact with Paul Beckmann; as a permanent member of the Consular Corps, and thus a 'Protected Person', he had been allowed to leave for Japan in September 1939. It was easy to intercept these letters. The contents did not appear particularly dangerous, unless there was some sort of pre-arranged code in them, but it was objectionable that Marsi was writing at all to a man who had been a Nazi leader in South Australia and on Ribbentrop's staff in London.

The first of the family to be interned was Heinrich Krawinkel, on 30 May 1940. In September, a woman close to the family reported that Herman had threatened to 'get even with McBride' because he was responsible for Krawinkel's internment. In fact, he was not. Senator Philip McBride became Minister for the Army only on 14 August 1940, after the previous Minister, Geoffrey Austin Street, had been killed in a plane crash, and he was replaced on 28 October by Percy Spender. However, McBride probably signed the Detention Orders for both Fritz and Hermann Homburg.

It took five months for Krawinkel to get a hearing before an Advisory Committee. Claims that appeals had to be made to a military tribunal are patently untrue. By regulation, a Committee had to be headed by someone who was, or had been, or was eligible to be a Justice of the Supreme Court, and most other members were senior legal men.[10] On 13 November, he was released under a Restriction Order after Homburg put up a bond of £500. By the time Krawinkel was released, Fritz Homburg had been interned. A case had long been building up against him. An intercepted letter said that 'the loyal inhabitants reckoned the Nazi element was still going strong in spite of lip loyalty and subscriptions to the Red Cross'. It was claimed that his children had been unable to speak English until they went to school. He had said that the war would not have happened if England had not intervened when Germany invaded Poland.[11] Then there was the mass of background material relating to his association with Becker and the editorial policy of the *Barossa News*. On 9 September, the army had recommended his detention, but he was not arrested until 29 October.

Fritz's appeal was heard within days before the same Committee. He denied that his children could speak German; neither could his wife, he said, although she understood it a little. He claimed he too could speak German very little. He claimed that he was very friendly with Becker, but had never heard him make any disloyal statements. Even though he had belonged to the *Fortbildungsverein* and possibly to the Friends of the Hitler Movement, he also claimed that he knew of no Nazism in the whole of the Tanunda district. Either he was naïve, or he had a very narrow concept of 'Nazism', or he was committing perjury.

One Anglo-Australian witness said that he had never heard Fritz Homburg say anything disloyal, and that he had 'practically made Tanunda'. Questioned by the Committee, he admitted that he was known as a loyal British subject, and that he would not expect a person to express disloyal sentiments in his presence. One of the grounds for internment was that a person's pro-German arguments were disrupting community morale, and in a solidly German environment where people expressed such views only within their own coterie, they were not creating a disturbance. On 8 November, the Committee recommended that Fritz Homburg be released unconditionally, and he was in fact released on 14 November.

Hermann Homburg was no doubt feeling pleased with himself that his influence had succeeded in having his brother and son-in-law freed, but a Detention Order for himself had already been signed on 14 October. His internment was delayed, as it was a sensitive case that needed to be checked. One woman, who would not have her identity disclosed officially because she was afraid of the consequences, said that only German was spoken in the Homburg house; almost all their friends were German; Hermann constantly 'ran down' the Jews and had brought up his children and grandchildren with the same attitude. This was confirmed by written material found among his papers when his house was searched.

A CIB officer complained that allegations that Renolf had served in the German army were unsubstantiated. They dismissed any sinister implications that the parties held on 17 March 1938 and 1939 were to celebrate Hitler's successes in Austria and Czechoslovakia, for Homburg's birthday was on that date. They did not give much consideration to claims that members of the family had been seen to give Hitler salute in public, for they were unlikely to have been so stupid and had probably just been waving. The inclusion of false claims weakened the overall case, and as a result two army officers were removed from the Intelligence staff and one police officer was relieved of his duties. Maud Prisk said that her brother had seen Homburg and Krawinkel burn a lot of books just after war broke out, and it was presumed that these would have been regarded as suspicious. She also said that when her son Gordon had appeared in uniform, Homburg had insulted him in such a manner that Gordon had refrained from hitting him only because he was an old man.[12] In a dossier compiled a little later, there were thirty-six separate accusations against Homburg. Whatever the truth of some private allegations, there was on public record material that justified his detention, and he was arrested on 25 November.

A few days later, Brigadier Sandford, the senior officer in South Australia, reported to the National Security Advisory Committee; he referred to 'Hermann Homburg, Fritz Homburg and Heinrich Krawinkel and a coterie of powerful and influential people of marked ability' and stated: 'The release from detention of Heinrich Krawinkel and Fritz Homburg is calculated to accentuate the anti-British feeling and the attitude of studied arrogance now existing which if uncurbed, may lead to conduct prejudicial to public safety and the defence of the Commonwealth.' An informant among the internees reported that Hermann Homburg had said: 'the only justice we will get is when Hitler and Mussolini come here'.

Homburg's position in politics and the legal profession meant that the members of the South Australian Advisory Committee disqualified themselves from hearing his appeal, and on 18 December he appeared before the Victorian Committee, which consisted at that time of Justice Fred Russell Beauchamp Martin, Justice of the Supreme Court of Victoria; Mr William Henry Sharwood, former Commonwealth Crown Solicitor, Victoria; and Dr Thomas Cornelius Brennan, King's Counsel since 1928, Senator 1931-37, and Acting Attorney-General of Victoria, 1934-37. These were the eminent legal men whom careless writers have dismissed scornfully as 'a military tribunal'.

Even when the obviously false or dubious accusations were rejected, there was still a substantial body of evidence. Homburg, like other internees, gave evidence under oath, and it was clear that he did not shrink from a little perjury. He denied knowing what the letters NSDAP represented, although he had addressed letters to Becker as 'Vertrauensmann der NSDAP'. Reading the transcript of the hearing is wearisome, for an experienced lawyer and politician had met his superiors in legal standing, and he could not deceive them as easily as he has pulled the wool over the eyes of historians. The Committee reported that Homburg's denials did 'not carry conviction', and his reasons were 'unconvincing'. It referred to his 'attitude of studied arrogance', adding that 'it would be unsafe to accept his sworn testimony where it conflicted with other testimony or natural inferences from facts… Too much reliance should not be placed on his public service in view of his desire for leadership'.

The Committee did not, as has been suggested, find Homburg innocent; it was in any case not its function to determine 'guilt' or 'innocence', but to assess whether the internee had demonstrated that it was 'neither necessary nor advisable' that he should remain in internment. The Chairman (Justice Martin) and Mr Sharwood favoured continued detention. The other member, Dr Brennan, agreed that internment was justified, but urged that Homburg be released on account of his age. All three of the Committee agreed that the internment of Homburg had been warranted, but they merely advised; the Minister for the Army decided. On 21 December, Percy Spender, who was allied politically to Homburg, ordered that he be released under restriction, and he was released to Melbourne three days later. One condition of the Restriction Order was that he should not reside in South Australia; approval was given for him to live at Ballarat in Victoria.

On 6 January 1941, the Army lodged an objection to the release of Homburg under any conditions. A letter from the public shortly afterwards complained: 'The Homburgs are too smart to let you get anything on them.' On 10 March, South Australian Headquarters protested 'in the strongest terms possible', as the release of Hermann Homburg revived the view that he was above the law, and his return would set a 'most undesirable precedent and endanger the State'. The release of both Homburgs had already reduced the amount of useful information being passed to the authorities, as the public felt it was useless supplying information when people like them could get away with absolutely anything.

A watch was maintained on the family in South Australia and on Hermann and Marsi in Ballarat. Krawinkel was seen burying cans of petrol under a tree at one o'clock in the morning, and he was reported to be breaching the terms of his Restriction Order by appearing in town with his appearance disguised. He was reinterned on 1 October 1941. This was a critical time when the German army was advancing on the suburbs of Moscow, and victory seemed within Hitler's grasp; some Australian Germans were becoming vociferously arrogant. His appeal four weeks later was unsuccessful, and he was not released until December 1944, again under restriction.

Much of the evidence against the Homburgs now came from their correspondence. Letters to and from Krawinkel were, of course, known to be censored, as was all internment camp mail. However, it was little suspected how much domestic mail was also intercepted under secret XRD orders. This was an expensive procedure taking a lot of time by skilled Intelligence personnel, so the power was not widely used. At various times all mail to the households of Hermann Homburg and Krawinkel was intercepted. For letters that they knew might be read – that is, the ones to Krawinkel – the family adopted a number of subterfuges. Some letters were sent as though from Peter to his father, in the hope that a child's letters might not attract serious scrutiny. In others, a system of code words was adopted, but this did not deceive the authorities. Among the code words adopted were 'armchair friend', 'R. Chee', 'May Chin' and 'Gardine'. The first two both referred to Archie Cameron, Liberal member for the electorate of Wooroora, former Minister for the Navy and member of the War Cabinet. 'May Chin' was Norman Makin, Labor Party member for Hindmarsh, current Minister for the Navy and member of the War Cabinet. 'Gardine', a German word for 'curtain', referred to Prime Minister John Curtin. Cameron and Makin were close associates of Homburg, and possibly felt that it might be in their long-term interests to assist a person who might influence the South Australian 'German vote' after the war.

The first step was to get permission for Homburg to return to South Australia. On 28 October 1941, Makin wrote to Frank Forde, who had become Minister for the Army and Deputy Prime Minister a few weeks earlier and was now responsible for internments and restrictions, suggesting that Homburg could be watched more effectively in Adelaide where he was known. At about the same time, the Army Intelligence Corps began to collect statements about Hermann and Marsi Homburg from its own personnel and from fellow guests in the hotel where the Homburgs resided. Hermann was said to attempt constantly to engage other guests in discussion about the war and to become abusive when they rejected his overtures; he also asked servicemen who frequented the hotel too many improper questions about their work and their postings. Marsi, who was described as 'an attractive girl of undoubted ability', drank very freely with RAAF men and also asked too many questions. Homburg's Melbourne dossier claims that complaints from an American unit stationed near Ballarat hastened Homburg's departure, but the Americans did not arrive at Camp Darley near Ballarat until February 1942. On 12 December, Evatt authorised Homburg's return to South Australia, and he was back in Adelaide six days later.

Homburg was ordered to live at his Dulwich residence; he was forbidden to have a telephone in the house, or any wireless except an approved one not capable of short-wave reception. He was also forbidden to receive visitors except members of his family. However, Homburg did not observe the restrictions to which he had agreed, and in his letters to Krawinkel he wrote frequently that he was flouting them. Krawinkel's letters were censored in the internment camp, as Homburg must have known. This correspondence attracted renewed surveillance, and it was found that visitors would enter Krawinkel's property through a side entrance, cross their backyard and reach Homburg's property secretively through a gate in the dividing fence. In addition, Makin, Cameron and Arthur Calwell,

Minister for Information, were calling on him openly, disregarding the restrictions imposed on him.[13]

In April 1942, Major-General Vasey recommended that Homburg be re-interned, but Forde refused to sign the order. In June, F. R. Sinclair, Secretary to the Department of the Army, wrote to Forde summing up the case; he criticised some of the evidence, criticised the Advisory Committee for rejecting other evidence, and recommended renewed detention. Still Forde would not act, and in August authority for detentions was transferred from the Minister for the Army to the Attorney-General, Dr H. V. Evatt.

In May 1944, Homburg was given permission to attend his office between 10.00 am and 5.00 pm. This made nonsense of the restriction on his home telephone, as he could use the office telephone. On 28 July, he was stopped in the street and asked to produce his identity card. This was a legitimate request, as everybody over fourteen had to carry an identity card at all times and to produce it on request.[14] Homburg complained about the indignity, as he claimed that everybody in Adelaide knew who he was. The police complained again that Homburg thought that he was above the law, and that regulations did not apply to him.

It was not the only case when Homburgs flouted the law. It was found that Renolf Homburg was registered neither with the military authorities nor with Manpower. He claimed he had posted the registration form on 22 December 1941 and had heard no more about it. The authorities did not believe him, particularly when he failed to respond to a further notice in February 1943 requiring him to enrol. There was a difference of opinion about the course to take. The army opinion was that it was doubtful whether there was sufficient evidence against him to formulate a charge. The Deputy Director of Manpower disagreed, writing that it was wrong that he could escape the consequences by claiming that he had posted the form; in addition Renolf had failed to produce his identity card when interviewed by Manpower. In fact, he did not possess an identity card; *nor did he have a ration book.*

One might concede that Homburg had returned his registration form and that it had been lost in the post, but failure to obtain an identity card or a ration book was deliberate and ongoing deceit with criminal intent. In October 1943, Renolf appeared before a court and was fined £15 for failing to register with the Manpower authorities, and a further £10 for failing to register with military authorities. This answered Marie Krawinkel's question to her mother in January 1938: 'If there was a war, who would Uncle Rene fight for?'

There could be no doubt that Hermann was behind Renolf's actions. He apparently managed to keep a report of the proceedings out of Adelaide papers, but he could not reach the *Canberra Times*. On 15 October (page 3, column 4) it carried a few lines on the case, and it was a piece of undeserved luck that the name was given as Renolf 'Hornbrum'. The fact that Renolf had no ration book would point to the likelihood that the Homburgs made up for this by dealing on the black market; they were wealthy enough to afford this.

As the restrictions on Homburg had become a farce, and the war situation had improved, a notice that the restrictions had been revoked was served on him on 19 September 1944. Other information that came in had nothing to do with the detention of Homburg and Krawinkel, for it arrived much later. A friend of Marie Krawinkel mentioned that he (the friend) had stopped calling on the family just before the war, owing to their disloyal attitude, and he had not responded to invitations; it was his opinion that Hermann Homburg was 'a dangerous fool'. On 20 April 1945, Homburg gave a small party, allegedly to welcome a new pastor. There was no telling whether the choice of Hitler's birthday for this function was a coincidence or a deliberate provocation.

Meanwhile, a deep-cover Military Intelligence agent had been inserted into Tanunda, one whose German credentials were impeccable. People spoke their minds in front of him, for he was not considered loyal to Australia. In public, Fritz Homburg had been fulfilling his civic duties. He was Secretary of a War Savings Group that had raised £2,475; he had organised a concert for the Red Cross; he had helped work out an evacuee reception scheme in case Adelaide had to be cleared of women and children. His private feelings were different. Within his own clique of close friends and extended family, he maintained that Germany was fighting for a righteous cause and would be reduced to bondage and slavery if 'the Jews' won.

Fritz Homburg had an excellent short-wave radio receiver, and he invited friends to listen to the news from Germany with him. One night, when the informant was among the group, they had discussed means to rectify the 'persecution' and 'unjust internments' they had suffered. They listened to the news in German at 10.30 and the German news in English at 11.30, and between times they rejoiced that the German army had halted the Allied progress.[15] They saw it as a sign of God's favour, just as Hitler's escape from assassination had been a sign of divine providence, and Roosevelt's death the following April was God's retribution on 'the Jews'.

Early in 1945, Fritz Homburg had said that people were seeing for themselves that National Socialism was the most workable plan ever thought out to overcome political problems. He still maintained that the war had been forced on Germany. The agent reported:

He said he would be the last man to lift one finger to assist Government requests in any shape or form whatsoever. He might, he said, outwardly be present at certain meetings, accept a nominal position on one or two but that his heart would never be in the work. He also said if the British Empire is bad enough to declare war on a nation which after all is only seeking her rights, only for the sake of monopolies in trade, then I am finished with this glorious thing they call the British Empire.

In March, he prophesied that the German Storm Troopers would convey Hitler and picked fighters to friendly neutrals to save them for future action. Germans abroad would not take Germany's defeat lying down, and there were Germans in Australia who had links with Nazis in Argentina. Some time after the war, Fritz Homburg was awarded a medal of the Order of the British Empire, which he probably had no hesitation in accepting from the Empire that he had so despised. When he died on 5 July 1970, his obituary in the Adelaide *Advertiser*, 7 July, bore the title: Grand Old Man of Tanunda Dies'.

In his last available report, made at the end of May 1945, the agent in Tanunda recorded that there was an atmosphere of gloom and resentment over Germany's defeat. He was probably withdrawn soon after this, for what the Homburgs and the Tanunda Germans thought and felt was now of little security significance.

After the War

Soon after the war, Charles Archibald Price, son of Sir Archibald Grenfell Price, wrote a Master of Arts thesis and published a book on the difficulties in assimilating German migrants. He appeared to work only from the limited sources then available to the public, but he had a vast store of background knowledge that he could not reveal, knowledge that he had gained as an Intelligence lieutenant in the South Australian Military District. Hence his facts are almost impeccable, although some of his conclusions can be disputed. If there is no official interference from Germany, German migrants assimilate more readily than most other non Anglo-Celtic groups, but some outstanding exceptions have been obnoxious.

In 1947 Homburg, seeing this book with some justification as an attack upon him in particular, published a booklet in response, denying that he or any other German-Australian had done anything objectionable and attacking those who had taken action against them. The booklet is not so much downright lies as a concoction of evasive and hypocritical lawyer-speak, politician-speak, omissions and evasions. The main misleading point is that he feigns to be pleading the case of others, while in fact almost all the instances he mentions refer to himself or his family.

Hermann Homburg pleads: 'If a century and more of residence in this land does not entitle them to be regarded as Australians, then how much longer must they sojourn here before they are?' Harmstorf paraphrases this: 'the question arises: when are people of a non-British background accepted as Australians?' One answer is that they would not be while they still put foreign interests before those of the Australian community in general, and certainly not while they had obeyed the Nazi injunction to 'think German, feel German, act German'. As far as Homburg was concerned: not while his sister's husband denounced him as a traitor and a bastard, and his wife's sister could say that Hermann had always been a traitor to the country of his birth. Apart from Hermann and Fritz, none of Friedrich Wilhelm Homburg's other descendants was in any obvious trouble in either war. Their treatment was a response to how they behaved, not to their German name and ancestry.

There was considerable annoyance when Hermann Homburg received an invitation to attend one of the functions to meet Queen Elizabeth during her 1954 visit, and a medal for services to South Australia. Even if it could be argued that his intentions towards Australia were not intentionally noxious, he had always been opposed to Britain and the British Empire or Commonwealth. As for services to South Australia, Homburg served only one cause: Hermann Homburg's ego, no matter what the cost to others, including his family. Any benefit to South Australia was incidental. He died on 12 December 1964, cocooned in resentment and self-righteousness.

Chapter 6

The Hired Hack

In the House of Representatives on 26 March 1947, Arthur Calwell, Minister for Immigration, said of John Sleeman: '[No] alien who ever came to Australia was more traitorous to Australia than Mr. J. H. Sleeman... There is no more dubious character, alien or British, in this country than the same Mr. J. H. Sleeman.' This was an oblique attack on Calwell's old enemy, John Thomas (Jack) Lang, and the story went back many years.

One of Japan's main aims concerning Australia in the 1930s was to convince influential and powerful Australians in politics, commerce and the media that Japan's intentions were peaceful, and that the war in China should not affect trade relations between Australia and Japan, because the war was none of Australia's business. This involved much effort, much smiling and smarmy persuasion, and a considerable number of tokens of their appreciation. In the case of John Harvey Crothers ('Jack') Sleeman, it was easier for them. Sleeman they had bought; to Sleeman they gave orders. He was well known as a scoundrel and a pornographer, but few realised how deeply and dangerously corrupt he was. He had entrée to high political circles, mainly but not exclusively Labor. Not only did he have friends in politics: he knew what sort of skeletons they had in their closets and he could threaten them. These contacts and this influence made him useful to the Japanese and potentially very dangerous to Australia.

The Journalist

Jack Sleeman was born at Dunolly (near Goldsborough) in Victoria on 28 January 1880 as the second son of John and Mary Sleeman. The first publicly announced discovery of gold in Victoria had been made at Clunes, being published in the *Geelong Advertiser* in July 1851. It was located in the so-called 'Golden Triangle', as was Dunolly, which lay just 15 km southeast of Moliagul where the massive 'Welcome Stranger' nugget was found in February 1869. However, the main reefs ran so deep that only large companies could afford the equipment to mine them, and to work the mines they imported skilled Cornish miners. Among these miners was John Sleeman senior, who arrived about 1875; on 22 June 1876 he married Mary Harvey.[1] Their first son, Bertram Harvey Sleeman, was born at Clunes in 1878, and died there eight months later. The Eureka Stockade rebel leader, Peter Lalor, had settled at Clunes for a time, and in keeping with the atmosphere of the area and times, Sleeman became a stalwart of the Labor movement.

John Harvey Crothers Sleeman (From *Beckett's Budget*, 28 September 1928, page 6.) (Courtesy of the National Library of Australia, Canberra)

The third son, Charles, who lived just one day, was also born at Dunolly towards the end of 1880, and Joseph Bertram, who appears in registration records as Jas Bertram, was born at Inglewood, County Gladstone, on 21 June 1885, where John was probably working on the Morning Star reef. There was allegedly a daughter named Emily, but no trace of her birth, marriage or death has been located in South Australia or Western Australia. On the goldfields, John must have come in contact with Chinese miners and merchants, although they were less numerous than at the more famous fields of Ballarat and Bendigo.

In the 1890s, the main lodes in the Golden Triangle began to peter out. Some of the Sleeman family had gone to Western Australia, and one, probably his uncle, was involved in copper mining at the Geraldine mine, east of Geraldton. Fortuitously, the massive goldfields extending out from Coolgardie and Kalgoorlie, the heart of the 'Golden Mile', were discovered around this time, and in about 1895 John Sleeman senior followed the gold trail and took his family to Western Australia. He worked in various mining towns: Day Dawn for a time, then at the famous Sons of Gwalia mine, just west of Leonora. Joseph became an office boy at Gwalia, then a storeman at Leonora and was head of the Leonora Volunteer Fire Brigade until he left for Fremantle, then Albany, then Fremantle again. Young Jack worked as a pupil-teacher, then as a clerk in a lawyer's office and an engine driver on the mines, as Secretary of Leonora hospital and reporter for the *Mount Leonora Miner*. He married Sarah Ann Dryden at the little settlement of Malcolm on 14 November 1905. As a reporter, he covered politics, racing, trotting and vice. He quickly gained a reputation for his florid, abusive, salacious style.

Joining the army in Western Australia on 19 March 1917, Sleeman was drafted to the Engineers as a sapper and transferred to New South Wales.[2] He was discharged at Sydney on 10 October 1917 as medically unfit and overweight. (The legend was circulated that he was a publicity officer for recruiting; this is repeated in the *Australian Dictionary of Biography*.) His father had died in September 1908, his mother in May 1918. Fairly soon after his discharge, he went to Queensland. Although his sympathies were with Labor, he became a publicity agent for the Northern Country Party in the Queensland election of October 1920. He first attracted a seriously adverse notice in 1922, when he and Edward Bernard Connolly offered Frank Brennan, Member of the Legislative Assembly (Labor Party), £3,500 to cross the floor on a 'No confidence' motion against Premier E. G. Theodore.[3] Connolly was a journalist with the *Daily Mail*, a Brisbane Labor paper controlled by John Wren, the Victorian racing magnate and political power-broker, while Sleeman worked for the Brisbane *Sun*.

Though Brennan was in financial difficulties and was suspected of sharp dealings, he had his eye on becoming a Justice of the Supreme Court. He trapped Sleeman and Connolly into committing themselves before hidden witnesses. In the Supreme Court in Brisbane in September, they were found guilty, sentenced to three months' imprisonment and fined £500, in default a further nine months. It was never officially discovered who was behind the bribe or who paid the fines. Sleeman said only that the man concerned was not a politician, though keenly interested in politics. It was suspected that this meant that the man was a supporter of the Country or National party, and the person who comes to mind is George M. Dash, a National Party official and managing director of the Brisbane *Sun*. At the time of the bribery attempt, Dash was negotiating with Wren over the future of the Albion Park racecourse. In view of the employment connections of both Sleeman and Connolly, this Dash-Wren connection might well have been behind the attempt, but hard evidence is lacking, and there were many other shady characters on the racing and political scenes.

On being released from prison, Sleeman apparently returned for a time to Western Australia, where he worked as a sub-editor on the Kalgoorlie *Sun*. It was said that he worked also for the (Liberal) National Party in that state, writing anti-Labor pamphlets for it. His younger brother Joseph, organiser of the Shop Assistants Union from 1920, became the Member of the Legislative Assembly (Labor) for the state electorate of Fremantle in 1924, a seat he held until 1959. Jack, however, had no loyalty to any party and would write for anyone who paid him. By 1927, he had moved to Sydney where he began to work for William James Beckett as Editor-in-Chief of *Beckett's Budget*. On 14 June, he brought out its first issue. It began as a fairly staid paper dedicated to presenting rural news, promoting the interests of primary producers, and maintaining the White Australia policy 'in the interests of racial purity'. A lot of space was devoted to racing news and tips, and the paper was spiced up with lottery advertisements, graphology and the promotion of some very doubtful share companies.

Dull, pompous and poorly composed, *Beckett's Budget* had little support from the rural community. Then, by the issue of 7 October, it had changed style and format. Its agricultural content shrank to one page; racing news became more prominent; but the biggest change was that it became a searing sleaze and scandal paper so obscene and scurrilous that it could make even the hard-boiled reporters of *Truth* and *Mirror* blush:

murder, suicide, rape, divorce – all the sordid details, including names and addresses of child incest victims. It pandered to the lowest instincts of the masses, and they loved it. In a few months, circulation doubled and trebled and doubled again.

From the beginning, *Beckett's Budget* was racist, with references to 'John Chinaman' and 'degenerate Dagoes' and crude anti-Jewish jokes. Large headlines proclaimed: 'Australian Beauty Soiled and Ruined in the Squalid Chinese Opium Dens of Sydney's Back Alleys - Behind this shutter a white girl lived with the lust of yellow men.' (14.10.1928) It was filled with references to 'wily Celestials', 'slant-eyed Chinks', 'opium-sodden, lascivious yellow men'. He published titillating details under the guise of fighting for women who were victims of incest, 'unnatural offences', seduction and abortion, who could get no justice from male judges and juries.

Newspaper owner Ezra Norton called *Beckett's Budget* 'vile' (17.2.1928). When Sleeman retaliated by claiming that Ezra's father, John Norton, had gained control of *Truth* by fraud, blackmail and murder (9.3.1928), he made dangerous enemies and, in publishing details of indiscretions and orgies in the exclusive Melbourne suburb of Toorak, he made new powerful ones. He now had almost total control of the *Budget*, with a regular signed column and the freedom to print whatever he liked.

Inevitably, Sleeman landed in court on charges of defamation and of issuing an obscene publication; early in 1928, the paper was threatened with deregistration. Sleeman began to take a political stance in the paper. For a time it was hard to make out a definite line amid the verbosity, but he settled down to outright support of Labor with no pretence of impartiality. Before the Federal election in 1928, he was preaching the Labor cause to a readership of 300,000. On 28 September, the paper published 'An Open Letter to Every Voter Who Loves Australia First'. Under Sleeman's editorship, however, the paper attracted a string of libel actions that helped cause its bankruptcy later.

In 1930, *Beckett's Budget* was sold, resuming publication as *Australian Budget*. Soon a close relationship developed between Sleeman and Jack Lang. Sleeman was a member of the Darlinghurst Labor League, which was in the East Sydney electorate of Edward John Ward. When Jack Lang split the official Labor Party and formed the Lang Labor Party, with its Lang-Ward-Beasley axis, Sleeman supported them. Before the 1930 New South Wales election, his editorial policy was: 'Vote for Lang and Labor as your answer to Nationalist misrepresentation.'

Chapter 6: The Hired Hack

Lang's lackey

In March 1931, the *Sunday Times* group folded, and with it fell the *Australian Budget*. Sleeman was jobless again. Not long after this, he was rewarded for being a leading sycophant in the Jack Lang admiration society and for having delivered to Lang the editorial policy of a paper with a large circulation: he became speech-writer and publicity officer for Lang; he probably did some writing for the *Labor Daily* in Sydney; and, according to L. F. Crisp[4], he helped concoct the notorious 'Lang Plan' to rescue the New South Wales Government from financial disaster.

Lang should have known that Sleeman had been imprisoned for corruption connected with an attempt to topple the Queensland State Labor government. Perhaps his lack of scruples suited Lang, for in 1932 Sleeman was in court again, this time in New South Wales in connection with the Judge Frederick Shaver Swindell case. Swindell came from America and the 'judge' title was equivalent merely to a Justice of the Peace. During the trial, which was referred to as a 'perjury marathon' and a 'labyrinth of lies', it was alleged that Lang had granted licences for greyhound racing and gambling machines ('fruit machines') in return for secret payments to the Lang Labor Party and the Trades Hall, which included an initial payment of over £3,000, which could have bought a modest house in Sydney at that time. Ten per cent of the gross takings from the machines was supposed to go to the Labor Party via Sleeman. Harold McCauley, Lang's secretary, had allegedly introduced Sleeman to Lang, and he too was involved in the court case. The feeling at the trial was that Lang was taking bribes, the aptly named Swindell was fleecing the public, and Sleeman, who held shares in the Shepherds' Bush Greyhound Racing venture, was making some crooked money out of everyone, although he denied that any money was paid to him.

Little could be proven, but a report called Swindell unprincipled, unscrupulous, sinister and crooked, and it was not without reason that Dr Evatt called Lang 'the biggest crook in the labour movement'. According to L. F. Crisp, Percy Coleman (ALP President in New South Wales) said that 'Langism' relied on 'graft, patronage and corruption', and members of the Inner Group of Lang's Executive, which included Eddie Ward and Jack Beasley, were 'vicious, mercenary, arrogant and immoral'. Sleeman was the man in the shadows of this unholy alliance.

Sleeman also wrote and published books. His most notable book was the savagely anti-Japanese *White China: an Austral-Asian perspective*, self-published in 1933 but undoubtedly financed by the Chinese community in Sydney. It was a very knowledgeable and informative book as regards Chinese history and tradition; in view of the nature of Sleeman's other writings, it is probable that some Chinese scholar gave him the information, and he simply put it into book form. Here too he attacked the Japanese. On account of this book, the post-war Chinese community have long regarded him as a great champion of China and a friend of the Chinese in Australia. They could not have known of his later work for the Japanese, but how could they have overlooked the infamous bigotry of *Beckett's Budget*?

Later in 1933, his book, *The Life of John T. Lang*, was published: a nauseating book in which he likened Lang to Sun Yat-sen, Gandhi, Mustapha Kemal, Pilsudski, Mussolini, Lenin, Moses, Spartacus, Cromwell and Napoleon, saying also: 'Socrates, a mason, Christ, a carpenter, St. Paul, a tent-maker, St. Peter, a fisherman, Lincoln, a rail-splitter, Lang, an accountant, guarantee that the people must evolve toward dignity and power.' He spoilt the effect of the eulogy by adding an epilogue:

> Personally, I agree with many of Labour's [*sic*] conclusions and policy planks, even though I recognise how impracticable, how fraught with terrorism, is its objective... The tragedy of the whole thing is that socialisation will give the workers as a whole, nothing more than a nationalised servitude.

Between what Sleeman was paid to write and what he thought lay often a vast chasm. He became a largely freelance journalist, writing, among other things, political gossip for the racing form weekly, *Newsletter*, conducted by T. J. Hopkins. In July 1939, Sleeman wrote for it a series of anti-British articles, copies of which he sent to Dr Seger, the German Acting Consul-General, who wrote in praise of them to the Foreign Office in Berlin. Unfortunately for Sleeman, this letter was intercepted in England early in the war. Sleeman was still associated with *Newsletter* in 1941, and on 29 October of that year he rang the office of Dr H. V. (Bert) Evatt, Attorney General since 7 October, while trying to obtain exemption from military service for Allan Hopkins, apparently the son of Thomas James Hopkins. Evatt's secretary would hardly have suspected that the telephone call came from the Japanese Consulate-General, but Military Intelligence had tapped the Consulate-General telephone line and noted the call.[5]

Sleeman and Evatt knew each other well. During 1928-29, Evatt had been one of the team representing Thomas Davies Mutch on two occasions regarding defamatory material in *Beckett's Budget*. There was more to this than meets the eye. In June 1925, Mutch had challenged Sleeman's patron, Jack Lang, for leadership of the New South Wales branch of the Australian Labor Party, and he had been defeated by only one vote. If he had won, it would have changed the course of Australia's political history.[6] Mutch served in Lang's Cabinet in 1925-27 as Minister for Education before being expelled from the party. It looked very much as though Lang used his conspiratorial financial and political dealings with Sleeman to get his revenge on Mutch.

Chapter 6: The Hired Hack

Japanese Agent

When did Sleeman begin to work for the Japanese? As he was often short of money, his pen was for hire to anyone. His lack of ethical principles, combined with his access to the press and his political contacts, were likely to make him a target for recruitment by some foreign power. He loathed the Japanese, but for money he became one of their most important hired agents.

As relations between Japan and Australia had become strained during the war in China, Japan's trade had suffered. To counteract this, the Japanese government and the Federation of Exporters allocated secret funds to be disbursed through the Consulate-General and the Japanese Chamber of Commerce in Sydney. An entry in consular accounts recorded the payment of £10 to Mr Sleeman on 26 November 1937 for his war pamphlet, *China and Japan*. The Japanese government provided the information and policy guidelines, and Sleeman wrote it up in pamphlet form, using the pseudonym Myles Cheguin. The Chamber of Commerce had thousands printed for distribution. He also wrote a booklet called *Australia and Japan* for Mitsui, which bought and distributed the total issue.

About March-April 1939, again as Myles Cheguin, he wrote a 60-page pamphlet called *Japan and the Japanese - What Australians should Know!* Written in Sleeman's florid style, it was published by the left-wing New Century Press Pty Ltd in Sydney, the printing of 3000 copies being financed by Mitsubishi. It gave current trade statistics that must have come from the Consulate. Recalling the war of 1914-18, Sleeman wrote: '[In] the dread years when the raucous War God's gong was menacing Australia and all that Australians hold dear, the Japanese were our chivalrous and courageous allies.' Of the period of Japanese isolation, he wrote: 'She has matured as the glorious pearl matures, imprisoned within narrow dimensions.' On Japan's policy in the 20th century: '[The] Japanese spirit hungers for peace… [The] War Lordism which has disgraced the last thirty years of Chinese history was the direct result of centuries of Chinese misrule.' On the last page, he came to the message Japan wanted conveyed: 'The duty that Australia owes herself is to remain on friendly terms with Japan.' At about the same time, he wrote another pamphlet, *Another Case for Japan*, of which no copy has been found.

Sleeman maintained his political contacts. Throughout 1937, 1938 and 1939, Eddie Ward condemned expenditure on defence on the grounds that Australian forces would be used only to defend the rich territories of other nations, and that there was no possible threat to Australia. Perhaps Ward quite honestly had in mind that the money could have been spent better on social welfare, but he would also have been listening to his mate Sleeman, who was doing Japan a great service. Soon Sleeman was receiving sixteen guineas a month from Japanese secret funds, paid about the last day of each month, while he continued to work for Hopkins or Lang. The first recorded salary payment of £8 for two weeks was made on 26 July 1938. The salary was supplemented by occasional extras such as: '22 September 1939: To Sleeman for secret information, £50.'[7]

What work was he doing apart from writing pamphlets? He analysed and reported on parliamentary proceedings and newspapers. He compiled dossiers on politicians; the Japanese were particularly interested in Cabinet Ministers of whichever party was in power at the time. He also gave Consul-General Masatoshi Akiyama information on the development of the secret service in Australia. This sounds sinister; in fact, he did little more than tell the well-known story of the egg thrown at W. M. Hughes during an anti-conscription demonstration in Brisbane in November 1917. He had his own desk at the Consulate-General, where he also compiled statistical and economic information, such as the location of kilns and the production of charcoal for use in car gas producers, the location and capacity of Broken Hill Pty (BHP) plants and the influence of BHP in politics, Imperial Chemical Industries production, and statistics on oil and coal. An informant close to him said that Sleeman had confided that he still hated the Japanese and had never given them anything of real value. However, Sleeman was a poor judge of what was valuable to a government planning a war.

In September 1939, Military Intelligence began widespread mail interception and telephone tapping, and Special Branch (State Police) shadowed Sleeman intermittently. Surveillance showed that he spent at least four afternoons a week at the Consulate-General, and he was found to be checking odds and phoning through the racing bets that consular staff made with illegal off-course bookies. Their bets were meticulously recorded in the watch logs of Military Intelligence. Thanks to Sleeman's racing contacts, several of the consular staff did very well by backing Skipton in the 1941 Melbourne Cup. Sleeman also had a free hand to use the phone for his personal business.

From January 1940, 'gratuities' to Sleeman were raised to twenty guineas a month, and there was still the occasional additional entry, such as: '30 March 1940: Allowance for Sleeman for secret information for the three months period: £64.' In June 1940, Vice-Consul Kenichi Otabe told Kenneth Easton Cook, a deep-cover Intelligence agent, that some politicians were not above accepting bribes (*What a surprise!*), and Joseph Lamaro, State Attorney-General in the Lang government, had a 'back door entrance' to the Japanese community, including the Consulate. Military Intelligence phone taps showed that Lamaro was a friend of Sleeman. Indeed, through Sleeman, several of Lang's colleagues in government were tainted with Japanese influence and money.

Chapter 6: The Hired Hack

Sleeman maintained close contact with Otabe, who had come to Australia from the United States. He was in frequent contact with David Hidemichi Tokimasa, the Japanese-American press attaché at the Legation. Also, from mid 1941, he worked closely with Taijiro Ichikawa, the former commercial attaché in Sydney, then in Canberra. Sleeman sent him political books such as *Scum of the Earth; Battle for the World*. Ichikawa addressed his letters to Sleeman care of the Japanese Consulate-General.

Ward and Sleeman were on 'Eddie' and 'Jack' terms, and, at some time in 1941, Ward was seriously considering appointing Sleeman as his publicity officer, until he was warned of Sleeman's activities in Queensland. (After the war, Ward made another unwise choice in appointing Jock Garden as one of his advisers to a corruption inquiry.) Sleeman took part in the Darlinghurst Labor League Speakers' Classes, for which he prepared a series of lectures. One advocated letting Japan have a free hand in China. On 10 September 1941, he gave a speech on the Asian-Pacific situation. He submitted both scripts to Otabe for approval, saying it was the only way to bring the question of relations between Australia and Japan under discussion. One may be the speech, of which a little more than one undated page is retained on file. This describes Australian public opinion as being manipulated against Japan for the benefit of other countries; it draws attention to the fact that the official Labor Party, if it stood behind a vigorous defence policy, would have to renounce its anti-conscription policy: 'If Labour [sic] decides definitely that appeasement is anti-Labour, then we must once again review the question of conscription.'

On 21 October 1941, the Security Service, Sydney, reported to Canberra: 'There are reasonably conclusive indications that SLEEMAN has been in possession of information which as a loyal British subject he should have passed to the Commonwealth Authorities, but there is no record of any attempt by him to do so.' This referred to the fact that, early in 1941, copies of *Action Post*, a strongly pro-Nazi pamphlet circulating in Sydney, were sent to the Japanese Consulate-General by 'Alexander Mortimer'. The consulate asked Sleeman to investigate and report. He said he would try to locate Mortimer, although the articles were not subtle enough to be of use; they simply antagonised people. There had been appeals in the papers for anyone who knew the identity of the author of *Action Post* to report the matter to Security, but Sleeman did not report what he knew of Mortimer. In fact, 'Mortimer' was a pseudonym, and Sleeman knew nothing of his true identity. Within the Security Service, it was suggested that an attempt be made to trace Japanese payments to Sleeman by checking bank accounts. However, payments were made in cash; the Consulate kept large sums of money on the premises in order to make untraceable payments.

Ten days after this report, Sleeman offered the *Sydney Morning Herald* 'confidential information behind the news' for a fee. Did he intend to betray the Japanese by selling information he picked up at the Consulate-General, or to pass on information the Japanese wanted publicised? Or did he mean to pass on information gleaned from Lang and Ward? This is unknown, as the paper did not take up the offer.

On 27 November Sleeman, using one of the monitored telephone lines at the Consulate-General, made a call to 'a woman, probably Mrs Sleeman' asking whether it was true 'about the loss of *Sydney*'. She said that Mrs Spender had confirmed it. Percy Spender, recently Treasurer and Minister for the Army in the United Australia Party of the R. G. Menzies Government and still a member of the Advisory War Council, had told his wife that *Sydney* had been sunk, and Jean Spender had told Sarah Sleeman. Sarah then told *her* husband, and Sleeman told the Japanese Consul-General. So much for keeping secret the loss of *Sydney*!

It had already been noted that the Spenders were indiscreet, that they were too close to the Sleemans, and that Sarah Sleeman was well placed to obtain confidential information from Members of Parliament. Sleeman cultivated all sorts of politicians, wrote to them and generally received polite though non-committal answers. He would then show the letters to consulate staff as evidence that his influence with politicians made him worth his salary.

The Internee

On Monday, 8 December, police were busy arresting Japanese nationals. Sleeman was left until the next day. He had barely been locked up before he had a letter of protest on the way to Dr Evatt, now Attorney General. After looking at Sleeman's dossier before the outbreak of the Pacific War, Evatt had commented that internment should occur where there was a definite fear of sabotage, otherwise 'prosecute and punish', but much of the evidence against him could not be produced in court without damaging the security system. Besides, Evatt had made such a fuss about the bugging of the Japanese Legation that it would have been unthinkable to let him know that the phones of the Consulate-General had also been tapped.

An enemy alien could be interned simply because of his nationality; he did not need to have done anything to harm Australia, nor even to appear as though he might. With a British subject, there was supposed to be evidence of some kind: not necessarily proof, but good reason for suspicion. On Evatt's orders, Mr A. R. J. Watt, KC, conducted a special examination of the case. Sleeman was interrogated on 19 and 22 December. He was loud in his protests and denunciations. It was all a foul plot by his political and journalistic enemies. He had never taken a penny from the Japanese. Didn't his book *White China* prove how much he hated them? Watt's report, submitted on 23 December, was summarised later in this manner:

Chapter 6: The Hired Hack

> [For] eighteen months Sleeman had been a regular salaried employee of the Japanese Consulate at four guineas per week (a fact which Sleeman strenuously denied during Mr. Watt's interrogation until towards the close of the examination)... his conduct and actions and explanation of his presence at and work for the Japanese Consulate (including his presence at the Consulate when Consular papers were being burned) left Sleeman, in Mr. Watt's opinion, open to grave suspicion. No definite evidence of subversive activities was available but Mr. Watt pointed out that no reliance could be placed on Sleeman's word.

Sleeman never admitted being paid for longer than 18 months, though there is evidence that he was receiving Japanese money regularly from July 1938 to November 1941, plus bonuses. In exculpation, Sleeman wrote a long screed to Watt in late December, saying that he had been arrested because he had dared to say that Australian troops had been sent into battle poorly equipped; that the stupidity of senior officers was responsible for this state of affairs; that Australian troops should not have been sent overseas; and that a policy of appeasement should be adopted toward Japan, as Australia's armed forces were not powerful enough to defeat Japan. However, this was not the reason for his internment. He was interned because he had been a paid agent for the Japanese, because he had given them secret information, and it was feared that he would do their bidding again, if the price was right. He wrote also that he got close to the Japanese in order to try to discover whether they intended to 'plunge the Pacific into war'; but if he discovered this, he did *not* report it.

One way and another, Sleeman obtained his release on 21 January 1942, under certain restrictions. No sooner had he agreed to the conditions of his release than he began to campaign against them, claiming he had been interned because he had unearthed a dangerous plot. He appealed to the Australian Journalists Association (AJA) for support, pleading freedom of the press. On 10 February, the secretary of the AJA reported that Sleeman had asked the Executive to protect him and have these restrictions repealed, while at the same time admitting that he had been paid by the Japanese.

He wrote on 28 January to Dr Evatt complaining about the restrictions. Evatt replied on 5 February that the matter had been the subject of an impartial investigation that he would not upset, although: 'I think myself that whatever you have done of an indiscreet character would not affect your loyalty to the country in the present crisis.' If Evatt described Sleeman's activities as merely 'indiscreet', the dossier he had seen must have been very incomplete. Indeed, Military Police Intelligence would hardly have let Evatt know that Sleeman's calls to him from the Japanese Consulate-General had also been intercepted.

On 17 March, Sleeman wrote to Forde, Minister for the Army, complaining again about his parole conditions and saying he would prefer to be re-interned if restrictions were not lifted. As he was not allowed even to talk to an alien or a naturalised British subject of enemy origin, he would be unable to interview persons in the news. 'If you will not favourably consider my request will you please tell me how or to whom one would surrender.' He probably did not expect to be taken at his word, but the situation had changed so much that on 18 March, the Base Commandant, Eastern Command (Major-General A. C. Fewtrell) had already recommended that Sleeman be re-interned, as he was now a real danger. Forde signed the new detention order, and on 2 April Sleeman was re-arrested and sent to Liverpool Internment Camp.

In March 1942, Sleeman had been the target of an exercise to train police cadets in shadowing techniques. They reported, among other things, that he had contacted Jock Garden and Federal Members of Parliament, and a senior officer concluded:

> There is a mass of evidence against this man, and his continued liberty is not only a disgrace but a grave reflection on the Authority responsible for his release from internment... Any protestations of loyalty or assurance of good conduct cannot be accepted from this renegade, and I submit that the security of our Country will be best assured if he is immediately re-interned.

Sleeman bombarded Ward with letters. Ward kept passing them to Evatt, after which Sleeman wrote directly to Evatt: long, indignant, piteous protestations of injured innocence, loyalty and persecution. It seems he did not ask his brother for help, although Joseph had been Speaker of the Legislative Assembly in Western Australia since 1939. Coming in contact in Liverpool with Harry Woodfield and members the Australia-First Movement, he collaborated with them in a scheme to take revenge on Lieutenant-Colonel Prentice for their internment.[8]

Appealing to Ward for help would not have earned Sleeman credit points with Evatt or Prime Minister Curtin. Ward had been imposed on Curtin by the Labor Party's factional system of appointing ministers, whereby the only option left to the Prime Minister was to allot the portfolios among the ministers selected by Caucus. Curtin distrusted and despised Ward, and allotted him Labour and National Service, Transport and External Territories. In 1943, he was left with only Transport and External Territories. Curtin allegedly said that the army had the transport, and the Japanese had the external territories, which limited the damage that Ward could do.

In August 1942, responsibility for internments was transferred from Military Intelligence to the Commonwealth Security Service, and the ministerial head was no longer the Minister for the Army (Forde), but the Attorney-General (Evatt). In a letter written to Evatt in August, Sleeman claimed he had uncovered a dangerous conspiracy by certain military

Chapter 6: The Hired Hack

personnel to damage Australia's economy by interning loyal citizens who were doing productive work. This was combined with scurrilous attacks on the morals of certain army officers, of the sort in which he had revelled in the days of *Beckett's Budget*. He refused to communicate his discoveries to anyone below Cabinet rank and demanded to see Evatt personally.

Although Evatt was rather a sucker for a sob story, especially when it came from someone who was apparently one of Labor's 'True Believers', he did not want to become involved with Sleeman. On 15 August, Evatt's private secretary, Dr John Burton, passed on Evatt's suggestion that William J. MacKay, then head of the Commonwealth Security Service, interview Sleeman personally. Taken to Police Headquarters on 17 August, Sleeman made a statement regarding people he claimed had been unjustly interned, while claiming that he was interned because he was an obstacle to the malevolent and treacherous plans of disloyal elements in the army. He wrote:

> I absolutely failed to understand why Prentice should be antagonistic against my case, for I knew it could not be over anything I had done, because my conscience was perfectly clear on the matter. I was, therefore, slowly forced to the conclusion that Prentice possibly believed that I had learnt something about him, (presumably at the Japanese Consulate), which he feared that I might divulge. Now I go further and suggest that the reason of this attitude was based on a fear that I might be an obstacle to his possibly treacherous activities.

Sleeman had a defective conscience and an imagination that quickly turned fantasies into fact. He claimed that his information was of such value to the nation that he should be released immediately and compensated. Evatt ordered an investigation into the accusations. In October he had a special inquiry set up under W. J. Bradley, KC, Dr F. R. Louat and Mr. J. J. B. Kinkead. Adopting the guidelines and principles outlined by Evatt in the House of Representatives on 10 September 1942, they reported that there were indeed cases of unjust internment, particularly regarding some Italians interned on the 'omnibus' order of 22 March 1942, and these men were released fairly promptly. In other cases, the persons concerned were lying as glibly as Sleeman, and thoroughly warranted detention. As for Sleeman himself, this inquiry found that his internment 'was and is justified', and he should not be released unless he accepted the restrictions that had been imposed previously. 'The conduct, actions, writings and circumstances on which SLEEMAN was originally interned arose from SLEEMAN's own voluntary acts, and substantially have been admitted by him.'

Meanwhile, Sleeman was causing a disturbance in Liverpool Camp. A report from the camp on 30 October said that morale was good, except for Sleeman.

> Amongst other things he has threatened to commit suicide. The execution of this threat is most unlikely and it is obvious that if any attention be given to the vagaries of people of this kind or to hunger strikers any Camp may soon become bedlam.

On 27 November, Beckett began a letter to Ward. Now aged 72, Beckett was General Secretary of Carlyle Stevens Ltd, sole distributors of the *Australian Blue Book*.[9] He pointed out that Sleeman was a member of the Darlinghurst Labor League, a fact of which Ward should have been acutely and painfully aware. He wrote that his patience had become exhausted over the past month. 'I now write to you on his behalf to give you some very definite evidence collected by me which undoubtedly proves Mr. Sleeman's innocence.' The only evidence he had was Evatt's letter; they 'could not expect Mr. Sleeman to have to appear before a board when the highest judicial authority in the Commonwealth had declared him innocent'. However, Evatt's letter had done nothing of the kind; rather had it implied that his sins would be forgiven if he sinned no more. Beckett might not have been a knave, but he was certainly a fool.

Beckett mentioned his frequent contacts with Allan Dalziel, Evatt's secretary, and said he had appealed to Jock Garden[10] of the Trades and Labor Council to place Sleeman's case before the Darlinghurst Labor League and ask them to appoint a deputation to wait on Evatt and demand his release. He did not send the letter until 2 December, when he asked Garden to put the matter before that night's meeting 'to deal with this matter in the only way I believe will bring relief to a political prisoner'. Again, Ward simply referred the letter to Evatt. After the second inquiry, Evatt ordered Sleeman released subject to restrictions. This was done on 23 December 1942. Sleeman told communist journalist Rupert Lockwood that he owed his release to Eddie Ward, and Lockwood included this information in a report he submitted to the Soviet Embassy, a report that became known as Document 'J' in the Petrov Royal Commission.

As the Japanese were no longer paying Sleeman, and he had never worked for love of them, he probably no longer wished to act on their behalf, but he was forbidden to publish anything without the approval of the Deputy Director of Security for New South Wales, and he was not allowed to broadcast. For an author and journalist, this was difficult. It was a long time since he had done any other sort of work. Although he signed a declaration agreeing to the order, Sleeman's word was worth little. Soon he was writing under aliases and sending material abroad for publication. One of the papers for which he was writing in 1943, in breach of the Restriction Order, was Lang's weekly paper, *Century*.

On 8 September 1943, Sleeman complained again to Evatt that he had been compelled to send two books abroad to get them published and asked to be released from restrictions. On the same day, Beckett wrote to Evatt asking that the restrictions be lifted. Brigadier William Ballantyne Simpson, the Director-General of Security, would not lift the restrictions, except under the condition that *everything* Sleeman wrote, whether as a book or an article, for print or broadcast, be submitted to the Deputy Director of Security for New South Wales. Evatt agreed to this.[11] In December the restriction was eased to the extent that everything Sleeman wrote, or with which he had assisted, had to be submitted to normal censorship. This restriction was not lifted until August 1945. When Sleeman died on 16 July 1946, an item was entered in his file with a note that no further action was required, as the subject was deceased.

A Controversial Legacy

There was a postscript to the story. Calwell introduced an Aliens Bill in the House of Representatives in March 1947. Jack Lang, denouncing it as containing provisions that were an infringement of civil liberties, said it would not be necessary if lax screening were not letting Nazis migrate to Australia. Calwell retorted that Lang had employed a Japanese agent as his publicity officer. Calwell's private secretary then wrote to the Security Service asking them to check Sleeman's file, as the Minister was expecting Lang to attack him on the subject at the next sitting of Parliament, and there was some concern about a letter from W. J. Beckett, who claimed he had a letter from Evatt saying there was no justification for Sleeman's detention. This was again the letter of February 1942. Beckett was loyal to an old friend, who was now dead, and from whom he could not expect to gain anything, but he was elderly and obsessed, and he had never known the depths of Sleeman's villainy. Neither Lang nor Ward said another word on the subject. The less said the better; perhaps members of the parliamentary press gallery might fail to notice the incident. Apparently they did. Two of Sleeman's friends, Beckett and Victor Francis Vincent, District Agent for an insurance company, could not leave well enough alone. They lobbied Evatt to compensate Sleeman's widow for the allegedly wrongful internment of her husband. They did not succeed.

While the information that Sleeman gave the Japanese was probably of no great significance, the thing that made him dangerous was his influence with politicians, especially Eddie Ward, whose intention to take Sleeman as publicity officer indicated that he had fallen for Sleeman's spiel on the good intentions of the Japanese, denouncing expenditure on defence when Australia was facing no military threat. Then, apparently without a twinge of embarrassment, he began in 1942 to denounce the previous Government for failing to provide for Australia's defence. To support his arrant hypocrisy, Ward perpetrated the 'Brisbane Line' scam, alleging that the previous Government had been willing to abandon the northern and western areas of Australia to the Japanese. His 'revelations' in Parliament, if true, could have given the Japanese valuable information about Australia's defence plans. If not true, they still provided valuable information on Australian morale.

This attack on the previous Government was ridiculous, for the Labor Government had been in power since October 1941, and it was unlikely that such a formal plan would have been approved before then. Obviously, it was impossible to defend the whole of Australia against a sustained attack, and an attempt would have to be made to preserve a heartland. If Ward had ever served his country in the army, or had the slightest knowledge of strategy, he would have known this. On 26 October 1932, he had said in the House of Representatives: 'I was not old enough to go to the last war, but even if I had been I should not have gone… I say frankly that no matter what the nation may be with which Australia comes in conflict, I shall not support the project.' The plan to try to defend the more heavily populated and industrialised regions of Australia, instead of losing everything by trying to defend everything, might well have existed in military minds, but it had not received political approval from any party. The gall of such a man in criticising anybody in connection with defence plans or lack of them is breathtaking, for adherence to the statement quoted here would certainly have meant handing the whole of Australia, not perhaps just part of it, to Japan.

As for Sleeman: technically he did not commit treason, but he was dangerous not so much because of any information he gave to the Japanese, because of the extent to which he corrupted the press and seduced leading politicians into holding views and taking actions that might benefit an enemy. Equally reprehensible was the way he seduced his friends into believing in his integrity and loyalty. This cynical misuse of the trust of his friends was contemptible.

Chapter 7

The Amorous Vichyite

The French Consul-General, Jean Gaston Gabriel Marie Trémoulet, who arrived in Australia on 13 July 1937, was known among the French community in Sydney as a *sale fasciste* (dirty fascist), a womaniser and a cad even before he became a lackey of the Vichy government. As Consul in Barcelona during the Spanish Civil War, he had twice refused to obey a French government order to issue visas to Republicans who wanted to leave Spain; these people had been turned over to Franco's Falangists and killed. Trémoulet was recalled to Paris and sacked from the diplomatic service, but fascist supporters in the French government had him reinstated.

Trémoulet, born on 14 December 1891, had studied law before the war. During the war he had won the Croix de Guerre while serving as an infantry sergeant; he had been wounded and was entitled to a 40% disability pension. His marriage in 1916 ended in divorce two years later. After the war, he occupied consular posts in Buenos Aires, Brussels, The Hague, Durban, Cardiff and Barcelona.

As he was *persona* very *non grata* in most of Europe, he was sent away as far as possible, being appointed Consul-General to Australia in April 1937. He hated Australia passionately, and it was an insult to saddle Australia with such a creature. He also hated Britain, America, Protestants and Anglo-Saxons; his dream was of a fascist, Latin, Roman Catholic *bloc* consisting of Italy, Spain and Portugal under the leadership of France. In August 1939, in connection with the embargo on the export of Australian iron ore to Japan, he asked politicians about compensation for Japan, although it was no business of the French. A representative of a country that was not involved in the affair should have kept his mouth firmly shut. Later in August, he visited New Caledonia, returning to Australia on 3 September.

Jean Marie Gaston Trémoulet (Courtesy of the Mitchell Library, State Library of New South Wales: PXE 789 (v.17)/18: French Consul Jean Tremouler, 12 July 1937, photograph by Sam Hood.)

Vichy Agent

Until June 1940, when France capitulated, Trémoulet's arrogance, bullying, rudeness and flagrant womanising did little more harm than to cause dissension, disgust and embarrassment among French residents in Australia; the terms of surrender included the occupation of part of France by German forces and the establishment of a theoretically autonomous French regime in southern France, based on the town of Vichy. Soon, when he was taking German orders relayed through Vichy, he became a serious threat to Australia's security.

French residents in Australia then complained that he was blackmailing them with threats that their relatives in France would be punished if they did not support Vichy. This was the case in particular with crews of French ships, who were told that their wives and children would suffer if they served on ships sailing under British orders. When the merchant ship *Commissaire Ramel* was requisitioned during the night of 23-24 July 1940 at the request of General de Gaulle, Trémoulet went aboard and reminded the crew that French law forbade them to sail under a foreign flag. Those who obeyed him were to be sent back to France or to Saigon, but as some of those threatened had no relatives in France and nothing to lose, his actions were reported to Free French representatives in Sydney and thence to the Commonwealth Investigation Branch.

After the French newspaper, *Le Courrier Australien*, reported on 19 July 1940 that banks could not negotiate cheques drawn on the French treasury, Trémoulet quarrelled with 'Magrin', the proprietor of the magazine; then he refused to allow him on consular premises. This was probably Australian-born Edgar Earle Magrin, who had lost an eye and suffered other wounds during the Somme offensive in July 1916; his two sons were serving in the Australian army in 1940, and he had a very low opinion of Trémoulet.

During the struggle between Gaullists and Vichyites for control of New Caledonia, Trémoulet tried to go to Noumea to support the Vichy cause; he had become very friendly with the Vichyite Commander Toussaint de Quièvrecourt of French sloop *Dumont d'Urville* when it visited Sydney, and in mid 1940 the ship was stationed at Noumea.[1] On 5 July, Commander Rupert Long, the Director of Naval Intelligence, asked Frederick Shedden (Secretary to the Department of Defence), the War Cabinet and the Advisory War Council, to take steps to prevent Trémoulet from leaving Australia for any French colonial possession. This was arranged with the Prime Minister Menzies and the Minister for External Affairs (John McEwen). On the same day, a censorship instruction was issued to the media: 'No reference is to be made to the position of the French Consul-General in Australia, especially with regard to his relations with the Bordeaux Government.'

Chapter 7: The Amorous Vichyite

When he was denied passage on any ship, Trémoulet tried to send a series of admonitory cablegrams to Noumea. As the French code was being read, the contents became known. The privilege of using a diplomatic code was withdrawn from him, and soon the cable companies were ordered to delay any cables to or from Trémoulet by a few days. His cables were vetted, and anything truly obnoxious would simply be lost. On 10 July 1940, an order was given that no cables by Trémoulet, cipher or clear, were to leave Australia, nor cables sent by others on his behalf, and he was to be prevented from leaving the country. By now, the French had completely lost control of the codes and ciphers in which they communicated with their ships and colonies; their 'secret' communications were being read in Singapore, Britain, Australia, Germany, even in New Zealand. As they could not distribute new code books, every word sent could be read, every move forestalled.

New Caledonia Powderkeg

New Caledonia was in a state of turmoil verging on civil war. Many of the 17,000 permanent settlers, both tradespeople and farmers (*colons*) supported de Gaulle, but they lacked a leader. Most of the public servants, Catholic missionaries and military and naval officers (*métropolitains* from France) supported Vichy, and the military commanders, Lieutenant-Colonel Maurice Denis and Captain Michel, were prepared to arm the natives to suppress the French colonists, who were outraged that a French Government was prepared to arm *kanakas* to kill white French citizens.

Then, as the Japanese consular codes had also been broken, it became known that signals from Masatoshi Akiyama, the Japanese Consul-General in Sydney, to Tokitaro Kuroki, Consul in Noumea, contained messages from Trémoulet to the Governor of New Caledonia. Trémoulet had earned the enmity of the Dutch Consul-General, Tom Elink-Schuurmann, and his French wife by telling her how pleased he was at the destruction of Rotterdam. Madame Elink-Schuurmann had access to French consular circles, and one of her confidantes was an undercover security agent. She said that her husband claimed to know beyond doubt that Trémoulet sent secret messages through the Japanese. His flat in Wentworth Place was only a few houses away from the residence of the Japanese Consul-General at 69 Wolseley Road, Point Piper, and he often paid long visits there; he had told her that the Japanese were right to take over Indo-China, as they needed bases there from which to attack Singapore.

The security services exploited Trémoulet's weakness for women and turned female agents loose on him. The agent mentioned above appears only as 'Mme X', who may have been Madame Elink-Schuurmann herself, but could possibly have been either Dorothy Jenner, who wrote for the newspapers under the name 'Andrea', or Amélie Tuband, who had worked in the consulate 1938-40 but was sacked by Lancial when her father was appointed to the Free French Committee in Sydney. Jenner spoke French, was a sympathetic listener, and often dined with Trémoulet. 'Madame X' said later that she was glad to play a role in Trémoulet's downfall, and he had no idea of her part.

The Commonwealth Investigation Branch tried to obtain acknowledgeable proof that messages were being passed over. It was difficult to keep the Japanese consulate under observation, as the Grace Building in which it was situated had exits on three streets (York, King and Clarence), so it was Trémoulet who was shadowed. On the afternoon of 2 August 1940, he left his house at Point Piper to keep a tryst with Vice-Consul Kenichi Otabe. They met to exchange *billets doux* in St Andrew's Cathedral on George Street; as neither was a devout Anglican, their attendance was obviously not related to piety. The contact was no great surprise, as Otabe was known to be the Foreign Office (*gaimusho*) agent for clandestine contacts with non-Japanese. On that same day, the High Commissioner in London (Bruce) cabled Prime Minister Menzies that it had been learned from 'most secret' sources, a circumlocution for decrypted wireless signals, that the Japanese Government had instructed Kuroki to obtain the entire New Caledonian nickel output; that the Vichyites in Noumea were negotiating for Japanese 'protection'; and that Vichy had ordered French colonies to detain British shipping pending German instructions. As Britain was reading the Japanese consular codes and ciphers, what the Japanese sent to and from Australia, and what Trémoulet and Vichy sent through the Japanese was also known.

After a bomb was thrown at the residence of Governor Georges Pélicier in Noumea, he sent for *Dumont d'Urville* and Quièvrecourt to suppress the Gaullists. When the captain's Order of the Day denounced the Free French as criminals who were taking foreign bribes, the council cabled Pétain demanding that Pélicier be dismissed. Pétain replaced him with the fanatical fascist Denis, who all but plunged New Caledonia into civil war. It was vital to keep Trémoulet away from Noumea; Denis, Michel and Quièvrecourt were dangerous enough, but Trémoulet would have put a match to the powder keg.

The Department of the Navy reported to Cabinet that the fact that Trémoulet was allowed to continue his activities was being interpreted as meaning that Australia did not support the efforts of French residents to oppose Vichy subversion. Those who were aligned with the Free French had practical worries that were largely solved when Britain guaranteed on 15 August to pay salaries and pensions, and to deport the Vichyites. De Gaulle asked the Resident Commissioner in the New Hebrides, Henri Sautot, to go to New Caledonia as Governor to rally that colony to the cause.

Chapter 7: The Amorous Vichyite

With more than a little help from the Australian navy, he arrived there on 30 August. Pélicier left a few days later. Sautot dithered, but with a bit of pushing from Australia, pointing out that it would supply New Caledonia with neither food nor coal if she declared for Vichy, which would cripple industry and make life very difficult, and some pulling from General de Gaulle, the situation was resolved slowly. When Colonel Denis ordered the fort to fire on the cruiser *Adelaide*, which had entered harbour, the troops refused. When Quièvrecourt sent a party from his ship ashore to enforce a curfew, they were stoned and beaten; being unwilling to fire on the settlers, they had to retreat to their ship. Quièvrecourt was brought to heel by some hard facts. One was that his crew was on the verge of mutiny; another was that the only practicable source of fuel for his ship was controlled by the Australian navy, and he would not get it unless he reconsidered his attitude. Then Sautot cut off food and water to the French sloop.

Code-breakers in New Zealand now found that Vichyites in Saigon were sending the sloop *Amiral Charner* to New Caledonia with one hundred troops from Indo-China. The idea of turning Indo-Chinese troops loose on the French settlers in Noumea was bizarre. It was a farce, for not only was everybody reading the French codes, but the Germans were reading the RAN cipher in which *Adelaide* was communicating, and this information was recorded in their intelligence reports. Germany had little interest in the Noumea tragi-comic opera, and probably did not pass the information to Japan. When it was intimated that the ship would not be allowed to reach Noumea, let alone land troops, she returned to Saigon. She would have been no match for *Adelaide*. The recent actions of the Royal Navy against French warships would have suggested to the Vichy Government that the threat that *Adelaide* would be prepared to sink *Amiral Charner* was not an idle one. Sautot had Colonel Denis and seventy-three of his troops arrested and put aboard *Pierre Loti* with their families. They were transported to Brisbane, whence they were forwarded to Saigon by *Tanda*.

With the situation in New Caledonia resolved, Trémoulet was no longer a menace, only a nuisance. Britain reported on 17 October that French consuls were reporting the movements of British ships, and code facilities should be withdrawn. In Australia, this had already been done on 18 September. Trémoulet also lost his censorship privileges. Even before that, he had tried to send letters to the Vichy governor of New Caledonia with the captains of French ships, but the captain of *Cap Tarifa*, who supported de Gaulle, reported the attempts to Naval Intelligence (22 August). He said that the letters would probably go by *Néo-Hébridais* (29 August), and suggested that the vessel be intercepted. A Free French supporter also reported on 21 October 1940 that Trémoulet had asked the Japanese Consul: 'Why don't you seize New Caledonia? You could do it in half an hour. Australia has nothing with which to oppose you, only wooden guns.' It was a step that Japan was not yet prepared to take.

Consular Changes

The report said further: 'Mr Trémoulet has not a friend amongst the French people in Sydney. All without exception despise him intensely. For them he is the symbol of all that is rotten and evil in France.' This may have been from the report that R. L. Loubère, a French consular official, is known to have made to Australian authorities on Trémoulet's state of mind and on conflicts within the consulate. In December, he resigned from his consular position, allegedly in order to join the Free French air force.[2]

The French Consulate was in dire financial straits. Consular funds were down to £150 by 25 October; staff had not been paid since August, and it would soon be impossible to pay pensions due to French civilians and ex-servicemen. On 9 October, the *Comptoir d'Escompte de Paris* Bank refused to allow funds to be transferred to Trémoulet. He opened an account in the Bank of New South Wales, Sydney, and the Japanese came to his aid; the Yokohama Specie Bank provided him with £6,000. It might have been a pay-off for Vichy aid in Indo-China, or it might have reflected Trémoulet's usefulness to Japan, or it might have been French or German money sent via Japan. As the Security Service was being supplied with information on the French consular bank withdrawals and balances, it knew how desperate their financial position was becoming.

Trémoulet tried to dissuade Frenchmen passing through Sydney from joining the Free French forces, threatening them with loss of citizenship. Early in November, he suppressed cables from the French community in Sydney offering their services to de Gaulle, but the cables from Dr Louis de Gellé, President of the *Alliance Française* in Perth, were beyond his control, and Gellé was appointed Consul for Free France.

In December, Censorship found a letter from a Frenchwoman to her husband in Hong Kong:

> He is the cause of much misery to all the free French - he threatens them and has even told them it is no good them thinking they will be able to return to France later on, as, if they did, they would be shot. He has even gone as far as saying that their families denounced by him are being martyred and sent to Concentration Camps.

The Free French and the Australian authorities put Trémoulet under increasing pressure and restrictions. He was removed from the presidency of *Alliance Française* early in December. During the first week in December, Trémoulet was seeing the Japanese Consul-General Akiyama almost daily on the pretext of arranging the repatriation of French officers in Indo-China. On 5 November, Sir Frederick Stewart, Minister for External Affairs, made a formal recommendation to the Full Cabinet that Trémoulet's *exequatur* be withdrawn. On 5 December, the king approved the request. This was not formalised until a cable from the Secretary of State for Dominion Affairs in London arrived on 12 December, and it was published in the *Commonwealth Gazette* that his consular recognition was withdrawn. Trémoulet was notified on 15 December, and he proposed to travel via Saigon to his new post as Consul in Canton.

He was replaced by Charles Emile Dominique Lancial, Consul in Melbourne since December 1939. Lancial, who had married the widow of a Russian consular official, had been consul in Leipzig before the war, but he had been genuinely anti-German until the collapse of France. Like Trémoulet, he took orders from Vichy; although he was not such an ardent fascist, nor such a cad with women, he too was unpopular with the French community in Sydney. They considered him 'a very poor specimen of a man, with bad manners and approach', although others described him as 'sound, placid and well-balanced', despite his well-publicised controversies with the Minister for External Affairs (Sir Frederick Stewart) and the Attorney-General (W. M. Hughes). He was no friend of the Japanese and was less of a threat to security, even though he had told a former Australian soldier:

> You have run away every time that you met the Germans… If the British ever land in France they will be chased out by the French population. There's not only this but other things that we French people have against the British and want to settle… You are a skunk like the rest of them.

Either France's consular corps was a rather inferior type of service, or the very worst of it was inflicted on Australia. Tens of thousands of Australians died fighting in France in World War I; they helped save France, even if their motive was not primarily love of France. Lancial did not have a monopoly on invective; he was the target of a lot of abusive letters of this type:

> Get out before it is too late. You bloody Bastards you kidded Britain to protect you buggers in 1914 & again in 1940 … rotten spies & cranks are selling loyal France [*sic*] people to murder. Get out of our country.

On 4 January 1941, the Secretary of State for Dominion Affairs (London) informed the Prime Minister's Department that it had been learnt 'from a most secret but certain source' (cryptanalysis) that the French Consul-General at Sydney had corresponded with his Government through the Japanese Foreign Office suggesting suppression of the Vice-Consul, whose sympathies were anti-Vichy. Trémoulet was ordered to leave Australia. He kept promising to leave, then cancelling his arrangements, under the pretext of having received no instructions from his Government.

In December 1940, businessman André Brenac was appointed Free French leader in Australia. The family had been established in Australia for many years, while senior consular personnel were recent arrivals with no affinity with Australia and little understanding of the country.³ Brenac had been editor of *Le Courrier Australien* from July to December 1940, but although most of the French in Australia supported de Gaulle many of them did not support Brenac, saying he had too great an opinion of himself. He asked that Trémoulet be sent to Indo-China, not America, and that he be sent out unexpectedly, so that he could not take out documents to the detriment of the Free French. It may have been partly coincidental that Trémoulet's censorship privileges were withdrawn the following day; such decisions are seldom made so quickly. Vice-Consul Frank Puaux took matters into his own hands; he removed sensitive documents from the consulate safe, lodging them and the key to the consulate safe in his own bank safe deposit box; then he went to Newcastle and took passage in *Cagou* to New Caledonia, where neither Trémoulet nor Australian courts could touch him.

Trémoulet's Last Australian *affaire*

Trémoulet had an Australian paramour, Cynthia Margaret Powell, whom he had been considering sending to America 'for a holiday', as he had some money there. Cynthia, born in Siam in August 1916, was recorded as a dress designer and photographic model, and her stated reason for wanting to go to America was to study as a beautician; her request for permission to travel was endorsed by Clive Evatt (Dr Evatt's brother). For a time, Military Intelligence tapped her telephone and intercepted her mail, in case Trémoulet tried to use her as a channel for forbidden communications. No evidence has been found that they tapped the phones of the French consulate while it was under Vichy control, but it would be surprising if they did not.

It was reported on 7 January 1941 that Trémoulet had not received instructions from his Government about where he should go, but had booked a seat on a Dutch plane leaving for Indo-China on 31 January, and a berth on a Japanese ship leaving for Manila on 1 February. A week later, he had still not received orders. On 1 February, he booked on *Atsuta Maru*, leaving on 12 February for Japan. On 3 February, the British High Commissioner, Sir Geoffrey Whiskard, passed on a message that Britain did not want Trémoulet to pass through Singapore; apart from security considerations, it was policy to make the movements of Vichy officials as difficult and circuitous as possible.

On 6 February, Brenac protested about Trémoulet's continued presence in Australia. Trémoulet had changed his mind about going to Saigon; now he wanted to leave for the United States by the next American ship. The Department of External Affairs told Trémoulet that if he did not leave then, he would be interned until he was put on a departing vessel. Trémoulet then said that he was booked to leave on 7 March. Australian patience (or dithering) lasted until Saturday, 22 February; he was arrested at 11 o'clock that night and interned in Liverpool Camp.[4] Both he and Lancial raised mighty howls of protest. He was released during the evening of 24 February, after giving a written undertaking to leave Australia by the first available ship; he now had a firm booking to leave for Los Angeles by *Mariposa* on 7 March. Indeed, he might have been waiting for this ship all the time, for he had already booked his paramour aboard. He claimed that he intended to marry her. The local French were flabbergasted. On the one hand, Cynthia Powell was young and pretty, while he was bordering on elderly, divorced, and a rather unpleasant character. On the other hand, they considered that she was not the sort of girl whom one married.

Trémoulet arranged for a cosy table for two in the dining saloon, and side-by-side deck chairs outside his stateroom, but they were 'just friends'. This grim little farce of Vichy's man in Australia drew to a conclusion, and one French resident in Sydney wrote triumphantly to a friend in Saigon that the 'beast of a Trémoulet' and his 'tart' had left for America. The liaison did not last. About a year later, she turned up in Portugal and appealed to a British consul for help to return to Australia via South Africa. At least Trémoulet was not such a cad that he left her stranded and penniless. Through the Australian High Commissioner in London, he sent her £200 for fares and upkeep. What happened to Trémoulet after he returned to France is not known, except that it was reported that he died in 1973. It is not part of Australia's story.

The Ousting of Vichy Agents

On 24 April 1941, it was announced that the Melbourne Consulate, which at that time was probably being run by Pierre Clémentel, would close, and French-Australian relationships resumed some sort of normalcy. However, Lancial carried on Trémoulet's work. Neither French nor Australians liked or trusted him; true, he had not been a tool of the Japanese, but he soon became closely associated with them. It was reported on 31 May 1941: 'The Australian authorities know that France is secretly using the Japanese Consulate. The only thing is to close the French Consulate.'

From February 1941 onward, Lancial was engaged in a battle with the Bank of New South Wales over the material that Puaux had left with them. This contained not only files, telegrams and confidential consular documents, but code books and the key to the consulate safe. In September, the case came before the courts in Australia. Puaux was now a judge in New Caledonia; he refused to recognise the legitimacy of Vichy, and threatened to counter-file a suit for unpaid salary before he would give the bank authority to hand over the material. No record has been found stating how or when the French Consulate-General regained access to its safe or Puaux to his arrears of salary.

On 21 October 1941, Admiral Darlan of Vichy demanded that all diplomatic and consular staff write out and sign a declaration of loyalty to Vichy, and threatened dissenters with punishment.

Once the Japanese came into the war, Lancial could no longer send coded messages through their consular service. The Security Service had somebody ferreting through the consular waste paper baskets, and Lancial was sometimes irresponsible enough to throw out secret documents instead of burning them. The Security Service patiently patched together scraps of torn letters, and did not like what was found. In February 1942, censorship found a letter that he tried to send to the Minister for France in Lisbon and withheld it: 'The writer must be credited with sufficient intelligence to be fully aware that his enclosures, openly intended for the enemy, were damaging to Australia.'

Australia showed great patience – or laziness and cowardice - with regard to the French. On 11 November 1942, the Germans began to occupy Vichy France, ending the bizarre charade that it was still independent and French. It was noted on 23 November 1942 that Australia was the only member of the Allied nations that still recognised Vichy consular representation, and all Vichy establishments should be closed. The king revoked Vichy *exequaturs* for Australia and New Zealand on 30 November, and Lancial was instructed on 8 December to close the Vichy Consulate-General immediately.

As the closing of the Vichy consular offices left the way clear for the 'Free French' representatives of de Gaulle, Brenac was appointed to look after French affairs. Lancial, however, continued to exercise some consular functions for another year or so, even without official recognition. Although Brenac was a rather difficult man who caused some dissension within the French expatriate community, he was no friend of the Japanese and no threat to Australia's security. In September 1944, he left for a Free French consular post in South Africa.

Besides being an unpleasant character, Trémoulet had been dangerous, because he encouraged the Japanese to seize New Caledonia – not that they needed much encouragement, for they had allegedly been scouting for submarine bases there by early 1940. A Japanese naval base in the islands would have threatened the sea links between Australia and North America. If the Vichyites had gained control of New Caledonia, the Japanese would have been welcomed officially, no matter how the colonists felt about them.

Chapter 8

The Bigamous Abortionist

The Commonwealth Investigation Branch and Military Intelligence spent a lot of time investigating the controversial Ross family in Queensland. Central to their enquiries was Dr Arthur John McLaren ('Jack') Ross. The CIB kept watch on him for some fifteen years. In the 1990s, some people in Brisbane still reacted to his name with: 'Ah, yes! Jappy Ross! Abortionist, you know. Killed a girl once.' If he did, that was not the reason for CIB interest in him, and the allegations that provided a pretext for his internment – that he was of partly Japanese ancestry and was working for the Japanese – were definitely not true.

Family Background

Many of Ross's troubles were of his own making, but some were the fault of his father. John Christopher ('Chris') Ross claimed he was born on 25 March 1866 on the island of St Vincent in the West Indies, of a Malay father and a Scottish mother, whose name he took. He also claimed he was the son of Robert Ross and Elvira Valadares, of mixed Portuguese and native South American parentage. These were the details declared when he applied for a passport, but obtaining proof from the West Indies was not easy. The CIB usually asserted that his father was Japanese. Although his passport photo shows a facial bone structure and eyes that look rather like high-class Japanese, and not at all Malay, few Japanese were allowed to leave the country before July 1866, so the birth of a half-Japanese child in the West Indies four months before then would need some fancy explanation.

Occasionally he claimed, in one of the Japanese clubs in Brisbane, that he had been born in Japan, which raised a remote possibility that his father was Scottish and his mother Japanese. At other times, the CIB reported that Chris was Australian, but his wife was Japanese, and therefore Jack was

Arthur John Ross (Courtesy of National Archives, Australia: D1901, R38: ROSS, Arthur John McLaren. [Portion of photo.])

'half-caste Japanese'. The more that Jack Ross denied Japanese ancestry, the more people wrote him off as a liar. An inquiry in 1943 decided that Chris Ross's father was West Indian or South American, and his mother part Portuguese. Whatever their origins, the family had enough money and social standing to give Chris a good education. He became a teacher, and about 1888 he allegedly married Imogene Florence Sharples. One son, Claude Vane Ross, was born allegedly on 4 June 1889 at Kingston, St Vincent Island. There were also two daughters: Alice Lalytha and Cecily. Jack was allegedly born on 18 July 1893 in London, but registrations in England show only one Arthur John Ross born in the third quarter of 1893, and he was born on 24 July, the son of John Arthur Ross and Elizabeth Hackett, while Cecily referred in one letter to *Aunt* Imo. It is possible that Cecily and Jack at least were the nephew and niece of Chris and Imogene Ross. That was ancient history, but they certainly had no Japanese ancestry.

About 1904, Chris went to Japan for a British engineering firm, and he soon set up an export business of his own. Either on the way to Japan or soon afterwards, he visited Australia, but for most of the next 28 years he lived in Japan.

Jack spoke Japanese fluently, but he probably could not read or write it. He studied medicine in Japan, at an institute that gave lectures in Japanese, but allowed examinations to be taken in English. He registered at the British Consulate as a British citizen on 8 October 1912, and soon afterwards, without completing his studies, he left Japan because of woman trouble. At times, he said he went to Australia as an acrobat and strongman with a troupe of Japanese jujitsu performers. At other times, he said he went as a farm labourer (possibly with the aim of eventually buying land for the family) and joined the acrobats only when a member of the troupe let them down. He worked for about six months as 'Kondo', the name of the missing man.

Jack left the troupe to work as a herbalist, again passing himself off as Japanese, this time under the name 'Kameda'. On 15 August 1916, in Adelaide, he married Phyllis Avice Parker, registering himself as Kuma Ross-Kameda, born Yokohama, son of Kosaburo Kameda. This deception came back to bite him 25 years later. Within a few months, Jack Ross left Phyllis and returned to Japan to complete his studies, graduating in 1918. In July he was ordered to report to the consulate to be returned to Britain for military service, but the war ended before transport could be arranged. Instead, he returned to Australia in 1919 and took up with Phyllis again.

How was he to earn a living? He could not practise medicine, as foreign medical qualifications were not recognised in Australia. It did not take long for Ross to get around that problem. Britain and Japan had a reciprocal arrangement regarding recognition of qualifications. Ross served as a ship's medical officer in the British merchant navy long enough to have

Chapter 8: The Bigamous Abortionist

his qualifications recognised in Britain, and Australia recognised British registration. Thus Dr A. J. M. Ross could set up practice in Brisbane, in Rothwell Chambers, Edward Street. As the only Japanese-speaking doctor in Brisbane, he served most of the Japanese community, which did not entirely please him, because they demanded a lot of attention and paid their bills slowly, and Jack Ross liked money. With his lifestyle and his obligations, he needed lots of it.

Claude Ross had worked for the Canadian Trade Commissioner and for Standard Oil Co. and other firms in Japan. He became a proof reader, then a sub-editor with *Japan Mail*, an English paper, then with *Japan Advertiser*, an American paper. From 1918 to 1923, he taught English, after which he worked in his father's export business. He had two sons and a daughter by a Japanese girl, daughter of a small landowner and a shopgirl. His wife died in 1921, and his daughter also died. In August 1926, Ross took his elder son George to Brisbane for schooling. George was the only member of the family in Australia who did have some Japanese ancestry. Claude worked in a Queensland sugar mill for several years. In 1928, he married an Australian girl whom he took back to Yokohama the next year. He obtained a teaching job at Mito High School and stayed there for ten years.

It is not known when Jack Ross and Phyllis split up, but in December 1929, he married Dorothy James (Jimsie) Sharp, a Brisbane girl some ten years younger than he was. This was another delicate matter. He and Phyllis had apparently not divorced; but then, had they ever been legally married? He had used a false name, while she had been married in England, under age and without parental consent, so had her first marriage been valid? There was no divorce, but had the marriage been annulled? Despite these irregularities, he continued to pay her an allowance.

At about this time, Dr Ross attracted the attention of the Security services. He had given up his Brisbane medical practice and was trying his hand as a business entrepreneur. While on holiday in New Zealand in 1930, he became interested in land on Sunday Island in the Kermadec Group belonging to New Zealand.[1] It was said that he had bought or was trying to buy 200 acres there. News of this reached a Goondiwindi chemist, a former soldier who was a friend of Claude's second wife. In 1931, he wrote to the Prime Minister of New Zealand, warning him of the sort of person he believed Ross to be. He said he wished strongly to remain anonymous, as 'I want to live a long time yet'.

New Zealand referred the matter to Australia, and in April 1931 the Investigation Branch in Brisbane reported to Canberra. Sunday Island was said to be good only for feeding goats. But it was about 650 miles (over 100 km) from Auckland, between New Zealand and the Friendly Islands (Tonga), in an excellent position to carry on the opium smuggling in which Ross was believed to be involved. Ross had set up the Barrier Reef and

Coastal Tourist Company and bought an ocean-going yacht *Stradbroke II*; at the time of the report, he was in Gladstone, running tours to the Barrier Reef.

The IB in Brisbane reported that Ross was badly balanced, irascible and at times 'non compos mentis'. He was a clever abortionist, using a Japanese method that took only about 20 minutes, and he had never lost a case. It was also claimed he was a drug trafficker, but the police could not catch him. He did so many abortions that the police should have been able to catch him at that if they had wanted to do so. While admitting performing abortions, he claimed that they were all necessary for the woman's health, and therefore legal. The report summed him up: 'All information about him is most adverse, and his name may be said to "stink in the nostrils" of respectable persons in Brisbane.'

Under Notice

As often happens once a person comes under suspicion, ulterior motives were ascribed to everything Ross did, including his Barrier Reef trips. It was thought that he was passing to the Japanese soundings of the reef further south than their sampans normally operated, and he could have been picking up drugs dumped at sea or cached on an island.

Ross's life was far from simple. He had had a row with his father over his demands that Chris, in order to get him out of trouble with the Taxation Department, make false statements that money sent to him from Japan was repayment of a loan. It was possibly undeclared income from his share in his father's business in Japan, but the mystery about its origin caused him more trouble than the Taxation Department could have given him, for Military Intelligence suggested that it could have been payment from the Japanese government for 'services rendered', i.e. espionage. This is highly unlikely; Japanese payments for espionage were concealed better than this, being made in cash through commercial firms in Australia, and the Japanese secret service was downright parsimonious in its payments to agents, few exceeding £25.

On 19 March 1931, Chris Ross wrote to Jack concerning finance, saying: 'Your share of Grandma's estate came to about £7,000.' He added that both the accountants who had been looking after Jack's financial affairs had died, and that all records had been lost in the fire that followed the great earthquake in September 1923. Chris, though he told some fancy fibs when it suited him, resented having his son demand that he lie for him.

During the same earthquake, Chris had received a severe blow on the head. Since then he had been subject to bouts of mania, and he had tried to commit suicide. Japan had no facilities for European mental patients, and his wife and daughters, unable to bear the strain of watching him constantly, asked Jack for help. Chris was 65 years old and in poor health; he was allowed entry into Australia only on condition that Jack take financial responsibility for him. Ross senior was virtually penniless and totally dependent on his son. Arriving in Brisbane in February 1932 aboard *Nellore*, Chris Ross settled in Toowoomba. Jack and Dorothy Ross had returned to Brisbane, but they did not want him with them, owing to the unwanted advances he made to their maid and receptionist and female friends.

In 1934, Dr Ross and his wife and son went on an extended holiday to China, Japan, Siam and Europe. On his return, he wrote an article for the Brisbane *Courier-Mail* about poverty and distress in Japan, about children being sold to factories, and the appalling conditions following a typhoon in July.[2] A Japanese agent in Brisbane sent a copy to Mitsui, and they gave it to the Consulate-General in Sydney. The Japanese did not like unflattering comments about their country.

His wife having died, Chris married Helen West, a retired hospital matron, on 17 April 1934. The marriage did not last long, for it turned out that he expected his wife and Jack to support him financially, while his wife expected him to do the providing, and Jack expected him to need less money. In May 1935, Chris Ross was committed to Goodna Mental Hospital, where he stayed for six months. His wife moved to Brisbane and refused to return to him.

Dr Ross came under Investigation Branch notice again in connection with G. Howard Robbins and G. M. Smerdon who were trying to make some dishonest money out of alleged ore deposits on Iron Islet. On 26 May 1936, Inspector Wake sent a report to the Sydney CIB, repeating allegations of abortions, drug smuggling and espionage, and adding that Ross was associating with Japanese from a company called Australian Mineral Deposits, and had recently entertained them at the Bellevue Hotel.

It was natural that Ross, as one of the few Caucasians in Queensland to speak really good Japanese, should be asked to help with translations and advice, but the CIB arranged to intercept his correspondence for a time in order to find people who would report on his activities. According to the subsequent report, his current mistress was too enamoured of him to be of much use, and she was in any case not very intelligent, but his previous mistress was hostile over the way she had been dumped and might be induced to talk.

In 1937, Chris Ross, now nearly 71, had delusions about going back to Japan to claim a share of his late wife's property and conduct some business; he obtained a visa and booked his passage aboard *Kamo Maru*. There were protests from his daughters in Yokohama, begging Jack to have their father certified as insane to prevent him from returning, as 'his breakdowns are getting more and more frequent and at very best in his comparatively lucid moments he is more than merely eccentric'.

Chris had been in a mental hospital for a second time after 1935. When the Consulate-General was informed, his visa was cancelled; a letter of 18 May 1937 said there was information from Japan indicating it would be inadvisable for him to go to Japan at present. He wondered if the 'information from Japan' was to the effect that he had taught English to the Soviet Trade Representatives in Tokyo for six months, and he protested to the Consulate-General that he was not a communist but a very keen member of the Douglas Social Credit Party. Suspecting that his children had intervened, he was bitter about their 'ingratitude'. The fact that he was living off Jack's charity did not prevent him from writing a rambling screed denouncing his son, and claiming that Dr Ross had been born in Georgetown in British Guiana. Jack Ross protested vigorously; as he had always said he had been born in England, this made him seem a liar.

Until then, the activities of Chris and Jack Ross had drawn limited public attention and low-level interest from Security and police. It was largely the fault of Dr Jack Ross himself that they became a massive public scandal. Ross became involved with the United Protestant Association and the weekly paper, the *Protestant Clarion*. Their initial aim was to counteract the excesses of a militant, bigoted section of Catholic Action. The first issue of the *Clarion*, on Thursday, 27 January 1938, stated its principles:

> Democracies must remember at all times that the price of liberty
> is eternal vigilance . . . In Queensland, Protestants have been
> asleep while Roman Catholic leaders have in accordance with a
> planned campaign, captured Parliament . . . Nurtured in tolerance,
> Protestants are apt to forget that Rome has never been tolerant, that
> she claims dominion over the whole world.

The *Clarion*'s business office was in the Country Press Chambers, 117 Edward Street, in the same building as herbalist Robbins, he of the Iron Islet affair. Management changed hands a month later, and the paper degenerated into vituperative bigotry over both genuine evil and imagined wrongs.

Ross was supposed to have financed the *Clarion*; of more than 10,000 shares issued, his wife held about a third, but he held only 253 in his own name. To edit the paper he picked Ernest Charles Ranger, who had a lot of debts and a series of convictions for trivial offences. Some of the Ross family had links with Christian Science, and the *Clarion* frequently featured reprints from the *Christian Science Monitor*; besides trade advertisements, it ran announcements for the Loyal Orange Lodge and British Israelites. When Prime Minister Lyons visited Pope Pius XII, it stigmatised the pope, not without some reason, as a friend of the Nazis. It stressed that the Nazi leadership was largely Catholic: Hitler was Austrian Catholic; Hess and Himmler were Bavarian Catholics; Goebbels was Rhineland Catholic and

Chapter 8: The Bigamous Abortionist

had trained as a priest. It unearthed widespread fraud in electoral rolls. It attacked the Catholic Church, especially the work of Catholic Action in stacking the Cabinet, the Public Service and the police force with a much greater percentage of Catholics than their numbers in the population would justify, and attacked the 'corrupt influence' of individual Catholics on the Labor Party and the Queensland Government. It attacked the virulent Father Cain, who publicly advocated that all Protestants be 'kicked out' of the Queensland Public Service.[3]

Its prime target was Edward Michael (Ned) Hanlon, later Premier of Queensland, claiming that he had 'dreams of being a second Mussolini'. As Minister for Health and Home Affairs, he was responsible for liquor licences, gaming and racing, and these were areas where money could be made from bribery and racketeering. He was Patron of the Returned Soldiers and Sailors Labor League Club, which sold liquor after hours and operated gambling machines. Its manager, John Quinlan, was a friend of Hanlon and was involved in running the Golden Casket Lottery, which was known to have been rigged occasionally. Many of the *Clarion's* accusations were true, for corruption in Queensland politics did not begin in the 1960s, but its savage style was counterproductive. The United Protestant Association helped form a Protestant Labour Party to oust the government of William Forgan-Smith, putting up George Sydney Webb to run against Hanlon for the seat of Ithaca, which Hanlon had held unopposed at the previous election. Labor could not afford to lose the funding that came from racketeering in licences, and Hanlon could not afford to lose his seat. According to Jack Ross, Hanlon initiated the Labor gerrymander of electoral boundaries and was the originator of police corruption in Queensland. The election of 2 April 1938 became one of the dirtiest and most savage ever held in Queensland.

During the evening of 1 April, a band of Hanlon supporters swept through Ithaca electorate, dropping in letterboxes a leaflet containing scurrilous accusations against members of the Protestant Labour Party. It claimed that Robbins, the organiser, was a herbal quack who had robbed the Catholic Church of £13,000 on the sale of his house in Kedron; that the President, Webb, an ex barrister, had been convicted of embezzling trust funds; that the secretary, Smerdon, a solicitor, had been struck off the roll in England for professional misconduct regarding clients' money; that the Patron, 'Jappy' Ross, had been responsible for the death of a young woman during an abortion.[4]

The pamphlet was illegal, as it did not bear name of printer and authoriser. Quinlan was seen putting these pamphlets in letter boxes, and it was taken for granted that Hanlon was involved. George Alfred Morris won the seat of Kurilpa for the Protestant Labour Party, and Webb polled well, but Hanlon was declared the winner in Ithaca. Webb challenged this, not just because of the leaflet and violence and threats to people handing out how-to-vote cards opposing Hanlon, but because Hanlon's men had removed ballot boxes illegally. The *Clarion* (7 April) offered a reward for proof of the origin of the pamphlets and called for money to finance the legal challenge. The court declared that Hanlon 'was not duly elected', and the election was 'void', but this was overturned on appeal, and Hanlon attacked his opponents under parliamentary privilege.

The pamphlet affair revived the interest of the CIB and Military Intelligence in Dr Ross, and Hanlon turned his police force loose on him. One case that added to the notoriety of Dr Ross was the disappearance of Marjorie Norval, secretary of the wife of Labor premier, Forgan-Smith. She took leave of absence from her job, saying she going to visit her sister, who was ill. A friend took her to the station to catch a train late on 11 November 1938, and she was never seen again. When she was reported missing, it was found that her sister was not ill, and the train she pretended to catch did not exist; but evidence was found that she had been about five months pregnant. There was a strong presumption that she had gone to have an abortion and had died as a result. People jumped to two not entirely illogical conclusions for which there was no real evidence. First, that Forgan-Smith was the child's father. Second, that the abortionist was Dr Ross, who usually did the abortions for the girlfriends of politicians, police and socialites. Her body was never found; but it was noted that Ross had an ocean-going launch, and the bay was full of sharks. The mystery of her disappearance was never solved.

Security estimated that in 1938 Dr Ross had a legal income of about £2,500 a year, and probably another £2,000 from illegal abortions.[5] He owned more real estate than even a well-paid doctor could have purchased from legal earnings: his house in Moray Street (New Farm), four blocks of flats, two other houses, three cottages, two building blocks.

World War II

At the outbreak of war, Dr Ross offered his services to the Citizen Military Forces. He was enlisted in the Army Medical Corps long enough to get a uniform, but was discharged when Security found out. Claude's son George also enlisted early; it is possible that, as was the case with several other part-Japanese Australians who enlisted in the army, he let it be thought that he was Maori. Chris was totally against the war. In October 1939, he wrote to George that killing was against God, and he was opposed to fighting for the British Empire. The only cause worth fighting for was the Social Credit Movement, and the only democratic country was Russia. Claude, however, gave his blessing.

Chapter 8: The Bigamous Abortionist

In Toowoomba, Chris Ross had been evicted from his boarding house in Clifford Street; his landlady complained that he came to breakfast only in kimono, demanded rice after every meal, and made disloyal remarks. He dossed down in the lending library that he ran in Empire Chambers, Ruthven Street. His rooms were searched during his absence, but nothing of security interest was found. He was a nuisance to a lot of people; Kyohei Sakamoto had driven him out of his laundry because of his harassment. A report said that Chris Ross was eccentric, an inveterate scrounger who wore second-hand clothes and hitched rides to Brisbane in trucks to save the fare, but he was a 'harmless old humbug'.

Losing patience over the damage done to him by Chris's ramblings, Dr Ross said he would refuse to continue to support him unless he left Queensland. Early in 1940, he took Chris to Sydney and found him accommodation in the Salvation Army Home in Thames Street. Chris was found dead a few weeks later and was buried on 30 January.

At about this time, Dr Ross visited the Japanese Consulate-General in Sydney and spoke to the Vice-Consul, probably concerning family affairs in Japan. In April 1941, A. L. Baker, editor of the *Queensland Producer*, reported this when, in his capacity as an executive of the Queensland branch of the Australian-American Association, he complained about an attack the *Clarion* had made on this organisation. Although Ranger was editor of the paper, Baker blamed Ross. The *Clarion* had written that Paul McGuire, a well-known Catholic lecturer and author, had visited Brisbane to help establish the Australian-American Association, and accused it of being 'Roman under cover', studded with Catholics in administrative positions. In fact, McGuire was strengthening links with America on behalf of Naval Intelligence and MI-6, and *Clarion* staff were meddling in things they did not understand. The paper kept up its anti-Catholic diatribes, many of which were banned by Censorship. The Reverend William Daniel McIlwraith objected that Catholics exerted undue influence in the Censorship Office and threatened to make a public complaint.

In June 1941, Censorship notified Military Intelligence: 'Censorship take a hostile view of this extremely scurrilous paper and has been in conflict with it from time to time.' It had been 'subjected at times to severe censorship by excision of articles considered subversive of the war effort'. The *Clarion* antagonised Labor supporters, Catholics, communists, police, politicians, the Intelligence services, even mainstream Protestants. Support came from Protestant extremists, Christian Science, Social Crediters and British Israelites, which was not enough when it came to a showdown.

Anonymous letters accused Dr Ross of being in secret communication with Japan; of using a wireless transmitter; of frequently expressing pro-Japanese sentiments. The Security Service noted that his brother Claude had arrived in Brisbane in April 1941. Commercial secretary Albert Hard in Tokyo had advised all Australians in Japan who could leave the country to do so. 'And go quickly!' he said. Claude, his wife, son Alan and daughter Cecily left Japan in the evacuation ship *President Cleveland*, and transhipped in Hong Kong to *Nankin*. His sister, Cecily Harrison, and Claude's son Jackie went to Shanghai, and unfortunately stayed there too long. Claude settled his family in Caloundra, initially in a house owned by Jack. Their other sister, Lytha, arrived on 16 May, visited Jack at New Farm, stayed for a while with Claude, then went on to Christian Science friends in Sydney. In Brisbane, a Security agent had followed Lytha from *Suwa Maru* to Jack's house.

As well as being stridently anti-Catholic, *Clarion* warned against the danger of an attack by Japan. Claude wrote some of these articles as 'The Trumpeter', or 'our special correspondent'. Defence 'experts' were saying that the Japanese did not make good pilots because they had poor eyesight and a poor sense of balance, and their forces were so heavily committed to fighting in China that they would not dare attack the mighty British Empire. An article on the Sydney *Daily Telegraph* in October 1938 proclaimed that Japan could not invade Australia: 'First of all, she would have to crush France's Indo-China, then the Singapore base, then the Netherlands East Indies - impregnable walls that would turn back the tide of aggression from Australian waters.' Ross said that they made very good pilots, and their army was so large that they could attack Malaya without depleting their forces in China, and they were very likely to do so. This was true, but it was not what Australian politicians and military experts wanted to hear. For this Ross was abused as being 'pro-Japanese'; but the blind arrogance of the 'experts' did the greater harm.

In August 1941, Professor Ryonosuke Seita, Japanese lecturer at the University of Queensland and close friend of Mitsuru Toyama (head of the Black Dragon Society), gave a party at which he tried to enlist Dr Ross's help in getting Japanese propaganda articles into the *Clarion*. Ross refused and reported the offer to Security. He received no appreciation for this; Security interpreted this as meaning that Seita must have felt confident that Ross would accept a disloyal proposition, so they put Ross's house under surveillance from 11 to 23 August.

Whatever the Rosses did, Intelligence could put a sinister interpretation on it. They had known Harry Woodfield in Japan, and had renewed the acquaintanceship in Brisbane, and Woodfield was also marked down as a villain.[6]

Dr Ross tried to buy property on Fraser Island in 1940, allegedly for a tourist resort and trout fishing. It was noted that some Japanese had been interested in the island, and the property Ross wanted to buy was near a point where RAN ships sometimes anchored.

Chapter 8: The Bigamous Abortionist

For the 1941-42 summer vacation, Dr Ross rented on Bribie Island a cheap house that was beneath the social standing of a doctor, but in a sensitive area from a defence point of view. It was found that this was the only place available at short notice and that, contrary to reports, the ocean could not be seen from the house. Ross was building a new house at Clontarf on a bluff overlooking Moreton Bay and Hayes Inlet. It was not sufficient explanation that this was a very attractive location; it had to be so that he could observe naval movements and report on them, or send signals to Japanese ships.

Neighbours saw kimonos in Mrs Ross's wardrobe, and Japanese sweets in the house. Cecily and Lytha had sent them as gifts, but they were taken as evidence of a preference for the Japanese way of life. Especially suspicious was the fact that the Rosses liked Japanese food and even bought dried mushrooms. At the Caloundra School fancy dress party in 1941, said an informant, Dr Ross's daughter had been dressed as a Japanese lady, and his son as Hitler; both had won prizes. In fact, Dr Ross's children did not attend Caloundra School; these were Claude's children, and the humourless Nazis would not have liked to see Hitler mocked.

An informant reported from Caloundra that Dr Ross was continually snooping in a prohibited area, wandering along the beach and taking photographs. His children had allegedly said: 'Daddy writes his letters by typing them and then writing in invisible ink between the lines.' It turned out that Cecily, *Claude's* daughter, had told a playmate her father typed letters; this friend had told her mother; the mother told a neighbour, who admitted that it was he who had invented the invisible ink to 'puff' the story.

On 8 December 1941, someone wrote to the Security Service in Canberra suggesting that the Rosses should be watched. Canberra passed this on to Brisbane. On 27 January 1942, Military Intelligence in Brisbane sent back an automatic and inane reply of the sort that lazy public servants hope to get away with; it stated that the activities of Dr A. J. Ross and his father were being closely watched. They were watching Chris Ross so closely that they did not even know he had been dead for two years. One report claimed that A. J. Ross was interned for sectarian activities and J. C. Ross for political activities. Chris Ross was not *interned* at all; he had long been *interred*. In Brisbane, Inspector Wake controlled both the Commonwealth Security Service and Military Intelligence; they were understaffed, but some of their work showed lack of intelligence and a surprising degree of ignorance as well.

However, there were reasons for genuine concern. Letters found among Professor Seita's correspondence confirmed Ross's visit to the Consulate-General in Sydney, and among the papers of suspected spy Kanjiro (Henry) Suzuki was a certificate from the Ministry of Foreign Affairs acknowledging a contribution of £1.10s to a Japanese Defence Fund from Ross. Later Ross said that Suzuki had withheld payment of a fee for medical treatment and had applied it without his knowledge.

The intensification of the investigation into the Rosses and action against them was the result of several factors: a number of letters of denunciation; the worsening war situation; a leaflet published and distributed by the Protestant Truth Society, but connected with the *Clarion*. Entitled *The Story of the Little Papal Flag and the Threatened Japanese Invasion of Australia*, this claimed that children in Catholic schools were being given yellow and white Vatican flags as a recognition signal to protect them from brutalities when the Japanese invaded, but nothing protected Catholic priests and nuns who were murdered in New Guinea.

In February a letter from Caloundra said of Claude: 'this Ross is of Jappenese decent', and 'others has seen him commin from the direction of the camp early in the morning. & also morse codeing all hours at night'. (The informant was as ignorant as she was illiterate.) Another, concerning Dr Ross, said that 'he has done abortions for so many prominent men that they now shield him and he can blackmail them'. In that there was some truth, but it was a matter for the police, not Security.

It was reported that he had a stock of petrol at New Farm, that he had visited Amberley district near the RAAF base and become friendly with servicemen and their wives, and that he used his position as proprietor of the *Clarion* to get information on the armed services. Someone at Clontarf had a grandson who played with Dr Ross's son Philip. The child claimed he had seen guns at home, and that Philip had allegedly said they could put out a signal for the Japanese.

Internment

From 28 March, his telephones were monitored: one in Clontarf and three in Brisbane. As is the case with many phone taps, nothing significant was overheard. On 4 April, Jack Ross was arrested at Clontarf and Claude at Caloundra, on an order signed by the Minister for the Army, Frank Forde, a long-standing friend of Ross's enemy, Ned Hanlon, a fellow-member of the Labor Party and a fellow-Catholic. Ross's houses at Clontarf and New Farm were searched, his premises in Rothwell Chambers, his caravan, his launch. He had one shotgun and a good wireless receiver, but no transmitter. The police seized correspondence, three diaries, *National Geographic* maps (hardly secret), two swords, and some communist literature.

Dr Ross's appeal against his internment was heard in Adelaide on 5 October. The Tribunal reviewed the allegations against him and set out its findings.

- *He was half Japanese.*

Conclusion: this was without foundation.

- *He had lived in Japan and knew the language.*

Conclusion: he spoke Japanese fluently, but apparently could not read it, and he had associated with the Japanese Friendly Society in Brisbane.

- *He had passed himself off as Japanese and had gone through a marriage ceremony under a Japanese name.*

Conclusion: true. '[This] will clearly demonstrate the internee's capacity for deception both as to his appearance, and also as regards the truth.'

- *He had engaged in subversive activities.*

Conclusion: he had been involved in the Iron Islet scheme, and was connected with the 'Styles case' in 1938, although he denied knowing Styles. In fact, Styles was connected with Chris Ross, but knew Jack only slightly.[7] No importance was attached to his proposed land purchases, but he was closely associated with Suzuki.

- *He would be willing to assist the Japanese.*

On this point, the Tribunal passed no judgment, but the report said that the case against Ross was weak, based solely on suspicion and the fact that he had posed as Japanese, and the question arose of wrongful internment through spite. Security in Brisbane said he had been interned because he caused sectarian strife. (In June 1941 he had called for the internment of Archbishop Mannix of Melbourne.) So were attacks on the Catholic hierarchy, even venomous ones, now to be grounds for internment? The judgment of the Tribunal was that Dr Ross had had 'so many associations with Japan and Japanese people, has engaged in so many activities which are open to suspicion, and is such an unprincipled person that it cannot be said that he can safely be at large'.

In February 1943, it was repeated that, if Ross were released, the sectarian issue could be aroused again. Censorship reminded papers that internees were not to be named, and no reference was to be made to the Ross case. Dr Ross was released in February 1944, but apparently required to stay out of Queensland.

Claude Ross, on the other hand, impressed the Appeals Tribunal. His son George had been with the AIF in Libya, Greece and Crete, and had been mentioned in despatches.[8] The Japanese had interned his sister and elder son in Shanghai, and the war had ruined him. For a year he had been secretary of the Association of Foreign Teachers in Japan; Captain George Caiger of Intelligence Section General Staff had known him well in Japan and vouched for his loyalty. It was considered that he had not engaged in subversion and was not likely to do so; nor would his release cause unrest in the community, so he was released on 12 November 1942.

After the war, Dr Ross wrote a text book on judo, conducted a judo school, and in 1956, aged 64, represented Australia in the First World Judo championship. He also allegedly spent some time in Goodna Mental Hospital, and a few years later opened a 'Japanese Centre' in Southport.

It is unlikely that Dr Ross had been any sort of spy; he was not even a significant 'agent of influence' for Japan. However, he was a mischief-maker and had few scruples about how he made money. The Japanese, via Suzuki and Seita, had sounded him out thoroughly, and if they had occupied a part of Australia where he lived, he might have become a collaborator. So would a lot of other Australians. Ross became a victim of his own petty deceptions. However, internment for slightly less than two years, which he probably did not deserve, was a cheap trade-off against a lengthy term of imprisonment, which he escaped but richly deserved, for fraud, tax evasion, medical malpractice and possibly drug smuggling.

Chapter 9

The Vodka Priest [1]

The poignant story of the Russian émigrés in Queensland in the first half of the 20th century has never been told properly. People outside the Russian community have had little idea of the personal dramas involved, and few would have had the ability to investigate the stories. Thus their history has been written almost exclusively by members of this community or those closely associated with it. Early attempts to cloak the tensions within the community in a dignified reticence have led to a perpetuation of inherited myths, and this has had unfortunate consequences. Just as the German-Australians had a vested interest in claiming that their community was treated with unwarranted harshness and malice during the war, so do the writers of the history of the Russians complain that they were persecuted simply because they continued their opposition to communism while the Soviet Union was a wartime ally of the British Commonwealth.

Most Russian émigrés were not a threat to Australia's security during the war, and most were not interned or molested in any way. Writers on the topic seem to have felt that, in order to protect the community, it was necessary to depict all Russian immigrants as loyal Australian citizens, or at least as harmless. A small and dangerous minority were not, and to deny this is not only an insult to the Australian authorities, but it also does an injustice to the Russians who tried to control the rogue elements in their midst without letting the dissent become public knowledge. The task was made most difficult by the fact that these elements were encouraged by their Archpriest Valentin(e) Andreyevich Antonieff. Their courage and desperation should not be underrated or trivialised.

Australia has been a haven for refugees fleeing all sorts of problems: economic, political and religious. Irish revolutionaries, German republicans in the mid nineteenth century, Eastern Europeans from Soviet tyranny after World War II, Hungarians after the uprising of 1956, Vietnamese, Lebanese, Iraqis, Afghans, Bosnians, Somalis; and for something like a hundred years Russians fleeing either Tsarist tyranny or Bolshevik savagery. In the late 19th and early 20th century there were anarchists and Marxists such as Nikolai Bukharin and Feodor Andreyevich Sergeyeff ('Artem', also 'Artyom') – transients who returned to their homeland when the Tsar had gone. After about 1923, there were White Russians, especially various groups of Cossacks, who settled mainly around Brisbane or in the cotton-growing districts around the Callide Valley. When one thinks of 'Russian' subversion in Australia, one tends to think of *Soviet communist* activities, but there was a genuinely *Russian* form of subversion that, for a brief period, also threatened to be dangerous. How a few of the Russians in Australia came to be working for the Japanese needs explanation.

There were many separate groups among the Russians who had settled in Australia. Prior to 1914, Marxists and anarchists who had taken refuge in Australia were closely associated with various Socialist Parties in Australia and the Industrial Workers of the World (IWW or Wobblies). The main such activist in Queensland was the anarchist Nicholas Frederick Lagutin, who arrived in Australia in October 1916, aged 39. He was the only member outside New South Wales of a so-called 'Secret Seven', who advocated armed revolution against the government and formed a 'Russian Liberation Army'. During the 1914-18 war, they linked up with Sinn Fein (the revolutionary Irish independence movement) and certain Germans to oppose Australia's participation in the war and to arrange and fund the printing of anti-conscription leaflets. Lagutin delivered inflammatory speeches at the Russian Association:

> The Revolution must come. The Red Flag is the Emblem of anarchy, riot, bloodshed and destruction. The Red Flag should be unfurled on public buildings in Australia and all national flags hauled down. (21 December 1918)

> Men in high places must be got rid of. I should like each man here present to find out where munitions and arms are kept and where judges and the chief politicians live. At some future date I will lecture on the making of bombs. (27 July 1919)

Lagutin proclaimed that all rulers would be guillotined if he had his way, and that he was obtaining help from an expert in Sydney who would help them make bombs and incendiary devices. These socialist-anarchists were not noble champions of the welfare of the workers; they were the urban terrorists of their day, and it was their activities that precipitated the so-called Red Flag Riots in Brisbane in March 1919.

Following the 1917 Revolution, many Russian exiles sought to return to the Soviet Union to aid the Bolshevik forces in the civil war. While Australia would have been glad to get rid of them, their presence in Russia was seen as a threat to the anti-revolutionary forces supported by Britain, so obstacles were put in the way of their departure. When the civil war ended in victory for the Reds, there was little point in hampering their movements, and many left Australia. Thus the problem of Russian communists in Australia became less of a threat. The danger from the revolutionary left wing came now from local Anglo-Celtic residents and occasional visiting Soviet agents.

Chapter 9: The Vodka Priest

Russian Emigré Community

After the war, the majority of Russian immigrants consisted of White Russians and Cossacks, who just wanted to be left in peace to put their lives together. Many arrived in Australia virtually destitute. Many worked first at seasonal cane-cutting and cotton-picking, then some took up cotton-growing land at Cordalba in the Callide Valley (south-east of Bundaberg), or at Biloela and Thangool (east to south-east of Rockhampton). Others worked on the Brisbane waterfront or the Mt Isa mines. Still others worked in George Bros furniture factory in Coorparoo or their retail store in Woolloongabba, in an area known for many years as 'Little Russia'. In exile they clung to the little that was left to them: their language, their Cossack identity and the Eastern Orthodox Church.

The White Russians who settled in Australia between about 1923 and 1940 had suffered a great deal and were often severely traumatised and emotionally unstable. Most were well educated, of good family, sometimes minor nobility, usually connected with the Russian Orthodox Church or the Imperial Army or both. After an early life of privilege and culture, they had been through a nasty war, a nastier revolution, and a truly terrible civil war. Many had seen family members butchered. The Cossacks were not mild-mannered Sunday School teachers, and they had responded in kind. With the progressive destruction of the White Russian forces, they had escaped to Manchuria or Mesopotamia (Iraq) with what they could carry, losing much to theft and bribery and leaving many friends along the way as victims of disease or brutal murder.

They were survivors, willing to do whatever was necessary, be it hard menial work in mines or road gangs or stoking coal aboard ship, to support themselves and their families and to send their children to university. They were mostly honest hard-working folk, and they were valued employees. Filled with an implacable hatred of the Bolsheviks, they hoped that Lenin and Stalin and their minions would be destroyed and were eager to help in this destruction. In fact, those allowed to enter Australia had probably been checked to ensure that they were hostile to communism. They had few true friends. France and the United States gave many of them asylum but little help, so some looked for help where they thought they could find it. Some looked to Germany, to fascism and National Socialism to help them oust the Bolsheviks, and after Japan overran Manchuria others were forced to look to Japan. Some of those who made their way to Queensland had left relatives in Japanese hands and, from inclination or fear, a small number were willing to work in the covert service of Japan.

The first organised group of about thirty persons arrived by *Tango Maru* on 16 July 1923 under the leadership of a 42-year old 'priest-monk' (*hieromonk*) Alexander F. Shabasheff. At Woolloongabba, he organised the first Russian Orthodox parish, St Nicholas. Land was purchased in Vulture Street through a nominee who was a British national.[2]

The impoverished parish operated under makeshift conditions; Shabasheff's parishioners could not afford to support him, so he had to work as a labourer. However, it was not exclusively financial problems that almost destroyed the parish. Part of the problem lay with Shabasheff's character and his alcoholism. Another factor was the arrival of several groups who had bore no allegiance to Shabasheff and who neither liked nor respected him. The second organised group, consisting of Ural Cossacks under General Vladimir Sergeyevich Tolstoff, their *ataman* (chief or general) since 1919, arrived by *Yoshino Maru* on 4 November 1923. (See below for details.)

Many former members of the defeated White Army had found work with the Chinese Eastern Railway or the South Manchurian Railway, but a series of secret agreements during 1924 resulted in these men being removed from their railway positions and having little opportunity to find suitable employment. At this point, migration of Russians from Manchuria to Australia increased sharply. In 1925, at least eight groups arrived, bringing people who were to play leading roles on both sides of the schism in the Orthodox Church and the community: in March, Michael Ivanovich Maximoff (*Tokyo Maru*), a captain in the Russian navy and outside the Cossack groups; in April, Alexander Alexandrovitch Gzell (*Tango Maru*); in May, Vladimir Modestovich Vitoshinsky (*Aki Maru*); in August, Dmitry Anisimoff (*Aki Maru*).

The census of 1933 showed that there were almost 5,000 Australian residents who had been born in Russia. It was estimated that there were about 1,500 in Queensland,[3] of whom 300 lived in the Brisbane metropolitan area. An Intelligence report claimed in 1939 that these 300 Brisbane Russians had formed fifteen separate associations. There were several groups of activist White Russians. The Russian Imperial Union was in contact with Paris and the United States. Imperialists, mainly in France, waited in sad and genteel poverty, eking out a living as waiters, musicians or teachers, selling their remaining jewellery, and hoping that the communists would fall so that they could return home. The Legitimists supported Grand Duke Kyril Vladimirovich as the rightful tsar, despite his German wife's early financial support for Hitler.[4]

In Queensland, their leader was Vladimir Vitoshinsky, who arrived in Brisbane in 1925 aged 27. He was said to have operated a printing press for the Russians. (In fact it was only a duplicator.) Among the Imperialists were Michael Maximoff, Vassily (Basil) Posharsky and the Logootin brothers, Stephan and Vassily.[5]

At some time during 1932-33, Vitoshinsky had discussed linking up with Adela Pankhurst Walsh's Women's Guild of Empire and

Chapter 9: The Vodka Priest

the Sane Democracy League, which at that time were merely anti-communist rather than pro-fascist. Prior to 1936, he had also been in contact with the *Fichte-Bund*, which distributed Nazi propaganda.

Captain Maximoff, who had a Polish mother and Russian father, was one of the few Russian naval officers in Australia. Having arrived in Australia in March 1925, he had picked cotton at Thangool, cut cane at Childers, worked as a seaman, then in Brisbane at odd jobs such as carpentry, painting and gardening. He tried to establish himself as an author, and from 1936 he had been running a group of the National Organisation of Russian Razvedchiks Scouts.[6] The group, founded in 1909 and with headquarters in Paris, had an alleged membership of about 90 youths, who were being trained to keep the Russian language and Russian culture alive in Queensland, in accordance with the old slogan: 'Faith in God. Loyalty to the Tsar. Help to Others.' Authorities had it marked as extremely nationalistic, but not fascist, and noted that Maximoff and Antonieff were personal enemies. It is not entirely clear from documents which Pretender to the Russian Imperial throne was supported by Vitoshinsky and Maximoff.[7]

The Cossacks, whose homelands were mainly in the east of European Russia but west of the Urals, stood apart from the French-speaking nobility, the barely literate peasantry, or the turbulent intelligentsia. They formed close-knit communities, prosperous, freedom-loving, independent-minded and proud, with a strong military ethic and a reputation as fierce, feared and fearless warriors. They also wished the communists to perdition, but they seem not to have cared much which Grand Duke became Tsar, as long as they had their independence, and they did not think it was a good idea to enlist the aid of the Japanese and Germans. There were two distinct groups of Cossacks in Southern Queensland. After Tolstoff's Ural Cossacks had cleared Bolsheviks from their region, Admiral Alexander V. Kolchak had promoted him to lieutenant-general, but the war was lost.

The Cossacks did not surrender; Tolstoff led his typhoid-ravaged troops and their families on a 6100 kilometre trek along the Caspian Sea, across the desert to Mesopotamia (Iran). Many died along the way or gave up and stayed behind; optimistic reports claim that 4,000 reached Teheran, and that some served in the Shah's army, while some continued on to Basra.

According to Jon Smele,[8] of approximately 12,000 who set out on this trek, only 214 reached Persia. An online article on the Siberian White Army claims that there were 162 "Cossacks" left, but this may refer only to the number of fighting men or to the few who continued on to Manchuria with the aid of the Royal Navy. Some of these traumatised survivors were the people who eventually found sanctuary in Australia. Tolstoff's group settled mainly in the Callide Valley, and as the senior officer in the Russian community he tried tactfully to patch up divisions in the community. His adherents included Stephan Andreevich Logootin, who became parish secretary; Roman Klementievich Emelianoff; and Peter Makarevitch Smikoff, a Don Cossack and former lieutenant in the White Army and with Kolchak's forces. They had little regard for Shabasheff, and later even less for Antonieff, although the Ural Cossacks provided a substantial part of the funds for the parish of St Nicholas.

Leader of the Orenburg Cossacks in Queensland was 'George George', whose real name was Gyorgy Ippolitovitch Uglichinin, son of their *ataman* General Ippolit Ivanovich Uglichinin. Smele names Alexander Ilyich Dutov, assassinated in China in February 1921, as *ataman* of the Orenburg Cossacks; Ippolit Uglichinin apparently led a group that remained in the Balkans. Gyorgy arrived in Queensland with his wife Elena in *Aki Maru* on 7 August 1927, and was followed by his presumed brother Sergei, who arrived in January 1930 by *Orsova* from Naples. (Sergei used the spelling 'Ouglitchinin'.) They had money and enterprise enough to set up a furniture factory in Woolloongabba to provide employment for their compatriots. Most of these held moderate views: they were Cossacks, not fascists. There would still be customers who remember the photos of Cossack officers on the walls of the small office at their retail store.

When they were settled, the brothers applied for their parents to join them, but the *ataman* died, apparently in Yugoslavia, before they could set out, and only Lydia, their mother, came in May 1932.

The Cossacks and some other former officers belonged to a group called the Russian General Military Union (ROVS; see end of chapter.), a broadly based organisation that admitted most eligible men. Former Lieutenant-Colonel Vladimir Petrovich Peshkoff held the registration forms and was in close contact with General Evgeny Karlovich Miller in Paris, but there were at least two full colonels in Queensland: Ivan Ivanovich Popoff in Brisbane, and Vsevolod Vasilievich Korzhenevsky in Thangool. Peshkoff had arrived in Brisbane in 1926 aged 34; he worked as a boot maker until he obtained a waterside worker's permit in 1928, and he was naturalised in 1932.

Being a ROVS leader could be dangerous. In January 1930, the Soviet OGPU kidnapped the leader General Alexander Kutepov in Paris. In December 1936 (or early 1937), the next leader, General Miller, was also abducted in Paris, taken to Moscow, tortured and killed. The Australian branch of the ROVS began to issue its own bulletins and orders in 1933, and they established contact with leaders of the former White Russian Army in Belgrade and Sofia. The main aim of the ROVS in Europe was the restoration of an Imperial Russia, but the overriding permanent order from leaders of the former White Russian Army was that they should be good citizens of whichever country offered them a home.

Chapter 9: The Vodka Priest

Russian Fascists in Queensland

The Russian Fascist Union (RFU) formed another group. It definitely existed, but it is highly likely that claims that it met on the top floor of 779 Stanley Street, Woolloongabba, were untrue; this was probably the Russian Club, which was concerned mainly with social activities. The RFU had about 20 members in Queensland, but probably none in other states. They were the ones who caused almost all the trouble instigated by Russians, and who got into trouble themselves. It was established in Harbin (Manchuria) as the Russian Fascist Organisation by 1925, and by 22 May 1931, at the First Congress, it was called the Russian Fascist Party.

Some reports say that it was renamed the Russian Fascist Union at the Third Congress at Harbin in July 1935, when its programme was approved, stating its main aim as 'the overthrow of the Jewish-communist dictatorship in Russia', which would lead Russian workers not back to imperialism and capitalism but to a socialist form of government similar to Italy and Germany. Another claims that it was renamed on 28 July 1937, St Vladimir's Day,[9] when connections were established with the Black Dragon Society of Mitsuru Toyama and a section of the Japanese secret service (the *tokumu kikan*) run by General Sadao Araki, who had been military attaché in Russia, spoke very good Russian and seems to have liked Imperial Russia but loathed the Soviet Union. Later, Araki was War Minister, and after the war he was tried as Class A war criminal. (Toyama died in October 1944.)

The RFU, with its headquarters in Harbin, was led by Konstantin Vladimirovich Rodzaevsky; born on 11 August 1907 in Blagoveshchensk, north of Harbin, he was a turbulent ambitious dreamer with a fragile grasp on common sense, and he saw himself as the *vozhd*, the leader or *Führer* of a Fascist Russia.[10]

The RFU was prepared to work with anyone who might overthrow the Bolsheviks, but its contacts were mainly with the Japanese. Toyama and Araki provided Rodzaevsky with financial backing, but this meant that he could barely scratch an itch without Japanese permission. The FBI reported: 'Japanese sources have never denied that the Russian Fascist Union plays a part in the plans of the Nipponese in the Far East.' It published two magazines: *Nash Put* (Our Path) in Harbin, and *Natsiya* (Nation) in Shanghai. (See Appendix 2 for a summary of the different fascist organisations.)

Most of the dangerous Russians in Queensland belonged to the RFU, the Brisbane branch of which was allegedly founded by Alexander Vitte (born 24 January 1881, Kooronia), who arrived with his wife Nina in September 1925 by *Mishima Maru*; they were naturalised in 1936. Little is on file regarding their activities, for they departed for Shanghai by *Kamo*

Maru on 3 July 1939, leaving behind their married adopted daughter.[11] He told relatives he had been offered a 'lucrative commercial position', but he would continue the work of the RFU. British Intelligence in Shanghai was warned to keep an eye on the Vittes.

Rodzaevsky had asked a number of other people, including Maximoff, to represent him in Australia. All refused, until he approached Ivan Pavlovich Rodjestvensky, who became Member No. 68 of the RFU. About 1934, the latter began to work actively for the Harbin fascists, whereupon he and about eight others were expelled from the ROVS in August for spreading fascist propaganda. Rodjestvensky, who ran a barber and hairdresser shop on Logan Road, Woolloongabba, had been a lieutenant-colonel in the Imperial Army. After leaving Russia, he worked with the Chinese Eastern Railway, Harbin, and the Manchurian Society of Research; in 1925, he worked briefly with the Portuguese Ships Police in Macao. He arrived at Thursday Island by *Mishima Maru* in August 1925, aged 30. By early 1937, this group allegedly had only eight members in Queensland and none anywhere else in Australia. In April 1938, Rodjestvensky wrote to his wife, who was visiting her parents in the Callide Valley, saying that he was sending money to the Fascist Centre in Harbin, that some Nazis from the German Club had invited him to the celebration of Hitler's birthday on 20 April, and that he intended to go for business reasons.

Despite this information on Rodjestvensky, it was suggested that Vitte had been replaced by Aleksei Nikolaevich Stepanoff, who arrived in Brisbane in September 1939, aged 31. Stepanoff and his wife had lived in Queensland previously. They had marital problems, and their travels between Australia and Asia, including Manchuria, led security to think they might be engaged in drug trafficking. Stepanoff gave his profession as motor mechanic, and he worked for a time with A. P. Uscinski, an engineering firm in Coorparoo. Then they moved to Newcastle, which did not fit in with the idea of Stepanoff as RFU leader in Brisbane. In addition, Peshkoff had warned the Russians in Harbin that Stepanoff was a communist, and Intelligence thought he might be working for Vonsiatsky rather than Rodzaevsky. It was all very confusing.

In Connecticut, USA, another Fascist group had arisen in 1933: the All-Russian Fascist Organisation. It was led by Anastase Andreevich Vonsiatsky and financed by his wealthy American wife as a hobby for him. He fantasised that the Nazis would liberate Russia and hand the government over to him as *vozhd*. He wore a fancy uniform with a swastika armband, and he had new words praising himself written to the tune of the Nazi *Horst Wessel* song. He decorated everything in his house with swastikas, from lampshades to waste paper baskets. He too published two magazines: *Fashist* in Connecticut, and *Russky Avangard*, edited by Konstantin Alexeyevich Stekloff in Shanghai. In these he published fanciful

Chapter 9: The Vodka Priest

accounts of the exploits of his mythical agents in the Soviet Union. At first, even *Ataman* Tolstoff cautiously supported the Vonsiatsky; a letter he wrote, eulogising Mussolini and Hitler as liberators of their countries, was published in *Fashist* in April 1934.

In October 1931, Vitoshinsky (in Brisbane) had asked Vassily Alexandrovich Prootkovsky to accept leadership of an anti-communist league in Sydney.[12] He too claimed to have been an officer of the Russian Imperial Army, commissioned in 1909. An imaginative character, he claimed that he had been a machine-gun instructor in France at a time when, according to Military Intelligence, there were no Russian troops in France, and a diplomatic courier between France and Petrograd in 1916, when there was no Russian diplomatic courier service, and his own documents showed he had been in Russia the whole time. He also claimed he had been a prisoner of war in Germany for several years and that he had been treated for shell-shock and deafness, but Security believed that he was probably a malingerer. Prootkovsky claimed he had met Trotsky, who had asked him to organise a division of the Russian army, and shortly afterwards he was fighting with the British against the Bolsheviks, and was awarded the Military Medal. Military Intelligence said he could not have met Trotsky under the circumstances he described, and he had no Military Medal. He claimed that all his family starved to death or were executed, but he was writing to a sister and brother in Leningrad. They appeared to be comfortably settled, and when censorship was introduced Military Intelligence read their correspondence.

Prootkovsky claimed he had served in the police force and had escaped to Shanghai on a Dutch ship, but there was a reluctance to believe anything he said about his activities before he arrived in Australia by *Aki Maru* in May 1926, aged 36. He worked as a cane cutter, and as a gardener, and at the time of the maritime strike in 1935 he was a seaman. While working between Sydney and Vancouver in 1936, he offered his services to Vonsiatsky's group as its Australian representative. He was described in the party's magazine, *Fashist*, as the party's travelling organiser in Australia, distributing propaganda and reporting on Russians in the country. A letter from Prootkovsky appeared in *Fashist* of November 1937; it said they were gaining new fighters to serve 'under the holy swastika'; that was sheer fantasy. In mid 1939, he reported that he had placed his cherished bound copies of *Fashist* in the library attached to Russian House in Sydney; early in 1940 he mourned that they had been burned along with all other fascist literature.

In May 1941, Captain B. Tyrrell of ISGS (Intelligence Section General Staff) wrote that Prootkovsky was 'somewhat eccentric' and the Russians in Sydney would not associate with him, while one prominent Russian called him 'a damned fool'. Unaware of the capabilities of the Security services, Prootkovsky assured Vonsiatsky blithely: 'Nobody can prove anything against me.' At the hearing of his appeal against his internment, he said that Vonsiatsky was 'all bluff'. It was a charade for which the participants paid dearly.

The leader in Queensland, in fact probably the only member, was Nicholas Gregory Pole-Rogan of Thangool,[13] who was also in regular correspondence with Vonsiatsky and Stekloff. It was said that he had once been a supporter of Trotsky, but by 1919 he had been an officer in Kolchak's White Army in Siberia. Then he had gone over to the Bolsheviks and by 1922 had become a lieutenant in the Red Army in the Far East. It is likely that at least part of this is wrong. It was also claimed that he had studied law in Vladivostok and had become a magistrate there. He arrived in Brisbane on 5 December 1925 by *Mishima Maru* without his wife, and apparently she never joined him. He had made two trips to China and Japan, in 1928-1929 and again in 1935, and he had probably met Stekloff during his 1935 visit to Shanghai. He was a frequent contributor to the magazine *Fashist*, writing under the alias of 'Fashkor 973'. (Fascist correspondent) It seems a little unusual that the proceeds of cotton share-farming at Thangool could have financed two overseas trips. There was apparently only one other member in Australia.[14]

The glue that held the disparate elements of the White Russian community together was a mixture of anti-communism and the Orthodox religion. Rodjestvensky wrote in December 1935 that there were four communist papers in Queensland alone, adding: 'Dark powers are against us.' Outside these two factors, there were many differing opinions and some bitter conflicts.

Role of the Orthodox Church

Cutting across the political divisions were religious divisions between Nikonians and Old Believers. When Shabasheff's character and alcoholism, rather than serious differences in doctrine, caused a church schism in Brisbane, a group that included Maximoff, Popoff, Vitoshinsky, Smikoff and Logootin asked Father Adrian Gheorgievitch Tourchinsky to set up an alternative parish called Our Lady of Kazan. With his wife and three children, he had arrived from Hankow, aged 41, aboard *Mishima Maru* in December 1924. Unfortunately, Tourchinsky died of 'consumption of the throat' on 4 September 1928; the fate of Brisbane's Russians might have been quite different and more pleasant if he had lived. Shabasheff's departure for the USA the following year was possibly connected with police investigations into some 40 pounds of opium (ca 20 kg) allegedly smuggled to him from China. There must have been something in this allegation, for later Alexander Gzell admitted that he had been involved

Chapter 9: The Vodka Priest

briefly in trying to sell opium on Shabasheff's behalf, and that he had been 'a fool' to trust the priest.

When Shabasheff left, a group of parishioners wrote to their former priest in Shanghai: Archimandrite Methody (Methodius) Shlemin, who agreed to go to Brisbane. Metropolitan Anthony Khrapovitsky (in Serbia) appointed him rector of St Nicholas as from 20 August 1929, and he arrived to take up the post in October 1929. He was greeted with joy, but he received little financial support from his parishioners, and for most of the time they paid him no stipend. On 24 December 1930, the parish of St Nicholas was incorporated, and the loan raised to buy land in Vulture Street, Woolloongabba, was paid off by the following year. Failing to heal the rift between the two factions in the Church, Methodius moved for a time to the Callide Valley; then in 1933 he was called to Sydney when their rector retired. This was Brisbane's loss and Sydney's gain. Methodius kept politics at a distance from the Napier Street church; the RFU did not take root in Sydney and, as far as can be ascertained, only one Russian from Sydney was interned. (Prootkovsky)

Antonieff's Era

The Russian community now asked Father Valentin Antonieff to act as their priest. His personal temperament and addiction to alcohol helped to split the Russian community in Brisbane in the 1930s and 1940s into bickering factions and contributed to the behaviour that led later to the internment of some of its members. While his appointment was being considered, the *hieromonk* Feodot Shaverin conducted services; he was a worthy man, but his lack of formal education made him unsuitable for a permanent appointment, and he felt this keenly. Born in Ecaterinoslav, South Russia, in March 1878, Antonieff had been ordained deacon in 1908 and priest in 1910. He had served as chaplain in the Russian Imperial Army since 1899. Wounded twice in World War I, he joined Admiral Kolchak's army as chaplain during the Civil War.

Details of Antonieff's movements are confusing. He arrived in Australia in 1923 with his son-in-law, Alexander Pavlovich Shevtzoff, possibly the only Russian air force officer in Australia. His family, accompanying the

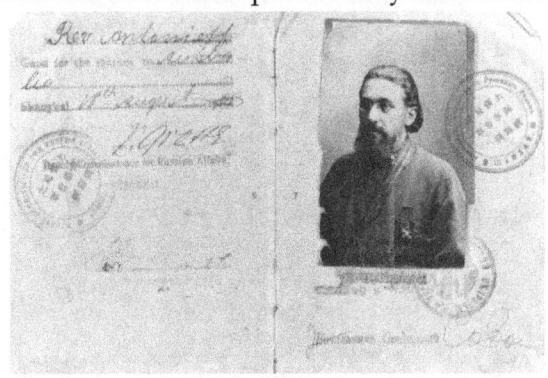

Valentin Alexandreyvich Antonieff (Extract from passport, courtesy of National Archives, Australia: A659, 1940/1/289: Antonieff, V A – Naturalisation)

Tourchinsky family, arrived in Townsville by *Mishima Maru* in December 1924: his wife, Maria Michailovna; his daughter Tamara Shevtzoff and her daughter; his daughters Militza and Victoria, and sons Andrew and Alim. He worked for the Queensland Railways, and as a ship's stoker, and for three years in the coal mines at Mt Mulligan. During the depression, he was on government relief for a time. The entry for Antonieff in the *Australian Dictionary of Biography*, Vol. 7, is neither frank nor entirely accurate; it pays tribute to his work for the church in Queensland, but does not mention his internment or his fascist activities or the trouble he caused within the church. It says he had four children, whereas he had five. It gives his birth year as 1877, and his arrival in Queensland as per *St Albans*, at Townsville, on 23 September 1923. However, his passport is stamped 'Seen by Customs, Thursday Island, 16 November 1923', and Townsville passenger lists show him landing from *St Albans* with Shevtzoff on 20 November 1923.

It might well be wondered why the parish had so much trouble finding a priest when a man of Antonieff's ability had been picking cotton, cutting cane, stoking coal and working down the mines for nearly ten years, but during his short stay in Shanghai he had been 'inhibited' from officiating as a priest by the Russian Bishop Victor, for reasons that are not recorded in available documents. As the problem of finding a priest to assume responsibility for the quarrelsome and ungrateful Brisbane parish had become acute, Antonieff accepted the rectorship on 22 July 1933, and the ban on his priestly activities was lifted in August. Michael Protopopov describes him as a man of strong character, energetic and firm in his resolve. A strong hand was needed in Brisbane but, like Shabasheff, Antonieff was addicted to alcohol and at times he was aggressive and abusive. There were rough times ahead for this 'turbulent priest' and his parishioners.

In theory, the Parish of St Nicholas, Woolloongabba, contained about 100 families. As Antonieff could not support his family on his stipend of £40 a year, he took labouring jobs and ran a small farm at Mitchelton, a suburb of Brisbane, and his sons later set up a furniture factory at Milton in competition with the factories of George Bros and Eduard Crafti.[15] The new Prior began organising energetically. He announced his plan to build an elaborate church in the proper Russian style to replace the converted house that had served them, and to honour the Royal Martyrs, Tsar Nicholas II and his family. With the help of a Government lottery and the generosity of the Callide Valley Cossacks in particular, funds were raised for the beautiful church of St Nicholas.

Although his grandchildren were not taught to speak Russian, Antonieff opposed assimilation into the community. He said in the 1930s that he would never become naturalised, because the King of England was a Mason, and the Governor-General (Sir Isaac Isaacs) was a Jew. Antonieff founded a women's group, a Russian Sunday School and a Russian library

Chapter 9: The Vodka Priest

attached to the church and run by Rodjestvensky and George Semen Volkoff, but his hectoring manner and his strong political opinions made him many enemies.

Antonieff's use of the pulpit for political purposes not only irked many of his parishioners but also attracted the attention of the Commonwealth Investigation Branch (CIB). The Minutes of the Parish Council of St Nicholas show that on 9 August 1935, they discussed a complaint against him by eleven men from the General Military Union (ROVS), the Russian Christian Workers' Movement and the Russian Imperial Union, presented by Stephan Logootin, secretary of the RIU. The Council resolved to ask Metropolitan Antony to tell him to desist, but the Metropolitan refused, as Antonieff was 'an ardent patriot, a convinced nationalist, and an implacable enemy of the bolsheviks [sic], and therefore we can in no way call his work harmful'. The problem for Security was that he was an ardent *Russian* patriot, a convinced *Russian* nationalist and a fascist, and in wartime Australia his loyalties would be called into question. Antonieff presented to the Parish Council a written complaint about Imperialist – but non-fascist – leader Vitoshinsky, who sued Antonieff for libel. The following year, while the case was in progress, the two men came to blows.

Antonieff had made a practice of allowing occasional plate collections for non-Church purposes. The ROVS had benefited from this practice, but when he held a collection for a new fascist organisation he incurred the opposition of almost every Russian group except the score or so of fascists. At a General Meeting on 31 January 1937, an attempt was made to take a vote on whether the Church had the right to interfere in politics; Antonieff refused to allow this. The Minutes recorded: 'The Chairman, Father Valentine Antonieff, declared that the struggle against the satanic power of the bolsheviks [sic] is not only the right but the duty of every clergyman and every religious association.' The extent to which it is proper for clergy of any denomination to impose political views of any kind on their congregations remains a contentious issue.

When Vitoshinsky's case came to court, the judgment went against Antonieff. As a result, parishioners had an 'Open Letter' of support for Antonieff, composed by a solicitor and signed by most of the adult members of the parish, inserted in the *Courier-Mail* of 7 September 1937. Vitoshinsky sued both the *Courier-Mail* and Rodjestvensky, who had circulated the letter, for maliciously publishing a statement that implied he had acted incorrectly in suing the priest. On 28 April 1938, the *Courier-Mail* reported that Vitoshinsky, painter and contractor of Thomas Street, West End, was claiming £1,000 each from Queensland Newspapers and Rodjestvensky. The judge ruled that the letter of support mentioned above was not defamatory, and awarded costs against Vitoshinsky.

The Harbin fascists appeared to have won, but the CIB had clipped out this letter and put the names on file, and on 20 February 1941, somebody who reviewed the file commented: 'This list can be taken as a guide to the sympathies of those who appear in it ...' However, the signatories were not only the usual fascist suspects such as Vitte, Rodjestvensky and Shevtzoff, but also anti-fascists; the list was headed by Tolstoff for the Ural Cossacks, and it included the Uglichinin brothers for the Orenburg Cossacks. Maximoff's name did not appear.[16]

In a bitter letter to Archbishop Victor in Shanghai, Antonieff accused Vitoshinsky of being a Soviet agent; he referred to 'the gangster brothers Logootin [sic]... the adventurer Maximoff... the atheist Drigin ... and the Mason Gzell', and he admitted that he was himself 'afflicted by a bad and generally known sin - the immoderate consumption of alcohol'.[17]

He wrote that Maximoff claimed falsely to be the illegitimate son of Grand Duke Nikolai Nikolayevitch, which may well be a mistranslation, as elsewhere it says 'godson'.

On 2 October 1937, General Tolstoff tried to exert his authority and ordered Antonieff to stop meddling in politics. Antonieff pointed to the RFU slogan on the wall: *God, Nation, Work*. This was a fascist slogan, not a Church pronouncement, but it was Tolstoff who caved in. Later, when Antonieff denounced the Cossacks, Tolstoff withdrew his support from the priest again, ordered his Cossacks to give up all posts in the church and tried to have a monk-priest, Lieutenant-Colonel Derevsky, sent from China. In April 1938 Paul Rodukoff, representing the RIU in Queensland, told Antonieff they would refuse to take part in the St Vladimir Jubilee, for Antonieff's activities were not religious.

In Australia, the Military Board told the Intelligence Section of the General Staff on 22 June 1939 that there were unconfirmed reports that the Japanese were putting pressure on White Russians in Australia, through threats to relatives in Manchukuo (Manchuria), to serve Japanese interests in Australia. It was also reported of the White Russians: 'All of them, whether honest citizens or bandits, hoped for German or Japanese intervention in Russia.' Lieutenant Reginald E. Finzel, one of the few trusted Russian experts and linguists available in Queensland, complained later that police reporting on the Russian community did not understand the situation. Small wonder! It was difficult to work out the differences between the Russian factions. Apart from Finzel's complaint, some police were not only ignorant but did not take their job seriously. One report mentioned a Russian called 'PISSOFF (or some similar name)'. Although the material actually concerned Shevtzoff, it was filed under 'Peshkoff'. This wrongly attributed information might have been partly responsible for Peshkoff's internment. The claim that Antonieff formed a fascist group at the same time as Hitler formed the Nazi Party is obvious nonsense, and the claim that it met in the German Club (416 Vulture Street) and saluted Hitler's portrait is also wrong.

Chapter 9: The Vodka Priest

The Russian Fascist Union distributed the papers *Natsiya* and *Novoye Slovo*. *Natsiya* had a swastika on the cover. They supported Germany and Italy as Allies, and advocated close cooperation with Japan. Military Intelligence recorded that articles published in *Fashist* established beyond doubt that the Far Eastern Fascist Party, Harbin, was a Japanese organisation, and that there were active members in Australia.[18] Books and magazines were received through 'a furniture factory'; it was assumed at first to be George Brothers in Woolloongabba, but it might have been the factory run by Antonieff's sons on Coronation Drive at Milton.

World War II

Information gathered by the Security services lay dormant for some years; in peace time, Australians were free to hold whatever political views they liked, no matter how outrageous or obnoxious; but in war time they were not free to advocate assisting the enemy, and the RFU's pigeons came home to roost. At the outbreak of war, the powers of the various Security services were vastly increased, and consequently the flow of information. Searches of the premises of interned Germans uncovered correspondence from Russian fascists. Overseas mail was censored; however careful the fascists might have become with the letters they now sent overseas, for several months letters addressed to them – but written before the war – revealed how closely some were associated with the Japanese. An article in one of the Russian fascist papers said that the names of representatives in various countries were being kept secret, which was futile when their correspondence was being intercepted. Supporting information came also from London, Washington and Singapore, from mail intercepts and code-breaking. The fascists were blissfully, smugly unaware of the amount of information that had been obtained concerning their activities.

The Censorship Office refused to allow admission of magazines bearing a swastika. The RFU in Harbin wrote to Rodjestvensky on 28 October 1939 to inform him that it would no longer send *Natsiya* to subscribers in Australia, as it was 'out of the question to alter our emblem'. This upset the plans of a missionary in Montreal, who had asked Rodjestvensky to obtain the magazine on his behalf, change the wrapper and forward it, as the 'Jews and Masons' were everywhere in Canada; censorship intercepted the letter, in which the missionary described Rodzaevsky as an extraordinary man and prayed 'may God give him aid'. The British system of exchanging information being as it was, the Canadian authorities were no doubt informed promptly of the missionary's request. It is probable that there was no RFU branch in Canada, for Rodzaevsky had written to Rodjestvensky early in 1940 that Australia was the only Allied country with a branch; and since there was no branch in any other State, Queensland was the only location on the *Allied* side that had this particular problem. When Rodjestvensky wrote that 'we band ourselves together to work for Germany' everywhere in the world, he was exaggerating, but he was revealing his own colours.

On 2 November 1939 a letter was picked up, written on 1 September by P. Patrikeyeff, Chief of the Shanghai Division of the RFU, to Rodjestvensky, whom he addressed as Chief of the Australian Division of the RFU. It said that 'brother-in-arms' (*soratnik*) A. K. Vitte and 'sister-in-arms' N. M. Vitte had arrived from Australia and had been registered under the assumed name of Aleksandrov. Security knew that Patrikeyeff was 'in complete liaison' with the Japanese, and Vitte was definitely working for them, and this focussed attention on Rodjestvensky.

Searches of the houses and business premises of Germans marked for internment brought in more information. H. L. Foote, the 'Russian expert' in the CIB, reported on 19 September that documents found in the possession of several Nazi officials indicated 'a strong liaison between the White Russian organisation and the Nazi Party' and that the Friends of the Third Reich (a group of people with Nazi sympathies but barred from joining the Party because they were not German citizens) were trying to use the White Russian organisation. This was somewhat misleading, because few except Rodjestvensky were in contact with the Nazis. However, an undercover agent in the Friends of the Third Reich reported that they had discussed using citizens of neutral countries to continue their work. The contact that they favoured in the Russian community was Nicholas Otto Peterson; there is little on record about him, except that he had subscribed to *Natsiya*, had signed the public letter of support for Antonieff in 1937, and may have been a member of the RFU. Whether they actually consulted him is unknown.

Among material seized from the German Consulate in Brisbane were letters to Consul Hugo Witte from Rodjestvensky, hand-delivered because he thought the material too sensitive to entrust to the post. Witte and Rodjestvensky might have known each other from Harbin, for Witte had served there as Consul before World War I, and it seems that he spent quite a lot of time there after the war. These letters were on the official stationery of the Australian Section of the RFU, and this too bore a swastika and the slogan 'God, Nation, Work'. It was suggested that simultaneous searches be conducted of premises of all RFU leaders to look for membership lists, or for a code that they might be using to communicate with Harbin. Among the books found in the Russian library was a copy of Hitler's *Mein Kampf* in Russian. In May 1940, more RFU material was found on the premises of Waldemar Sommer, who was the first person to try to found a branch of the Nazi Party in Brisbane, but whose efforts were rejected because legally he was Czech. Sommer too had links with Harbin. Taken prisoner by

Chapter 9: The Vodka Priest

the Russians while fighting in the Austro-Hungarian Army, he had then fought in the Czech Legion, first against the Germans, then against the Bolsheviks. He arrived in Australia in June 1924 from Shanghai.

Another consequence of the outbreak of war was that many immigrants thought it wise to become naturalised. Among those who applied in September 1939 were Antonieff and Maximoff, who were naturalised a few months later. This would have left the way open for Antonieff to have been imprisoned as a traitor, not simply interned, but bringing evidence before a court would have revealed the identity of sources of information. In 1940, Maximoff disbanded his Russian Scout Group. Owing to the pact in August 1939 between Stalin and Hitler, the White Russians felt betrayed and for a time Antonieff kept fairly quiet, except that in mid 1940 he ordered (not advised) people to hide badges, swastikas and flags. Later in the year, Fashkor No. 973 (Pole-Rogan) wrote that 'the Harbin Fascists disappeared from the horizon from the first day of the war...'

At about the time when Finland was negotiating a treaty with the Soviet invaders, the Brisbane *Telegraph* (27 February, p. 12) published a cartoon entitled: 'He'll Have Something on His Hands Then'; it showed a bear labelled 'Russia' with its paws in honey pots labelled 'Finland' and 'Turkey'. Antonieff responded with a letter, published on 5 March, in which he wrote that the USSR was not Russia, and they should have put a 'hammer and sickle and five-ended star' over the head of the bear. Military Intelligence misinterpreted this, commenting that only an anti-Semite would think to use this association of a star. This was one of the mistakes made by the usually reliable Finzel. The Star of David was blue and white with *six* points; it was the communist Red Star that had five points. Still, this was but a minute fragment of the evidence against Antonieff.

Letters continued to be exchanged with the Harbin fascists. In theory, all overseas airmail was censored, and random samples of surface mail were taken, especially of letters posted to or from sensitive areas. Routine Orders of the RFU were intercepted. Domestic mail was intercepted only to (and if possible from) suspect persons, under a special XRD order. Little second class mail was monitored, owing to the volume of material, but delivery was so slow that most information sent in this manner would have been obsolete before it arrived. Phone calls could be intercepted. Evidence of the extent to which these powers were used in Queensland early in the war is lacking.

Unable to keep the Antonieff dossiers in order, a CIB agent reported that 'the Archpriest' was a sergeant in the army. It was Alim, one of his sons, who been conscripted, despite the priest's protests; Antonieff senior was well over 60. Antonieff knew he was under suspicion. He claimed that communists were telling lies about him. However, the police and Naval Intelligence had several informants in the White Russian community. One was Captain Maximoff; another was Alexander Gzell, treasurer of the Russian Club. In November 1940, accompanied by a police constable, Gzell called at Victoria Barracks, made a statement and handed over a partial list of members of the RFU; the names were already familiar to both police and army. He said that Rodjestvensky had prepared a list of anti-fascists, who would face retribution when Germany won the war; the list was allegedly headed by Gzell himself. One Security agent commented that Gzell was obviously intelligent and well educated, but after more than ten years in the country he could still understand hardly any English. It was noted that he had fallen out with some Brisbane Russians because he opposed the formation of Russian organisations with political aims, and he tried to ban extremists from the Russian Club.[19]

Another informant was Eduard Crafti, a leader of the Aid to Russia Movement. Crafti had arrived in Brisbane from Shanghai in June 1912 aboard *Eastern*. Born at Sebastopol in April 1888, he had gone to Harbin at the age of 16. He was naturalised in 1914, and re-naturalised under new regulations in 1925. His younger brother, Nisan, who arrived in April 1928 by *Commissaire Ramel*, was naturalised in 1934.

A fourth informant, said to be manager of 'a large retail business' in Stanley Street, Woolloongabba (George Bros furniture retail store), seems to have been Alexander Antropoff. Another source was Antonieff's wife, who may not have been deliberately informing but rather gossiping indiscreetly, but her friend, Evgenia Emelianoff of East Brisbane, passed her information to Detective Constable W. J. Clark. Between statutory declarations, confidential verbal information and casual chatter, the Russian Fascists did little that was not reported promptly to one of the Security or Intelligence services.

In May an agent showed Security a swastika-bedecked 1940 Russian calendar from the RFU in Harbin. Either censorship had overlooked it or had decided to let it through, or it had been smuggled into the country. In November, another reported that there was a pro-Nazi cell in the White Russian community, and 80% were disloyal to Britain. As late as January 1941, copies of Russian Fascist magazines were coming from Shanghai, and even magazines from Berlin were still finding their way into Australia somehow.

In 1940, it was decreed that nobody, including waterside workers, would be allowed on the wharves without a permit from Security. The Naval Intelligence Division kept dossiers (NI prefix) on seamen and wharf workers, much of the information coming from an agent about whom the only certain information is that he was born in Odessa. On 26 September, at the request of the CIB and NID, permits were withdrawn from eight Brisbane wharf labourers, four of them naturalised Russians. Jim Healy, General Secretary of the Waterside Workers Federation (WWF), threatened

Chapter 9: The Vodka Priest

industrial action on the waterfront if they were not restored, and the Australian Council for Civil Liberties in Melbourne also protested. It was suspected that some had been the victims of communist denunciations for political reasons, so it was ironic that a communist-controlled union was coming to their defence.

Three of the men appealed, and Posharsky (NI 33) and Peshkoff (NI 37) had their permits restored. Peshkoff was lucky, for his dossier contained an unsourced allegation that he had claimed that he had killed more than 50 people, some shot, some buried alive, and had said that not enough Jews had been killed and they should be killed in Australia too. Peter Smikoff (NI 63), another Cossack veteran of the Russian Imperial Army, the White Army and Kolchak's army, and of the escape route through Vladivostok, Harbin and Shanghai, did not appeal. He was secretary of the church in Woolloongabba, and for a time closely associated with Antonieff. Like Antonieff, he had a son in the Australian army. Edward Conrad Englart, Secretary of the Brisbane branch of the WWF, said later that the executive was of the opinion 'that Posharsky has subversive tendencies and was a definite menace to the waterfront'. Some thought that, until Germany invaded the USSR, Englart was a greater menace. The name of the fourth Russian who lost his permit is not evident in reports. Rodjestvensky also had an NID dossier (NI 108), perhaps because he had apparently worked for a time as a seaman.

In the Brisbane censorship office, the translator for Russian was a Yellow Cab driver, George Alexander (Yuri Alexandrovich) Zuckschwerdt. He was of German ancestry but born in Estonia in 1898 while it was under Russian hegemony, and he had been an officer in the Imperial Army, the Czech Army, and the White Russian Army. He too held a wharf permit in his capacity as a taxi driver. He had been a member of the German Club since 1932 (which gave him the right to park in the club's parking area in Vulture Street, Woolloongabba) and he was allegedly a member of the Russian Fascist Union. While Zuckschwerdt was a Lutheran and had no time for the Archpriest, his wife supported Antonieff for a time, telling her husband that whatever Antonieff had done, he was still a priest, but by about 1938 she too had had enough of him. Zuckschwerdt apparently did a good Security job as censor, passing over such things as a list sent from Harbin naming Queensland members of the RFU, but the appointment was unwise. Owing to his links with the German Club, it was a risk to have Zuckschwerdt in such a sensitive position, and in addition there were complaints that he had disclosed the personal content of letters that passed through his hands.

Early in 1941, Vonsiatsky warned Stekloff in Shanghai that he might have to take over leadership of the fascist organisation, as things were becoming difficult in America, and soon after Germany invaded the Soviet

Union, Stekloff told Pole-Rogan that he should be ready to take over if anything happened to him (Stekloff). It was more than somewhat bizarre to imagine the Thangool cotton farmer taking over such an organisation, particularly when Prootkovsky was available in Sydney, but it was enough to get the seemingly innocuous Pole-Rogan interned later. At roughly the same time, and still seriously out of touch with reality, Stekloff wrote: 'National Socialist Germany with heroic self-abnegation threw herself on the violators of Russia... The sword of the crusaders was not lifted against Russia or against Russian territory, but against the usurpers of holy Russia.'

After Germany invaded Russia, it was no longer quaint to have Antonieff praying from the pulpit for the death of Stalin; it became objectionable. An NID agent reported to Lieutenant-Commander I. Pryce Jones of Naval Intelligence on 27 June 1941 that Rodjestvensky had said: 'we band ourselves together to work for Germany'. He had admitted they got directions from Harbin, and sometimes from Sofia (Bulgaria). The Russian fascists expected that Soviet Russia would be beaten in three weeks, and that the downfall of Britain would follow.

The CIB reported on 8 July 1941 that parishioners were saying that if Antonieff made any remarks in church about the advantages of German rule for Russia, as he has been in the habit of doing, certain members intended to 'treat him with violence' while he was in church. The Cossacks in particular were outraged. Antonieff had said: 'Hitler will conquer Russia and then we'll go back. It is the duty of loyal Russians to help Germany as much as possible.' It was of no consequence to him that, when he was naturalised, he had sworn allegiance to Australia. Antonieff pointed out that a hundred years ago, Saint Sarowsky had prophesied the Revolution, the murder of the Russian Royal Family, and the suffering of Russians under the yoke of the godless. He also prophesied that their rule would be destroyed in the middle of summer, and the free Russian people would sing a second time in the same year: 'Christ Resurrected'. He exhorted them: 'I ask you to pray now to our God to make it possible for the Russian people to sing "Christ Resurrected" in the Summer.'

In July, the 'Secretary of Australian-Russian Association' (Crafti) told an MI agent that Antonieff had inquired about the objects of the association. On being told that they were to promote diplomatic, cultural and trade relations between the two countries, and that the discussion of politics was barred at meetings, Antonieff not only challenged his right to prohibit politics, but questioned Crafti's credentials as a Russian. Crafti told Antonieff that he traced his 'blood line' in Russia back at least four generations, and reminded him that he had helped Antonieff's family by employing his daughter for three years when they first arrived in Queensland, and also his son, and it was an impertinence to suggest that he was not a true Russian. Furious, he told Antonieff that 'you and your gang of Fascists' wanted to see Russia defeated, and that would mean the defeat of Britain and Australia. Antonieff's temper and bullying made more enemies than he could afford to have. The point here was that the Crafti family was Jewish, and Antonieff detested Jews, even though Finzel had been wrong about the 'five-ended star'.[20]

On 10 August 1941, after Antonieff had again asked the congregation to pray for the overthrow of communism in Russia and the death of Stalin, a meeting was held at his house, allegedly to celebrate the day of his patron, Saint Valentine.[21] Among those present were Rodjestvensky, Posharsky, Smikoff and Peshkoff. It may have started as a name-day feast, but it became a political discussion. Antonieff's wife Maria told Evgenia Emelianoff, who reported to Detective Constable Clark, who passed it to Pryce Jones: 'The resolution arrived at was to the effect that they would do all in their power to aid Germany to victory against her enemies.' They either did not realise, or did not care, that German victory meant Australian defeat, and they maintained their protestations of loyalty to Australia. Crafti, who had not been present, obtained and passed on similar information.

Rodjestvensky, who had written for the Berlin paper, *Novoye Slovo*, wrote in the fascist paper *Nash Put* that Russian Fascists must support Japan. Naval Intelligence reported that he had said, soon after Germany invaded the USSR, that 'we are affiliated... to all those elements who are friendly to Germany and who are naturally enemies of the British Empire'. When 'the day' came, they would be ready to do their part. There is evidence that Rodjestvensky was associated with a Japanese agent, Henry (Kanjiro) Suzuki, and the extent to which the Japanese were recruiting Russians for espionage was glimpsed when Kenzo Doi, in a moment of misguided zeal, tried to recruit Rastislav Boris Fedoseyeff, who had lived in China for seventeen years with his mother and a French stepfather. However, Fedoseyeff was already working for the Chinese; he passed on this information and Doi left Australia in a great hurry.[22]

As the Soviet Union fought for its existence, the Russian fascists in Queensland rejoiced at the prospect of its defeat. Late in September, Smikoff and Posharsky started a 'whispering campaign' that Moscow communiqués were false, and the Germans were advancing everywhere. Antonieff again asked his congregation to pray for the death of Stalin. Naval Intelligence reported on 21 October that there was a closer association now between the fascists and the local Japanese. Rodjestvensky had said: 'We have been in close touch with Mr Suzuki who has a very intimate knowledge of Japanese affairs and who is in close contact with Japan.' The report added that the local White Russians would have 'scores to settle'.[23] Rodjestvensky had also said that countless millions would live to bless Hitler, while an article in *Nash Put* said: 'History will write on the pages of Russian history the name of Adolf Hitler as liberator of Russia.'

Since the German invasion of Russia, the delusional Rodzaevsky had been sending letters around the world asking some of his followers to return to Harbin to prepare to join his Cabinet when the Germans turned the government over to him. On 29 October 1941, Michail Grott-Spassovsky wrote to Rodjestvensky, asking him or his deputy to go to Shanghai at once; the 'firm' would pay expenses. 'The affairs of our firm,' he wrote, 'do not admit of any delay.' He added the cryptic initials CP to his signature. This transliterated into SR – *Slava Rossii* – Glory to Russia, though some of the dimmer luminaries among the Security personnel thought it stood for Communist Party. By the time the letter reached Australia, the Pacific War had begun, and nobody would be going from Australia to Shanghai. It merely incriminated Rodjestvensky further, for the 'firm' was no doubt the RFU, and it might have been Japan that paid the expenses. The activities of the Russian Fascists raised not only the question of disloyalty to Australia, but also of their sanity, for they must have realised that overseas mail was censored.

In November, a fund was set up ostensibly to buy warm clothing for Russians in German-occupied territory. The main collectors were George (Grigory Petrovich) Pavlenko and the churchwarden, Victor Lolua, aided by some charitable muddle-heads who had little connection with Russians or fascists and did not stop to wonder how the clothing would reach the people for whom it was intended. By then it was known how the Germans conducted themselves in Russia, even in the Ukraine where they had at first been welcomed. The tragic siege of Leningrad, and the heroism of its defenders, inspired the Allied world. Only a few RFU fanatics were still enthusiastic about seeing Russia 'liberated' by the Nazis.

For several days after the Japanese attack on Pearl Harbor, police were fully occupied rounding up Japanese, including Rodjestvensky's contact, Suzuki. On 18 December, they turned their attentions to the Russian Fascists. St Nicholas Church, the Russian library and Antonieff's house were among premises searched that day. Antonieff admitted to searchers that he wanted Hitler to win the war, but he denied that a swastika flag had hung in Russian hall next to church until evidence compelled him to admit it. Then he claimed that the swastika had 'another significance'. A vast amount of fascist and Nazi material was found in the possession of various Russians, including speeches by Hitler and Goebbels translated into Russian. At about this time, searchers found an item they wanted badly: the list of subscribers to *Natsiya*. Many were in Darwin; between communists and fascists, it was no wonder there was trouble on the Darwin wharves.

When Peshkoff's house was searched, police thought they had found evidence of his association with fascists but, as Finzel had said, they did not understand. In a four-page inventory of documents, books, pamphlets and letters taken for examination and translation, there was not one scrap that came from the RFU, Harbin, the Japanese or Berlin; most of it was ROVS material from Paris or Brussels. Available evidence indicates that Peshkoff should not have been interned, being a victim of police ignorance or of malicious denunciations that could have come from either communists or fascists. After more than a year in internment, he was even more disenchanted with the RFU, referring in November 1943 to 'a lot of hooligans from Harbin and Brisbane under the wing of the Archpriest'.

On 6 January 1942, another undercover agent (probably Antropoff) reported that Antonieff had reprimanded him for not listening to the news in Russian from Germany, as it was the only reliable source, and the Australian press, controlled by Jews, printed lies. He said he had always known that the Nazi system was the best in the world. A barber shop was a good place to pick up information, and from which to start pernicious rumours. On 16 February, some agent reported again; when he had gone to the barber, Rodjestvensky had greeted him:

> I haven't seen you since before our Allies, the Japanese, came
> into the war, you remember what our friend SUZUKI said, well,
> everything is going according to plan - first Malaya and the North
> through Burma, and, later on linking up with the German Army
> beyond India.

Another suspicious meeting was held at Antonieff's house, about 18 March, allegedly to celebrate his birthday. The NID agent reported again, though there is no detail on this meeting. He said also that, on 13 March, Rodjestvensky had for the first time asked him to obtain specific information: the name, type and description of planes around Brisbane. Rodjestvensky had been very happy and excited, for he had heard that *Queen Mary* had been sunk with 3000 troops.

Internment

Authorities now stated that the Russian fascists were showing themselves to be 'sufficiently dangerous for precautions to be taken to keep them under surveillance and control'. On 23 March it was reported that some of the Russians were taking an undue interest in the American troops and their equipment, and it was deemed that there was adequate evidence on which to intern the leading fascists and their close associates. The Russians under suspicion in Brisbane were arrested on 18 April 1942 and a few in the Callide-Biloela-Thangool area few days later. Posharsky was picked up while working at Dalgety's Wharf. They were held for a while at Gaythorne camp before being sent to Loveday in South Australia. Rodjestvensky protested: 'I have been living in Australia as a law-abiding citizen and I never did anything against Australian Government or people of Australia and I never will.' He denied that he knew Suzuki, or any Japanese in Queensland; it was known that this was a lie.

Antonieff's daughter Tamara blamed her father for the internment of her husband, Shevtzoff, who had been Secretary of the RFU. Antonieff blamed the Bolsheviks for his plight: 'It is very silly on Tamara's part to say that I am responsible for Alex's internment, on account of my very doubtful life and work in the past... The Bolsheviks are responsible for my presence in this camp...'[24]

In fact, it was Antonieff who bore practically the entire responsibility for the development of the RFU in Brisbane, and it was RFU activities that led to the internments. In Sydney, where Shlemin did not give the fascists any overt encouragement, there was no RFU branch, and only one Russian was interned. Prootkovsky, leader in Australia of the pretentious and futile Vonsiatsky group, had been arrested on 19 March. Police were puzzled: he had bought a camera in September 1937 and an enlarger the next month, and he was buying photographic supplies until 1941, but in 1942 he had neither camera nor enlarger; he did not even have an album of photos. Might he have bought the goods for some Japanese who did not want his interest in photography known?

A petition was raised protesting against the internment of the Brisbane Russians. One of the organisers was George Volkoff. Reports on him gave conflicting evidence; one said he was a friend of Antonieff and Rodjestvensky, a librarian at the Russian library, and one of the leaders of the RFU, and he was lucky not to be interned himself; another said that he was 'associated' with the RFU, but not a member. One man who should not have been interned was George Pavlenko senior; he had served the tsar for 21 years, as a sergeant not an officer, and was neither a communist nor a fascist. Over seventy, in ill-health, with his daughter Leonella married to Sergei Ouglitchinin, he seems to have done nothing worse than collect second-hand clothing for Russia.

Protopopov writes of the internment of Russians:

> However, with the advent of war, Fr Valentin's outspokenness resulted in his, and some of his parishioners, falling foul of Australian authorities. Valentin and most of his parishioners were uncompromising anti-Communists. They loudly condemned the 1939 Pact between Germany and the Soviet Union, seeing both regimes as equally evil. However, when the Soviet Union joined the Allies in 1941 and the Brisbane Russians continued to condemn "Uncle Joe" Stalin, then their utterances became an embarrassment to the Australian Government and all ex-Russian nationals became akin to "enemy aliens." Consequently, in March 1942, they, and Russians in other states, were rounded up and interred [sic] in various camps around the nation.

This is exaggerated and misleading. Of the thousands of ethnic Russians in Australia, only 27 in Queensland and one in Sydney (Prootkovsky) were interned. Not one was interned in other states. They all went to Loveday Camp (South Australia) except Pavlenko, who was sent to hospital in Sydney before going to Liverpool Camp and being released. They were not interned because they were anti-communists; they were interned because

Chapter 9: The Vodka Priest

they advocated or were suspected of advocating assisting Japan. Despite the prodigious amount of work Protopopov did among Church records, he apparently did not consult a single file on Russians compiled by the Commonwealth Investigation Branch or Military Police Intelligence or Naval Intelligence in Brisbane, Canberra and Sydney, nor internee records in National Archives branches in Adelaide and Melbourne. This is hardly a solid foundation on which to make comments on internments.

The number of interned 'Russians' is slightly higher if one counts Latvian-born Arnold von Skerst and a few other persons born in the Baltic States when these were part of the Russian Empire. However, Skerst was a German national, interned because he was a member of the Nazi Party and editor of the weekly Nazi magazine, *Die Brücke*. At the same time, he was still the secret representative in Australia of one of the pretenders to the Imperial throne, Grand Duke Kyril and, after the death of Kyril, of Grand Duke Vladimir. Although this was another example of how close some Imperialists were to the fascists, this was not the reason for his internment. Another internee of dubious national status was the Estonian Lutheran Pastor, Kurt Gielow, but he was interned largely because he had been, for several months, the acting leader of the Nazi Party in Australia, not because he had served in the Imperial Russian army.

Appeals by the Russians against their internment were heard during September 1942, and Antonieff said at his hearing on 10 September:

> Malaria is used as a cure for syphilis; they are both bad. Both eventually die after the patient has been cured. I use this simile in relation to Germany and Russia. Germany is malaria and Bolshevism is syphilis. Russia will eventually be restored free and whole.

The weakness in Antonieff's metaphor was that the patient often died. As a result of the appeals, ten men were released before the end of the year. The plight of the White Russians in Australia deserved sympathy, but some of them were nonetheless a threat to Australia's security in 1942. Some internments may not have been *just* or *necessary*, but most were *advisable*. However, it is doubtful whether it was necessary to keep interned anyone except Rodjestvensky, Antonieff and Prootkovsky; a rooster does not flap about for long with its head chopped off. On the other hand, the Japanese had no doubt collected information about the former Harbin Russians, and they would have known how to exert pressure on them. Some of the internments may have seemed – and may have been – unduly harsh, but it has been estimated that as many as a million Eastern Europeans – White Russians, Ukrainians, Latvians and others – served in the German armed forces, many of them in the *Waffen-SS* – and some of these were Cossacks and ROVS members who, after General Miller was kidnapped and murdered, had moved to Belgium. At the Resurrection Church in Brussels their chief spiritual adviser was that same Father Alexander Shabasheff who had left Brisbane in 1929 and arrived in Brussels via America in 1933. Here he collaborated apparently willingly with the occupying German forces during the war, although he may still have been an Australian citizen.[25] He died in January 1956. Suspicions concerning what the Russian fascists in Brisbane might do, given the chance, could not be disregarded.

In addition, the case of Anna Volkoff, daughter of a Russian admiral, had shown that there were Russians willing to spy for Germany. In 1940, using Italian diplomatic bags, she was sending to Germany secret material obtained from the US Embassy in London by a clerk named Tyler Kent.[26] In November 1942, the German blockade runner *Ramses* was scuttled by her crew when intercepted in the Indian Ocean by HMAS *Adelaide*. Among her nominal crew was a diplomatic courier who still had a notebook containing the names of secret German couriers in the USA, and two of the major contacts were Russian. The courier himself, Wilhelm Ewert, had been born in Russia of a German father and Russian mother, and his father ran a shoe store in Harbin.

Another four Russian internees were released during 1943, and antagonisms worsened inside the camp. Posharsky wrote to his wife in October 1943 that 'Antonieff and his friends' were doing dangerous work spreading pro-Nazi propaganda, that Antonieff's preaching was racial and anti-Semitic, and that he associated with German Nazis. Smikoff, who had been a great friend of Antonieff, turned against him. Only about four men still adhered to the RFU. In Manchukuo the Japanese tired of the bickering Russians, and they wanted calm there when things were going badly in the south. In July 1943 they shut down the RFU in their territory: the headquarters in Harbin, and the offices and papers in Shanghai. In December 1944, Rodjestvensky made a statement from Loveday camp that the Japanese did not give money to Harbin Fascists, and there were no Japanese members of the Russian Fascist Union, which was bending the truth more than slightly.

During 1944, the war situation improved to the extent that most Russians were released under restriction, the last being Antonieff in July 1944 and Rodjestvensky in January 1945. It has been reported that, during the absence of Antonieff, the parish of St Nicholas was served by Feodot Shaverin, but he was old and often ill. Some Russians attended Divine Services in the St George Greek Orthodox Church, and the Russian choir enriched the services there. Protopopov writes that his parishioners received Antonieff with great joy: 'Many saw his internment as a form of martyrdom for the anti-Communist views which he had openly expressed... A feeling of renewal became evident in the parish.' It must be stressed again that it was not simply because Antonieff held 'anti-Communist views' that he had been interned. Apart from his tirades against 'the Jews', his exhibiting swastikas on church premises, and his inclusion of *Mein Kampf* in the Russian library, he had prayed for Hitler's victory and urged his congregation to assist in this.

Although Antonieff was allowed to return to Brisbane, he was forbidden to preach or to speak in public. At first his congregation looked forward to the time when he could take up his priestly duties again. He was released from restrictions in May 1945, but within a few months his 'propensity for causing dissension amongst his people and his tyrannical government of Church affairs' had split the parish again. A Security Service report of 9 October said that the greatest attendance at the church in the past six weeks had been seven, many preferring to go to the Greek Orthodox Church. The choir walked out; its conductor, Dmitry Anisimoff, remarked that people said of Antonieff: 'I cannot call him Father; he is not a religious man.'

After the War

When the Pacific War ended, the congregation tried to get another priest from Shanghai. Alexey Godyaev was appointed in September 1949. A new parish called Saint Seraphim of Sarov was formed in March 1950 and Archimandrite Methody Shlemin returned as rector until a younger, permanent priest could be found. Antonieff left a lasting legacy in Brisbane in the form of the beautiful St Nicholas Orthodox Church in Woolloongabba, but the essence of a Church is a community of people, not a building.

Australia's Russian fascists fared better than their Harbin leader, Rodzaevsky. Lured back to Moscow, he was subjected to a show trial and shot in a Lubyanka cellar. In America, Vonsiatsky was released from prison on parole in February 1946. Rodjestvensky was released from internment under restriction on 17 January 1945. In November 1946, he applied for a position vetting potential White Russian immigrants from Shanghai; he did not get it. Later he moved to Sydney where his fascist activities were not common knowledge, and he became a prominent figure in church affairs there. A Security Service officer wrote in October 1945:

> My own opinion, however, is that the majority of the Fascist members of the Russian Community, realising that we have won the war, and that it would not pay to pursue their previous activities, had suddenly decided to become good Australians, and have dumped ANTONIEFF and his immediate supporters to free themselves of any suspicion to the contrary.

Tolstoff, the last *ataman* of the Ural Cossacks, died in 1956. Losing hope of seeing communism in Russia overturned in their lifetime, members of the Russian communities settled down to being good citizens of the countries in which they had taken refuge. Few indeed of those who fought in the White Army in 1920 lived to see the Soviet Union self-destruct in 1991, and probably none to see the fascist Young Guards rampaging through the streets over a decade later, giving the fascist salute, assaulting foreigners, shouting 'Death to Chechens' and reviving and degrading the old slogan: '*Slava Rossii*'.

Appendix 1

Russian names are transliterated in the manner used most frequently in documents or by the persons themselves; that is, in particular, -off and -eff instead of -ov and -ev, while the use of -vich and -vitch, or -eeff and -eyeff is inconsistent in sources. This is often not the way in which they would usually be written in English at the present time. Generally, the feminine forms of surnames have not been used. Note that some dates are given in original records by both the Julian and the Gregorian calendar; some are given only one way, but it is not clear which way. The difference of only 13 days is not important, but it should be realised that documents might show different dates for an event, mainly a birth in this context. For example: Antonieff gave his birthday as 4 March [Julian] or 17 March [Gregorian], written as 4/17, which does not indicate 17 April. For more detailed information on the Russians in Australia and the activities of the Russian Orthodox Church, see the works of Michael Protopopov, but take note that he writes hardly anything on the *political* activities of individuals, the Church or the community as a whole.

Chapter 9: The Vodka Priest

Appendix 2

White Russian Russian Fascist Organisations Represented In Australia:

The nomenclature and orientation of the Russian organisations overseas was a Byzantine muddle, with organisations changing their names frequently, and the same name being given to different organisations at different times. This overview is approximate. An earnest student of Russian organisations overseas would need to study the matter more closely.

Russian Fascist Organisation (RFO): founded in Harbin about 1925. (Российская Фашистская Организация: *Rossiyskaya Fashistskaya Organizatsiya*). By 1932 it was led by Konstantin Vladimirovich Rodzaevsky.

Russian Fascist Party (RFP): formed at the First Congress of Russian Fascists, 22 May 1931. (*Rossiyskaya Fashistskaya Partiya*) Chairman: General Vladimir Kosmin. General Secretary and real controller: Rodzaevsky. Published two magazines: *Nash Put* (Our Path) in Harbin, and *Natsiya* (Nation) in Shanghai. The name was transferred later to Vonsiatsky's organisation. Kosmin headed a group of several hundred Russians who fought in the Japanese army in Manchuria.

All-Russian Fascist Organisation (ARFO): founded in Connecticut, USA by A. A. Vonsiatsky. (*Vserossiyskaya Fashistskaya Organizatsiya*) It published two magazines: *Fashist* in Connecticut, and *Russky Avangard*, edited by K. A. Stekloff in Shanghai. Australian representatives: V. A. Prootkovsky, Sydney; N. Pole-Rogan (Poliakoff) Thangool (Q).

All-Russian Fascist Party (ARFP): founded at Second Congress, Harbin, in April 1934, to try to unite the Harbin and American parties (*Vserossiyskaya Fashistskaya Partiya*).

All-Russian National Revolutionary Party (ARNRP): founded by Vonsiatsky in 1935 when the ARFP split. (*Vserossiyskaya Natsionalno-Revoliutsionnaya Partiya*).

Russian Fascist Union (RFU): allegedly so named at the Third Congress, Harbin, in June-July 1935. (Русский Фашисткий Союз: *Russkiy Fashistskiy Soyuz*) Its Harbin leader was K. R. Rodzaevsky. It claimed to have affiliated groups in Japan, China, Java, Persia, Australia, North and South America, England, Germany, France, Italy, Czechoslovakia, Yugoslavia, Bulgaria, Poland, Estonia and Finland. It took over publication of *Natsiya* and *Nash Put*. Known in the Russian community as the RFS (РФС), and to the Security Services as RFU, it was the main Russian Fascist organisation in Australia.

Brisbane leaders: President: I. P. Rodjestvensky; Secretary: A. P. Shevtzoff; Treasurer: B. F. Naggih.

Russian General Military Union (ROVS): founded in Yugoslavia in 1924 by General Pyotr N. Wrangel. (Русский Обще-Воинский Союз: *Russkiy Obshche-Voinskiy Soyuz*; also translated as General Association of Soldiers, or Combined Services Union.) It was an association of former White Russian military personnel living outside the Soviet Union; it was anti-communist but not tied to any particular political grouping. Queensland leaders: General V. S. Tolstoff, V. P. Peshkoff, I. I. Popoff, V. V. Korzhenevsky. Although its influence had diminished by 1939, it was not dissolved until 2000.

Russian Imperial Union: Worked for the restoration of a Tsar to the Russian throne. Brisbane leaders: V. M. Vitoshinsky, S. Logootin, M. I. Maximoff, P. Rodukoff.

Russian Imperial Order – Australia: (Affiliated 2005 with the Legion of Frontiersman)

Chapter 10

The Shanghai Gang

In mid 1941, Albert Hard, commercial secretary at the Australian Legation in Japan, wrote from Tokyo: 'A lot of these so called English up here would think nothing of joining up with the Nips to save their skins.' There were Australians with the same attitude. The persons considered here were not *in* Australia, but they were Australians who could have been a danger *to* Australia. At the very least, they were an annoyance to many of those who knew of their activities.

Prisoners of the Japanese obeyed orders or died; indeed, often they died even if they did obey orders. Those who broadcast propaganda for them were rather special cases. The story of Major Charles Cousens, born in India of British parents, is well documented. Apparently he was not a particularly admirable character in some respects, but he was not a willing traitor. Captured in Singapore, he was taken to Tokyo and was forced to broadcast propaganda largely because, before the war, he had done some radio work and had co-authored with one Kennosuke Sato a book on relations between Japan and Australia, so he was known to the Japanese. He has been compared with William Joyce (Lord Haw-Haw), but the cases were very different. Joyce went to Germany voluntarily at about the outbreak of war. Cousens was captured while serving in the AIF and compelled to broadcast.

The case of New Zealand-born Lieutenant Arthur Finlayson (Bill) Rodie, who broadcast from Java, is less well known. The Japanese identified him as a broadcaster and demanded his services. His commanding officer gave permission for him to broadcast, and he tried, with only occasional success, to use the job as an opportunity to gather information to pass on to Australia, and to make disappear documents that could have resulted in repercussions on fellow prisoners. After the war, he worked as an informant for ASIO within the media, and when this was suspected he was hounded mercilessly by Rupert Lockwood and other members of the executive of the Australian Journalists Association.[1]

Persons such as Cousens and Rodie worked in more comfortable conditions than the prisoners of war who slaved on the Burma Railway or in the mines in Japan, but they too were subject to brutality and danger, and to similar compulsions: Obey or die. Some heroic souls chose death. Most chose to obey, although that did not ensure their survival. This story is not about those who worked for the Japanese under compulsion, but some Australian collaborators in Shanghai, who worked for the Japanese willingly before the war, continued working for them during the war, and escaped without punishment and with their public reputations more or less intact: Alan Willoughby Raymond; John Joseph Holland; and Wynette Cecilia McDonald. All three also had irregularities in their backgrounds, were careless with other people's money, and scandalised contemporaries with their sex lives.

Alan Willoughby Raymond

Violently anti-British and anti-Semitic, Alan Raymond was the leading figure in this group – violent in rhetoric and, if his claims were true, physically violent as well. According to the passport he obtained in 1931, he was born in Melbourne on 27 February 1909, the son of Alan Raymond, who was born in England and died in 1911 at Chatswood, and Irene, née Johnson. Security claimed that his mother had been born at Tulle in France in 1888, and that the family arrived in Australia in 1891.

In 1931, it was not necessary to present a birth certificate and other official documents to obtain a passport, but when he applied for a new passport in 1949, he was confronted with evidence that he did not exist officially, for there was no such birth registration. His solicitor produced 'evidence' that he had been born in Sydney on 26 November 1910. Again, there is no such registration, but there is a registration for the birth of an Allan M. Johnson, son of James G. Johnson and Irene F. Johnson, née Richards, registered at Mosman (Sydney) early 1911.[2]

Alan Willoughby Raymond (Portion of a cutting from the *Shanghai Times*, courtesy of National Archives, Australia: A989, 1943/235/4/8: Defence Subversive activities – "The Break away from Britain League" concerning Allan W. Raymond.

A feasible explanation is that Irene Johnson, either before or after her husband died, took up with Henry Raymond, whom Alan may have believed was his father. Indeed, it is possible that he was, but there is no record of a marriage between Henry Raymond and Irene Johnson or Irene Richards. When Henry died on 23 December 1914 after a car accident, his funeral notice gave his wife as 'Irene Raymond', for that was the name under which she had been living. However, his will, which was a legal document, left his estate to his 'good friend' *Mary* Johnson. This would be a long shot, except that they had been living in *Willoughby* Street, Naremburn. Alan Raymond's mixed-up records seem to have been the result of Irene's attempts to cover the tracks of infidelity. (At times he also used the name Alan Willoughby.)

Chapter 10: The Shanghai Gang

Security reports suggest that Raymond had some Asian ancestry, but a blurred newspaper photo of him neither supports nor disproves this conclusively. They claim that at an early age he went to Sydney with his father and mother and two sisters. Henry Raymond had two daughters, Rita and Ada, by his late wife, Eva, but in 1917, Irene, using the name 'Irene Raymond', married William K. Spice, and it was known that Alan Raymond had two other 'sisters', Jean Poppy Spice and Dorothy Joyce Spice, who sometimes used the name 'Raymond', and for whom no birth registration can at present be found under either name.[3] It does not matter greatly where or when he was born, except to indicate that from early childhood he was apparently surrounded by a web of parental deceit, setting a pattern that he followed.

About 1927, Raymond allegedly left for Melbourne, where he had worked for Coles before moving back to Sydney. In February 1931, aged twenty-one, he left Sydney for Shanghai aboard *Buffington Court*. In Shanghai, he held positions with several small firms. He had already come under notice while working briefly for a British firm, Harvie Cooke & Co., and as an agent for the Sydney firm of Young & Co., from whom he received 'certain moneys' for which he failed to account. From 1932 to 1935, he worked with Jacob Wong of Shanghai Marble Co. as Foreign Manager and correspondent, travelling widely in China and Japan. After he left Wong, he dabbled in real estate sales and advertising, then he set up his own marble business, but he was stranded in Japan for three months when a business venture failed in 1936 or 1937.

He attracted early police and security attention in Shanghai and Hong Kong when he tried to found a 'Break Away from Britain Movement' among expatriates in China, an organisation that was quickly banned in Hong Kong. It was reported that he did not bear a good name in the British community, as he mixed mainly with Japanese, Germans, and 'low type' Chinese women, and he incurred business and personal debts that he did not pay. He became associated with horse racing, but he was forced to resign from the Shanghai Racing Club, where he was 'posted' for unpaid debts.

When the war in China resumed in July 1937, he made his way inland, then to Hong Kong as Chinese forces retreated. He was soon in trouble there, and after some incident at the Macao races, he was warned off both Macao and Hong Kong courses. He picked up various odd jobs. At one time he worked as sub-editor on an English-language newspaper, and at another as a clerk in a stock-broking firm dealing in American and Philippine stocks and commodities and Singapore rubber. He was probably in Singapore for a while, for he boasted later that he had 'stove a Jew's head in' at Singapore.

He allegedly returned to Shanghai in 1938 and discharged some debts before returning to Australia. It is more likely that this was, in fact, in 1939, and one might wonder how he obtained the money to do so. It is possible he was already being paid by the Japanese, for they valued any initiative aimed at removing Australia from the British political and commercial spheres of influence, and consequently from British support. He is next recorded as arriving in Fremantle from Singapore aboard *Centaur* on 6 December 1939. On the passenger list, he described himself as a journalist. During his brief stay in Perth, he visited Melanie O'Loughlin at Nedlands; she was the local organiser of the German propaganda organisation, The Link, and she had had some contact with visiting Japanese naval officers through an innocent interest in *bonsai* trees. At her house, Raymond met with certain persons who later became notorious in connection with the Australia-First group in Perth: Laurence Bullock and others. Bullock was involved in a variety of fringe political movements, including Social Credit, and early in the war he had written to the United States asking for German propaganda material and expressing his willingness to commit sabotage and carry out 'blood purges' in imitation of Hitler. He was also an admirer of the Japanese Black Dragon Society and its leader, Mitsuru Toyama. Early in 1942, he was the key organiser of a quartet of nitwits who devised some grandiose and noxious but woolly-headed plans to surrender the state to the invading Japanese and set up a fascist government in Western Australia under Bullock's leadership.

The question arises: how had Raymond known of the existence of these people and of a way to contact them? A friend of O'Loughlin, Veronica Margaret Connolly, had been secretary-mistress to one of the Japanese agents connected with a scheme to mine iron ore at Yampi Sound for export to Japan, and it is feasible that information about a small group of people who were friendly to Japan had been passed back to a Japanese political or military authority, who instructed Raymond to call on them. Evidence of connections at this level of secrecy would be almost impossible to obtain, but there is no indication that Raymond had any other means of knowing of O'Loughlin's existence.

Raymond must have been on an eastbound train within days, for he arrived in Melbourne on 11 December, and by 8 January 1940 he had reached Sydney, where he took a flat at Potts Point. He applied for a position with the stock-broking firm of Ralph W. King in Sydney, using a reference from Payne & Co. in Hong Kong. As this stated that he had been employed by them from 1 April 1938 to 30 November 1939, and described him as being of steady and sober habits and high integrity of character, it is likely that he had forged it, and obviously he had had access to the stockbroker's stationery while working for them as a clerk.

He asked Frank Cade, sub-editor of the *Sun News Pictorial* in Melbourne, to 'use the full power of your journalistic talents in a description of my unique and unrivalled abilities and reputation in Hong Kong (the better side of course)' if Ralph King should enquire. One way or another, he

Chapter 10: The Shanghai Gang

obtained a position as clerk with King, but it lasted only a few weeks, as he clearly did not know the job. At the same time, he applied for the vacant position of Australian Trade Commissioner at Singapore, again giving Cade as a referee, as well as one Donovan, Financial Editor of the same paper.

It would have pleased the Japanese greatly to have one of their agents as Australian Trade Commissioner, but this position required a person with some social and commercial standing, and Raymond had neither, as the Australian Government, through its British contacts in Hong Kong, could readily have found out and probably did. Raymond wrote an article called 'Business Robbery' for the Sydney *Bulletin* of 22 May 1940. In this he attacked the Australian trade representative in Shanghai (at that time, Vivian Gordon Bowden)[4] and urged recognition of the fact that the Japanese had been completely successful in China and that General Chiang Kai-shek would not be able to regain control. The Japanese sometimes paid both writer and publisher well for this type of propaganda, though the Australian records of secret Japanese payments do not include payments to either Raymond or the *Bulletin*. Bowden, who later obtained the position of Trade Commissioner at Singapore, complained to the Department of Commerce that an Australian paper should not have given prominence to an article by a man of Raymond's type.

Security tried to discover whether there had been any contact between Raymond and the Australia-First Movement clique in Sydney, and whether he had written for their monthly magazine, the *Publicist*. He said later that he had no contact with them, even though its later president, Percy Stephensen, lived near him in Potts Point, and Raymond must have been aware of this propaganda. However, no evidence of contact was found, nor did he write for the *Publicist*, unless it was under an alias.

Raymond left Sydney on 2 June by *Kitano Maru*. The Security Service reported later that he had been in financial difficulties in Sydney and had been trying to borrow money, and he had returned to Shanghai to avoid military service. Trying to borrow money was not unusual for him, and he did apparently leave in something of a hurry, as his name had been added to the ship's supplementary passenger list. He described himself as a clerk, and he travelled third class. Europeans of any standing did not travel third class on Asian ships, so he must have been short of money; it is possible that some Japanese agency paid his fare. Somewhere he must have changed ships, for he arrived in Shanghai on 3 July aboard *Husimi Maru*.[5]

He used the address of the Park Hotel in Shanghai for his mail; however, he never resided there, but with one of his shady racing colleagues. His mother followed him to Shanghai, leaving Sydney by *Taiping* on 7 November 1941. She was listed as Irene Raymond, divorcee. It was a name to which she had no legal right, unless she had changed her name by deed poll, for she had not married Henry Raymond.

Raymond's case and subsequent career illustrate the effect of *Publicist* propaganda on some people, and the betrayal that occurred in Shanghai was what Military Intelligence feared might happen in Australia. Although the Australia-First people in Sydney knew little about what was happening in Western Australia and nothing of the situation in Shanghai, copies of the *Publicist* reached China and gave moral support to Raymond and others.

John Joseph Holland

Another Australian who broadcast from Shanghai was Jack Holland, born on 5 July 1907 in Kanowna, Western Australia, the son of the local doctor. Father and son did not get along amicably. Like Raymond, he had an unenviable reputation in business and personal affairs. He worked as a car salesman for a time and was imprisoned for cheque fraud in 1932. On 19 September 1932, he married Queensland-born Emily Muriel Valentine Radecki in Sydney. She was born at Mount Morgan on 29 May 1902, but when she enlisted as a clerk in the army (NF409526) on 29 June 1942 she called herself Boris Emily Radeski and alleged a birth date of 1905.[6] In August 1937, Holland left for China as a greaser aboard *Marama*, which was to be sold to Japan for scrap.

From Shanghai, he undertook a difficult and dangerous transport job to Nanking for the Chinese, for which he was paid very well. He worked as a correspondent covering the Sino-Japanese War, and later he broadcast from Shanghai. At another time, he allegedly bought the radio station belonging to the *Shanghai Times*, acting as an agent for the Japanese. Holland travelled widely in Japan, Indo-China, Thailand, Malaya and the Netherlands East Indies, and he could speak several Chinese dialects. For a time he was in Hong Kong, which he left suddenly and secretly in October 1938, leaving behind a pregnant Chinese girlfriend and some large debts. He apparently went to Shanghai again, then to Peking, and by mid 1940 he was in Singapore, where Boris joined him in August. He joined the local Aero Club and obtained a pilot's licence, and allegedly served in the Volunteer Air Corps before being 'turfed out' for making slighting comments about the British. Accounts differ as to whether he was still in Singapore when the Japanese arrived, or whether he had already returned to Shanghai by December 1941. In any case, he was in Shanghai when he came to notice as a broadcaster for the Japanese.

Wynette Cecilia McDonald

The third Shanghai character of interest in connection with Australia-First was 'Wyn' or 'Gwyn' or 'Gwen' McDonald, allegedly born in Melbourne on 24 October 1912. In view of the way these people fiddled with their identities, it is not surprising that there is no such registration. In fact, it appears that she was born in Melbourne on 23 October 1916, and registered as Winifred Alice McDonald, daughter of Ewan Cameron McDonald and Winifred Grace Le Blanc. It is not known whether some clerk in the Registry Office made a mistake in the name, or whether she chose to call herself by a different name.

She said later that she had been married to a John Porter, and records show that in 1935 John Albert Porter married Winifred Alice McDonald. It was reported that her mother was of 'mixed French parentage'; that was the Le Blanc ancestry. There are statements alleging that she might have been Eurasian, and that she had adopted the Buddhist religion.

About 1939, after Wyn and her husband parted company, she took up with H. Olof Lindquist, who was of Swedish origin and much older than she was. They travelled around Australia together for about a year before they entered into some sort of commercial arrangement with Serge Wittouck, a Belgian of part-Russian ancestry. He was Managing Director of Asia Investment Company, Manila, and British Intelligence reports called him 'unscrupulous'. One of his deals concerned obtaining Timor oil for Japan, and this might have been the start of her association with the Japanese. Lindquist held a Swedish passport, issued in Sydney on 19 August 1935; Wynette obtained a British passport in Darwin on 29 July 1940, and both had obtained Dutch visas for the East Indies. However, by the time they arrived at Soerabaya, there was news that Wittouck had committed suicide in Manila. They had little money, and their contacts were suspect, so they were refused permission to land, but they were allowed ashore in Batavia before being deported by the Dutch *Tjibadak* on 8 August.

They arrived in Shanghai on 27 August, virtually destitute. Rumour had it that they had more money than they could account for legitimately, but Bowden, then in Shanghai, had to advance them money for accommodation and sustenance until Wynette found a position teaching in a nursery school. She spoke good Japanese, and she and Lindquist associated mainly with Germans and Japanese. Sometimes they claimed to be man and wife, sometimes 'just friends'. British residents of Shanghai disliked them and considered that Lindquist was 'a common confidence trickster'.

Wynette claimed that a friend was going to smuggle money to Manila for her, so that she could go to America. When she wrote to Bowden threatening libel proceedings against anyone who 'maligned' her, he reported that she was 'not quite normal mentally'. One day when she was absent from her teaching job, a member of the school staff found a coded naval telegram in her drawer. This was taken to the British Consul, who told Bowden they were in a secret navy code and had probably been obtained by Lindquist from a ship in which he was working.[7] On 27 December 1940, Bowden reported this to Colonel Jones of the Commonwealth Investigation Branch in Australia, but no action was taken against her.

Collaborators

Many British in the Shanghai International Concession collaborated with the Japanese, more or less *per force*, but some collaborated willingly, even enthusiastically. The first evidence that some Australians were involved in propaganda broadcasts came not directly from these broadcasts, but from a telegram from Britain, dated 15 March 1942, which said that in a broadcast by the German *Deutsche Welle* on 11 March it had been reported:

> Recently an Australian independence movement was founded in Shanghai under the leadership of Alan Raymond. Raymond stated that Australia will demand complete independence, in so far as she is able to determine her own destiny at the conclusion of the present conflict. Raymond made the announcement that he would appeal to his fellow countrymen in Australia over the radio.

It added that at the first meeting of the movement, held in Shanghai on 7 March, it had been resolved to approach the Japanese Government with a view to securing leniency for Australia, which, they said, had been tricked into the war by Britain. According to Domei's Shanghai correspondent, Raymond had said: 'Since the Japanese Government has intimated its desire to save Australia from the horrors of war the Commonwealth should negotiate for an honourable peace.' It was thought that there might well be a link between the Shanghai group and the Australia-First Movement, and it was not entirely a coincidence that it was indicated in the *Publicist*, discussed at the Yabber Club, and mooted at public meetings that Britain and the United States had involved Australia in their war, and that Australia should make a separate peace.

The story is complicated and reports are sometimes contradictory, so it is not possible to be certain of details, but the general trend of the reports was this. An association called at various times the Break Away from Britain Movement or the Independent Australia League was founded on 7 March 1942; it was obviously backed by the Japanese, who let them use the Astor Park Hotel for meetings. The latter name echoed that of the Independent India League, which was also sponsored by the Japanese. The committee consisted of Alan Raymond, Wynette McDonald, Olof Lindquist, Petersen (possibly not his real name, as he was allegedly using stolen papers), and a couple named Everett.[8] Although the group was started by Australians and aimed at Australia, it was joined by Britons and Americans who hoped to gain some advantage through it, and allegedly it eventually numbered about three hundred. Apparently it did not last very long, for the Japanese found they were not gaining much benefit from it.

Official news broadcasts from Germany, Japan and Italy described Raymond as President of a league that aimed at promoting a separate peace with Japan, and soon Raymond's broadcasts over the Japanese Shanghai

Chapter 10: The Shanghai Gang

station, XMHA, were urging Australian listeners to demand that the Australian Government contact the Japanese Government with a view to negotiating for peace. If Australians threw off the British yoke and made peace with Japan, they would find a freedom not enjoyed under Britain. Australian listening posts were soon monitoring, recording and transcribing Raymond's broadcasts, but the reception from Shanghai was so poor that few people would have had sufficiently sensitive equipment to receive it intelligibly, or the patience to persevere with the attempt. The only Japanese station that could regularly be picked up intelligibly in Australia was Singapore (then called Syonan, or Shonan), and its propaganda team was relatively ineffective.

Raymond's acquaintances in Australia turned against him; it is doubtful whether any could ever have been real friends. The *Sun News Pictorial* of 18 March ran a London report that the Japanese claimed they had discovered a Quisling to betray Australia, and Raymond's name was mentioned.[9] The *Bulletin*, which had published an article by Raymond nearly two years earlier, mentioned on 1 April 1942 that Raymond was broadcasting for the Japanese.

Raymond also wrote for several English-language Japanese papers. During 1942, he wrote a regular column called 'An Aussie's point of view' for the *Shanghai Times*. On 10 June 1942, the illustrated periodical called *Freedom* published an article on Raymond, with photograph, and called him the leader of the Break Away from Britain Movement. He wrote for the *Shanghai Evening Post* and had another virulently anti-British article in the *Time and Advertiser* of 25 July. He had a special article on page 22 of the 6 July 1942 issue of the *Shanghai Evening Post and Mercury*, celebrating the 'Double Seventh Anniversary', the fifth anniversary of the Lukouchiao (Marco Polo) Bridge incident that had re-kindled the Sino-Japanese War. His writings here accompanied those of Wang Ching-wei, leader of the Chinese puppet government under the Japanese, and Heinrich Georg Stahmer, German Ambassador to the Nanking puppet Government since October 1941, and Ambassador to Japan after 4 February 1943. This issue announced also the surrender of the Americans at Bataan.

When diplomats and some civilians were exchanged in August-September 1942, some of Raymond's articles were carried to Australia and Britain by repatriates. The Department of External Affairs had some by October, and in December the *Daily Mail* in London carried an article on Australian traitors led by Raymond.

The tone of the broadcasts changed as the war turned against Japan. On 22 May 1944, Raymond referred to the battle between the newspapers and Calwell concerning political censorship, saying that a small group of people 'with one foot in Australia and the other in England' controlled the papers, and victory for the newspapers was a defeat for the people of

Australia. On 14 November 1944, in a broadcast that smacked somewhat of desperation, Raymond said:

> The fight against Japanese soldiers will be of a fierceness and intensity never before experienced. All the more reason to employ Dominion shock troops. Australians and New Zealanders will be used wherever there is danger, in accordance with past experiences.

The more the Japanese emphasised the fierceness of the battles to come, and the casualties that the Allies would suffer, the greater the likelihood that America would use atomic bombs to end it all, and to that extent their propaganda backfired and in a collective sense they brought the sufferings of a nuclear holocaust upon themselves.[10]

John Holland worked first for the German station in Shanghai, broadcasting under the pseudonym of David Lester. In a letter to his father in Perth, dated 25 July 1942, he said that he was broadcasting over XGRS, Shanghai, adding: 'I belong to an Australian Political Party here which is interested in endeavouring to promote a separate peace with Japan.' This was apparently smuggled out with one of the exchanged repatriates. When one of his sisters passed this information to the authorities, she said that he had done difficult and dangerous work for the Chinese, and would be broadcasting for the Japanese only under compulsion. However, even before the Pacific War he had also been employed by the Japanese on secret work.

When Holland disappeared from XGRS in September 1942, it was thought at the time that he had been taken off air because he had admitted by inference that an Allied victory was possible. In fact, it was a personal industrial dispute. Holland wanted more money than the Germans were willing to pay him, so he offered his services to the Japanese. He left Shanghai in September 1942, arriving in Tokyo at the end of November; he broadcast from there until 18 March 1943. He did not get along well with his new employers, who arrested him on suspicion of being a Russian spy. He was put on trial, found guilty and imprisoned under brutal conditions in Hokkaido.

After Singapore fell on 15 February 1942, McDonald and Lindquist were the only non-Japanese invited to attend official Japanese celebrations. It was presumed that they had provided services that warranted this reward and were pleased about the British defeat. McDonald – Wynette, Winifred, Wyn, Gwyn or Gwen – broadcast for the Japanese from April 1942 to April 1943. In one broadcast she claimed that the current Prime Minister, John Curtin, had murdered a former Prime Minister, Joseph Lyons, by giving him poison.[11]

There was a close association between McDonald and Suyana, Chief of Police in Shanghai, and Hayashi, who later became Camp Commandant. McDonald and Lindquist handed over records and photos of their travels

Chapter 10: The Shanghai Gang

in Northern and North-Eastern Australia, which would have been of considerable use if Japan had decided on invasion. She also worked for the Germans. In 1941, she and Lindquist had approached Baron Jesco von Puttkamer, head of the German Propaganda Department in Shanghai, June 1941 – May 1945, with a proposition:

> The Swedish man undertook, if the German Propaganda Department would provide him with the necessary small craft, to take propaganda material such as pamphlets and books and land them in Australia. Wyn McDonald stated that she would undertake the distribution of this propaganda material after it had been landed in the said Commonwealth of Australia. Wyn McDonald was presented to me by the said Swedish man as his wife. The offer of distributing propaganda material in Australia after delivery by small boat was considered too fantastic by me and I refused to consider the matter.[12]

McDonald and Lindquist did rather well for themselves. In a letter home, written on 19 May 1943, she wrote: 'Olof and I are quite well.' The despatch of a letter was not unique, but the Japanese allowed very few letters or cards out of their prison camps. One New Year's night, she participated in an 'escape' allegedly arranged by Hayashi and lived quite comfortably before returning to camp. That she survived was in itself unusual; most recaptured escapees were tortured and killed.

Much information was collected about Raymond, Holland and McDonald. Through External Affairs in Canberra, the Chungking Embassy arranged for the Nationalist Chinese Secret Service to report on Australian collaborators and to supply copies of their articles in English-language Japanese papers. More information was obtained when diplomatic personnel and civilians reached British territory late in 1942, after an exchange of protected persons and some internees. The loathing of Shanghai internees for Raymond's group was deep and bitter.

After a farewell broadcast on 20 July 1945, Raymond disappeared temporarily. He claimed later that everything he had broadcast had been intended for Australia's benefit. Some Australia-First members also perhaps believed sincerely that Japan would be a more benevolent overlord than Britain, and that they were the true patriots. Holland too claimed that he believed what he had said, and that it was for the good of Australia. Indeed, many of their predictions came true later. The main thrust of broadcasts was that Australia needed to become totally independent of Britain, to cease being 'a puppet of British imperialism'. Australia needed to break ties with United States, and to be politically and commercially independent of both. Some Australians believed this even then, and many now expound a similar line in different circumstances. So what was wrong with their broadcasts? During the war the result of this would have been to shift Australia from a comparatively benign dependence on the goodwill of either Britain or the USA, and turn the country over to a Japanese military dictatorship. The ideological link between the Independent Australia League in Shanghai and the Australia-First Movement in New South Wales and Victoria encouraged the Japanese to believe that there was more support for them than there actually was, and that an anti-British attitude was as wide-spread and keenly felt among Australians as it was among Indians and Malays.

From Raymond's broadcasts, the conclusion may be drawn that the Japanese already had someone in mind as their puppet governor of Australia. Not necessarily Sir John Latham, as was secretly discussed by Australian politicians as the least worst of possibilities if Australia should be defeated and occupied, but possibly Eddie Ward, for 'Mr Ward' attracted noticeably frequent praise in Raymond's broadcasts. Ward had been under the influence of the Japanese agent, John Sleeman; he had fought hard for many years before the war to minimise Australia's military capacity by claiming that Australia had no potential enemies. He proclaimed that Britain and America were to blame for the war. He had created potential military problems with his accusations of a political motive behind an alleged 'Brisbane Line' strategy. However, his reaction to any suggestion that he might be a puppet Prime Minister or Governor for the Japanese cannot even be imagined.[13]

As the inept Japanese propagandists never really understood the psychology of individual Australians, nor the structure of Australian society, the effect of their propaganda broadcasts ranged from mildly irritating to hilariously ridiculous. In addition, they were so boringly repetitive that reading through the transcripts on file is as good as a sleeping tablet. If any of those who broadcast for Japan had had their hearts in the job, and had been given free rein, they could have done a much more effective job, although ultimately it would still have been futile. It would have done nothing whatever to enable Japan to win the war.

Repercussions

After the war, all available information on Raymond was sent to the Attorney-General's Department to determine whether he should be brought back to stand trial for treason.

On 24 October 1945, Sir George Knowles, the Solicitor-General, wrote a report in which he discussed whether there was sufficient evidence to justify bringing him back. He wrote that, if there was evidence that Raymond had broadcast over XMHA or written for Japanese papers, 'that would support a charge of treason'. However, if it could not be established that he did this with the *intention* of assisting Japan, the charge of treason would probably

Chapter 10: The Shanghai Gang

fail. It was remarked that his broadcasts were in general not notably anti-Australian or pro-Japanese: they were anti-British. They followed the Japanese aim of creating enmity between Australia and Britain: poor little Australia, duped by wicked Britain. It was further suggested that enquiries be made concerning the charges being laid against William Joyce (Lord Haw-Haw). However, Britain was able to arrest Joyce in Germany, while Raymond was in Shanghai, out of Australia's reach.

In November, Captain W. R. Blacket of the Security Service went to Japan to inquire into the activities of collaborators. Visiting Shanghai as well, he interviewed Raymond, who was studying psychology at St John's University, and was expected to graduate in January. Raymond claimed that he began to broadcast only after Singapore fell, that he had never been under any form of compulsion to make the broadcasts, and that he had received no preferential treatment. He said that his work had allowed him to support himself and rescue his mother from internment, and enabled him to trade as a broker on the Chinese stock exchange. How many other Australians in Japanese-occupied Shanghai enjoyed this privilege?

In May 1946, three British 'collaborationists' were arrested in China, and the Chinese wanted reciprocal treatment for Chinese in Hong Kong and Malaya. The latent question of the fate of Raymond was raised again. The British were powerless to take action against him without cooperation from the Chinese, who would regard any unauthorised action as an infringement of their sovereignty. To other British subjects who had suffered internment during the war, it was 'galling' to see that Raymond, who had done so much to assist the enemy, was still at liberty. As Raymond's British passport expired on 7 April 1946, he needed a new one. A telegram from the Legation in Shanghai on 1 May stated: 'This man showed himself to be a traitor during the war and it is felt he has forfeited all claims to be granted travel facilities as an Australian citizen.'

An Australian repatriated from Shanghai late in 1946 said that Raymond had tried, during the war, to contact all Australians in Shanghai and persuade them to join the Independent Australia League, but he received little support. He added: 'He was a traitor of the worst kind, and the fact that he is still in Shanghai enjoying a full measure of freedom is a gross miscarriage of justice.'

In February 1947, Raymond applied to the Australian Consul-General in Shanghai to have his passport renewed, and to have his full-blood Chinese wife and their son registered as Australian. Both applications were refused. The only offer was of a travel document to enable him to return to Australia, but he was faced with the prospect that he could be detained in Australia, while his wife was refused admission. He ranted and blustered, threatened the Consul-General, and showed no repentance for his wartime activities.

By 1949, now in Hong Kong, Raymond was desperate. Despite his work for the Japanese, Raymond got along well with the Nationalist Chinese, but he was afraid of what would happen to him under Mao's communists. In addition, he had a job with an airline, and in this position he needed to travel abroad. It was fairly easy now to deny him a passport, for his mother's indiscretions came back to haunt him, and he apparently was genuinely not sure where or when he had been born, nor under what name his birth was registered. He said he had no choice but to believe what his mother had told him, and she had apparently died during the war and could not be consulted. A solicitor in Sydney obtained apparent evidence of his birth details, and a new passport was issued. At this point, the dossiers on Raymond cut out, and his eventual fate cannot be determined.

Wynette McDonald went to Manila in October 1945 (as McDonald), and she had returned to Shanghai by mid January 1946 (as Mrs Lindquist). She returned to Australia voluntarily and boldly, leaving Hong Kong on 7 February 1946 by *Bonaventure*. She was reported to be living in Belgrave on a property owned by her sister's husband, 'Group Captain' Squires, son of an Australian father and a German mother. Like so much else connected with the Shanghai group, this also does not quite tally with records.[14]

She claimed that her 'friend' Lindquist was killed by Japanese while in command of Swedish ship on the Yangtse, but those who knew them doubted this. She planned to leave Melbourne for Sydney in April, allegedly for a well-paid job as a wool buyer for a Chinese firm, which had provided her with plentiful funds, though there was no indication that she knew anything about wool. McDonald, who had adopted the Buddhist religion, claimed that she intended to marry an officer from *Bonaventure* in May, and to return to Hong Kong. There was speculation that she would be acting as an informant for the Kuomintang Government.

In July 1947, Wyn returned to Australia with the latest claimant for the status of being her husband: Carlos Henrique Ozorio, born in Swatow, China, of Macao-Portuguese parents, but holding British nationality by virtue of his father's birth in Hong Kong. Carlos said they were married in January 1943, in a small church outside Lung Hua internment camp, but he did not hold a certificate; Wyn said they married on 3 January 1944 at Nanking. When a European Catholic priest refused to marry them, as she could not produce a baptismal certificate, a Chinese priest had married them, but had not given them a certificate. They lived for a time with her parents in St Kilda (Melbourne), and were married officially on 29 September 1947 at St Mary's. Was she free to marry? What about John Porter, and Olof Lindquist, and the officer of *Bonaventure*? Probably the only man she had really married previously was John Porter. He enlisted in the AIF in June 1940 and was assigned to the 2/21 Battalion; in December 1941, this was sent to Ambon as 'Gull Force'. He is registered as having been killed on 20 February 1942, but that is only somebody's guess, for he was among a group of over 300 men captured while guarding Laha airfield. Between 5 and 20 February, they were all murdered by their Japanese captors, and there was nobody to record the dates on which individuals had died. In Shanghai in December 1945, Wyn had told a representative of Military Intelligence that as far as she knew she was still married to Porter, although he might have divorced her. She did not have proof, but as the Japanese, whom she admired so much, had killed her husband, she was indeed free to remarry.

Ozorio obtained a position in Rabaul as a radio technician with the Department of Civil Aviation. In 1955, Carlos and Wyn applied for permanent residence in Australia for themselves and their two children. A report said that, as she was born in Australia and he was a British subject, there were 'insufficient grounds' to refuse this. In 1964, Ozorio, now calling himself Charles Henry, applied for Australian citizenship for himself and on behalf of his daughter and his second son, although he already held a *British* passport. (The first son was Australian-born.) He was still working for the DCA, but then stationed in Cairns.

Even the most noxious members of Shanghai group were barely inconvenienced and attracted minimal press attention. They did not seem to be in any way ashamed of their conduct, and only John Holland faced a court. Despite the evidence against them, it was difficult to get them and possible witnesses to Australia, and difficult to formulate a charge. The American Counter Intelligence Corps arrested Holland in Sapporo in northern Japan, as was reported by the Melbourne *Herald* of 28 September 1945. He was returned to Australia after being imprisoned in Yokohama and later being held under open arrest for several months on Manus Island. Released on bail while a case was prepared, he did not wait to be tried, but left Fremantle on 7 September 1946 as emergency replacement crew in *Tai Ping Yang*. He left the ship in Marseilles, and he was found while visiting relatives in England.

As Britain was more resolute than Australia in exacting retribution, Holland was put on trial at the Central Criminal Court, London, on 25 March 1947. As the court thought that Holland had left Australia with the consent of Australian authorities, and the sufferings that he had endured in a Japanese prison were taken into consideration, he was simply bound over to keep the peace for five years. The Lord Chief Justice warned him he was lucky not to have been charged with high treason and said: 'You did a dastardly act against your country.' Holland returned to Asia, where he married a Japanese woman before returning to China. They were divorced, and a few years after that, in July 1972, he died in Hong Kong.

Australia had never had laws adequate to deal with treason, espionage and threats to national security. Events in the first decade of the twenty-first century are showing that the laws are still flawed.

Sources: The Vindictive Metallurgist

The main sources for this chapter are the archival files:

A367: C1511 PART 1: Burkard, Louis.

ST1233/1: N25708: Louis Burkard [Investigation Branch file]

C415: 5A [PART 2]: Louis Burkard.

C415: 5A [PART 3]: Louis Burkard [Ex 244461] [*Contains passport*]

Publications:

Desmond Ball and David Horner, *Breaking the Codes. Australia's KGB network*, (pp. 220-31 for material on W. S. Clayton; pp. 240-44 for A. T. Hughes. See also Index of book.)

Sunday Telegraph (Sydney), 28 July 1946.

National Archives Australia:

A3201: TE284: Burkard, L.

A6335: 1: New South Wales Police Organisation – ramifications and branches of "The National Socialist German Workers Party" in Australia and Germany. [*dig.*]

A6202: J: Records of the Royal Commission on Espionage – Carbon Copy of document typed [and composed] by RE Lockwood. [*dig.*]

A6202: H: Records of the Royal Commission on Espionage – Character reports including biographical details on Australia journalists typed on three blank pages by Fergan O'Sullivan. [*dig.*]

AJCP: Reel M277: (M277 is an NLA Canberra accession number.):
L940/L269873: Asmis to Auswärtiges Amt, 25 March 1941.
L940/L269915: Paris, 23 August 1941: German Embassy.
L940/ L269997: 15 January 1942. Vichy.

Endnotes

[1] He was probably still in the Reserve, as he held the rank of lieutenant and was aged only 35, but he had not performed the annual training required.

[2] The majority right-wing party at that time was the United Australia Party led by Joseph Lyons.

[3] By 'fatherland' he meant Germany.

[4] Köhler had been a prize officer aboard the World War I commerce raider, *Möwe*.

[5] The wording, of course, comes from somewhat clumsy translations by various translators for one of the security services; Burkard wrote in German.

[6] It was the French Government in Noumea that had arrested Burkard in the first

Sources and Endnotes

instance.

[7] In Document "J", one of the exhibits in the Royal Commission on Espionage – Petrov case – in 1954, Rupert Lockwood described Pearl as a Trotskyite and 'one of Packer's most miserable bootlickers'. In Document "H", Fergan O'Sullivan described Fitchett, then 'Head' of the *Age* in Melbourne, as 'gross in physique and thought'.

[8] If any reader really needs to know whether Burkard's family survived the war, this could probably be deduced from his will. (NSW Probate 403906, 1952.) I was not willing to pay the exorbitant fee required.

Sources: The Fake Alien

The main sources for this chapter are the archival files:

A1533: 1955/4136: BRUNDAHL, Lars. [*dig.*]

A6126: 31: BRUNDAHL, Lars Gustav.

B741: V/4272: Brundahl, Lars Gustav.

C329: 118: Lars Gustaff Brundahl.

MP508/1: 255/702/32: Brundahl, Lars Gustoff – Objection against internment.

SP1714/1: N38981: Lars Gustaff Brundahl (Part 1). [*This contains the October 1939 report on his early life in New Zealand.*]

Publications:

Argus (Melbourne), 27 April 1949.

Daily Mirror (Sydney), 30 October 1951.

Daily News (Sydney), 7 January 1939.

Die Brücke, 11 December 1937.

Sun (Sydney), 6 September 1948, 14 October 1948.

Sunday Telegraph (Sydney), 15 May 1949.

Sydney Morning Herald, 22 November 1947.

Commonwealth Parliamentary Debates, (Hansard), House of Representatives, 7 September 1948.

National Archives Australia:

A367: C67248 PART 3: [Von Skerst, Arnold]. [*Report of interview, 23 November 1942*]

A437: 1946/6/205: Von Skerst, Arnold – Alien control.

A439: 1951/11/7589: Becker, Johannes Heinrich

A439: 1952/11/3007: Brundahl, L. – administration.

A472: W31449: Dr J H Becker, ex-internee. Request to remain in Australia.

A1838: 1477/1/33: Deportation - BRUNDAHL, Lars Gustav

A9108: Roll 21/18: Brundahl.

D1915: SA19060: A VON SKERST. [*Interview with Security Service, 22 November 1942*].

D1915: SA22353: NSDAP Landesgruppe Australien

BP25/1: BRUNDALL L: Brundall, Laurence – Nationality: American – Arrived in Sydney on flight VH EBC 21 May 1961.

SP1714/1: N39593: Nazi Party [Auslands, NSDAP, Concordia Club] membership lists.

AJCP: Reel M272 (NLA Canberra): pp. L940/L269007-18: General-Konsulat Sydney, at Batavia, October 1939. (*Seger letter*)

Endnotes

[1] Peter's birthplace was actually Sundsvall, but old registrations are riddled with spelling errors. It can be presumed that 'Agustoff' was a clerical error, and that his name was meant to be either Gustaff or Gustav, but 'Brundall' is correct. Peter M. Brundall died on 30 November 1891, and Melinda J. Brundall on 29 May 1921. She had four children from her first marriage, and Lars was the fourth of five Brundall children.

2 At this time, Brundall was not yet twenty. This information must be regarded as approximate and not entirely reliable.

3 She had been a widow, but there is no indication that her first husband had any connection with Canada. He was born in New Zealand and was working in the mines at Clunes, Victoria, when he and Melinda married in 1869.

[4] It is impossible to work out precisely how many of these contradictions in names were the result of Brundahl's propensity to tell lies, how many were due to errors by registry office clerks, and how many to the faulty hearing or memory of Security officers. Melinda Jane Scantlebury's first husband was William Alfred Bullen, so the names appear in some variant and in different sequence in many claims.

[5] If he had been working as a seaman, he might have arrived in Australian ports on several occasions, and it is vaguely possible that he had been in San Francisco at the time of the earthquake, but in 1906 he was supposed to have been still in New Zealand.

[6] See Chapter 3.

[7] The adviser did not know the extent of Brundahl's perjury at his Appeal

Sources: The Card-Carrying Spy

The main sources for this chapter are the archival files:

A367: C67579: Gunther G. T. Dorn, Internment and Deportation. [*dig.*]

A367: C68562: [EUGEN MATHY].

A9108: Roll 9/3: German intelligence service and espionage service in Australia. [*Formerly A784; There are two separate reports with the same title – 'Etappenorganisation der Kriegsmarine (Marine-Sonderdienst)' – in this file.*]

B741: V/19711: DORN, Gunther.

Publications:

Overlack, Peter: 'The Imperial German Navy in the Pacific 1900-1914 as an instrument of Weltpolitik, with special reference to Australasia in its operational planning. (Unpublished Ph. D. thesis, 1996. UQFL)

Laughlin, Austin: *Boots and All,* Melbourne, Colorgravure, 1951.

Moses, John A., with Gregory Munro, *Australia and the 'Kaiser's War'. On Understanding the ANZAC Tradition.* Arguments & Theses, Broughton Press: St John's College, St Lucia, QLD 1993.

Tampke, Jürgen, ed., *'Ruthless Warfare'. German military planning and surveillance in the Australia-New Zealand region before the Great War.* Canberra, Southern Highlands, 1998.

McKernan, Michael, *The Australian People and the Great War.* West Melbourne: Thomas Nelson, 1980. (p. 169)

Fischer, Gerhard, *Enemy Aliens and the homefront experience in Australia 1914-1920.* St Lucia, Qld: University of Queensland Press, 1989. (pp. 124-25)

Chapman, John (editor), *The Price of Admiralty: The War Diary of the German Naval Attaché in Japan, 1939-1943.* Volumes 2 & 3: 23 August 1940 - 9 September 1941.

De Jong, Louis, *The German Fifth Column in the Second World War.* London: Routledge & Kegan Paul, 1956 (p. 280).

Die Brücke, 26 May 1934, 2 June 1934. (*Freyberg*)

National Archives Australia:

A367: C1511 PART 1: Burkard, Louis.

A367: C68565: Von Bohn, Richard Rudolf. [also known as Richard Alexander Nikolai, Richard Von Arco].

A367: C68585: HANS H.F. RENZ.

A367: C18000/29: Objection No 1/41 – Josef Janssen – Advisory Committee.

The Most Dangerous Man in Australia?

A9108: Roll 8/5: Nazi activity in South Australia. [*Formerly A774, Part 2*] [*dig.*]

D1915: SA16752: Dr O E Seger (SS2286) [Copy of record seized from German Consulate at outbreak of WW2]. [*In Canberra.*]

D1915: SA19060: A VON SKERST. [*Interview with Security Service, 22 November 1942*].

ST1233/1: N39085: Frederick Wilhelm Kirchner. [*re election of Mathy and Hardt to Chamber of Commerce positions*]

A3201: TE990: LOHMANN & Co. [*Letter, 21 October 1914, from G. F. Schloetelberg, Seattle*] [*dig.*]

AJCP: Reel M272 (NLA Canberra): pp. L929/ L265229-266: Abteilung IIS. Akten betreffend: Die Jahres-Schiffahrtsberichte des K. Konsulats in Brisbane. Band 1. Schiffahrt Nr. 12. Von Januar 1907 bis 21.2.1914. England. (Consular shipping reports)

National Archives and Records Administration, Washington: RG38. E-6-A. 21753. Box 630. C-243. (Report on the organisation of the Etappe based on German files. Written June 1947.)

Internet:

König, Paul. *Die Fahrt der Deutschland*, 1916. (pp. 4-8). See Google:

http://www.archive.org/stream/diefahrtderdeut00kngoog/diefahrtderdeut00kngoog_djvu.txt

On *Zeitungsdienst Graf (Hans) Reischach*: http://www.oac.cdlib.org/data/13030/bn/kt7s2036bn/files/kt7s2036bn.pdf.http://www.teli.de/geschichte/2007-teli-unterm-hakenkreuz-web.pdf

For Gustav Hardt and Walter Darré, see Wikipedia.

Endnotes

[1] Alfred Lohmann was the son of Johann Georg Lohmann, Director of NDL 1877-1892, and he later became a director himself. It was he who first introduced freight-carrying U-boats as blockade runners.

[2] Plate's dossier was probably not available when McKernan was writing, but it should have been available in 1989 when Gerhard Fischer repeated this claim.

[3] The word *Nachrichten* means information or news, as well as secret Intelligence, and it may have been a misleading translation.

[4] It may well be only coincidence that there was a Heiler (not Willi) who provided a cover address for German espionage reports sent to Portugal.

[5] The classification he named, 'ganz geheim' [totally secret], was even more restricted than 'streng geheim' [strictly secret].

[6] See chapter on Homburg.

[7] These dates do not support a consistent story, but if there is one consistent thing about Dorn's documents it is that they are inconsistent and sometimes apparently contradictory. The story of the *Nerother* League is interesting, but too complicated to analyse here; it googles well.

[8] In fact, rolls were closed to adults resident in Germany from May 1933 until mid 1937, but it was possible for youths to join at 18, and for adults under special circumstances. Normally, male Aryan Germans going overseas at this time were compelled to join the Party.

[9] This press agency provided news items and photographs for the Nazi press, and its overseas branch was staffed largely with dedicated Nazis. The material they sent was, of course, available for military purposes as well.

[10] In fact, *Manunda* left Melbourne on 29 August. It is not known whether there was an error in the report, or whether *Manunda's* schedule was changed.

[11] The entry in one in Dorn's dossiers, saying that he was bound for India, was another piece of nonsense; his aim was to get clear of British territory.

[12] Was it an automatic pistol? Automatic revolvers existed, but by 1938 they were no longer the weapon of choice, nor very common.

[13] The *Abwehr* was the nominally 'counter-intelligence' organisation headed by Admiral Canaris.

Sources: The Neurotic Chameleon

Publications:

Hans Rothfels, *The German Opposition to Hitler: an Assessment*, London, Wolff, 1961. [p. 51, (re 'the "Avengers of Röhm" known as the "R.R.s"')

National Archives Australia:

A367: C68565: Von Bohn, Richard Rudolf. [also known as Richard Alexander Nikolai, Richard Von Arco] [*Report of Aliens Tribunal No. 4 (Victoria) 17 June 1941*]

A659: 1939/1/15127: Von Arco-Bohn, R. – Naturalisation [includes passport].

A1068: IC47/22/8/72: Passports – Italy. [*Title lists names, including Von Bohn Boham, Sophie A J O*]

D1915: SA3347: Von Bohn, Richard August Heinrich (Count).

MP529/3: TRIBUNAL 4/ VON BOHN: Transcript of evidence of objection by R R von Bohn, German internee.

MP1588/11: WHOLE SERIES: COIC Appreciations, Sep 1940 – May 1942. [*re Yoneda*]

ST1233/1: N11632: Richard August Heinrich BOHN. (Investigation file)

Endnotes

[1] The name looks like 'Johanes', but the stroke above the 'n' means that the letter should be doubled.

[2] There is not enough information available either to prove or to disprove any of these claims.

[3] The 18th Cavalry Regiment was based in Stuttgart-Cannstatt, but no evidence has been found that Rommel was there at the time, except perhaps as a visitor.

[4] Later Bohn said that when Hitler came to power in 1933, his prison sentence was confirmed.

[5] Hitler and Goebbels were Catholics; Göring was not.

[6] Perhaps he had in mind G. Sydor Stoler, a representative of the Red International of Labor Unions and nephew of Alexander Lozovsky, general secretary of Profintern. He visited Australia in 1928-29.

[7] Freyberg had retired in January 1933, as a lieutenant-colonel; he rejoined the armed forces later. His visit to Australia is not mentioned in his service history on Internet at http://www.oocities.com/~orion47/WEHRMACHT/LUFTWAFFE/Generalmajor/FREYBERG_EGLOFF.html

[8] Bohn could not go anywhere outside Australia legally, as his passport must have expired in 1931.

[9] She discontinued the suit in November 1939.

Sources: The Attorney-General

The main sources for this chapter are the archival files:

A367: C65376: HOMBURG, Hermann and Marsi (daughter) – Internment. [*dig.*]

A367: C68820: HEINRICH KRAWINKEL.

B741: V/24713: HOMBURG, Hermann, and Marsi (daughter) – paroled under National Security Regulations. [*Formerly MP798/1*]

MP508/1: 255/740/10: HOMBURG Fritz – Detention – release – inquiry.

C123: 10900: Homburg, Hermann (German)

D1915: SA2813: Homburg, Fritz.

Publications:

Price, Charles, *German Settlers in South Australia,* Melbourne: Melbourne University Press, 1945.

Homburg, Hermann, *South Australian Lutherans and Wartime Rumours.* Adelaide: Hermann Homburg, 1947.

Harmstorf, Ian & Michael Cigler, *The Germans in Australia.* Australasian Educational Press, Melbourne, 1985.

Leske, Everard, *For Faith and Freedom. The Story of Lutherans and Lutheranism in Australia. 1838-1996.* Adelaide, Openbook Publishers, 1996

McKernan, Michael, *The Australian People and the Great War*, West Melbourne: Thomas Nelson, 1980.

Fischer, Gerhard, *Enemy Aliens and the homefront experience in Australia 1914-1920,* St Lucia, Qld, University of Queensland Press, 1989.

"Adelaide Law School 1883-1983", by Victor Allen Edgeloe. See Internet:

http://digital.library.adelaide.edu.au/dspace/bitstream/2440/43920/1/alr_V9n1_1983_EdgAde.pdf

Adelaide *Advertiser*, 25 March 1912, p. 3.

Canberra Times, 15 October 1943, p.3. Electronic copy at:

http://newspapers.nla.gov.au/ndp/del/article/2653310/683181?zoomLevel=3

National Archives Australia:

A9108: Roll 8/4: Nazi activity in South Australia. [*Formerly A774 File 1*]

A9108: Roll 8/5: Nazi activity in South Australia. [*Formerly A774 File 2*] [*dig.*]

A9108: Roll 8/6: Nazi activity in South Australia. [*Formerly A774 File 3*] [*dig.*]

(*These three rolls should be obligatory reading for anybody misguided enough to imagine that there was no disloyalty in Tanunda.*)

MP742/1: H/5/563: HOMBURG, Renolf Mr – Failure to enrol for service.

D1915: SA18743: German Historical Society of SA.

D1915: SA19132: Heinrich Krawinkel: [*Dossier is in five parts.*]

D1915: SA23349: Homburg, Herman Robert. [*sic*]

D1918: S1523: Dossiers – all parties [political – communist, fascist]

Endnotes

[1] One source claims that the he arrived in Melbourne by the vessel *Godeffroy;* however, *Godeffroy* did not call at either Adelaide or Melbourne – Port Phillip – in that year, but he probably arrived by a ship of the Godeffroy company.

² The 1912 obituary for Robert Homburg senior states that they arrived in South Australia in September 1857.

³ Thusnelda's birth is registered as 'Homberg'.

⁴ They were probably the Georg and Caroline Fischer, who arrived by *Heloise* on 17 March 1847.

⁵ Hansie married Clifford Henry Cornish; Gerta married the well-known musician, Hooper Josse Brewster-Jones; Gretchen died unmarried in 1937.

⁶ As far as can be ascertained, neither Hermann nor his brother Robert took out the standard Bachelor of Laws degree, but only the 'Finished Certificate', the minimum requirement at that time for obtaining registration to practise law: Hermann in 1896, Robert in 1897.

⁷ Hardie, DSO, had been Deputy Assistant Adjutant General for South Australia since October 1914; no doubt he knew Homburg well and he would have been an appropriate person to interview Homburg. Gumpl and Kleinig report that Ian Harmstorf claims that the party was led by a 'Major Logan', whom I cannot identify. My evidence indicates otherwise. Ref.: NAA B741: V/24713: Hermann Homburg. Harmstorf does not indicate an authoritative source for his claim.

⁸ Many years later, this was seen in South Australia as a contender for the new National Anthem, but it was not known widely enough outside that state.

⁹ No record has been found that Renolf Homburg contested any parliamentary seat for any South Australian or Commonwealth election between 1927 and 1939. Either he failed to obtain pre-selection for a seat, or he resisted his father's urging and the reports were simply wrong.

¹⁰ The Committee that heard Krawinkel's case consisted of Edwin Erskine Cleland, Justice of the Supreme Court of South Australia; Andrew D. Young, President of the Stock Exchange and Director of the State Bank of South Australia; Sir Edward Lucas, Member of the Legislative Council, for the same party as Hermann Homburg.

¹¹ Did he consider that the war would not have happened, at least not at that time, if Germany had not invaded Poland?

¹² Staff Sergeant Dudley Gordon Prisk died in Japanese captivity on 22 August 1943.

¹³ Calwell in particular, being a Victorian, had no business interfering in Homburg's case.

¹⁴ The age had originally been sixteen, and the provision did not extend only to persons of alien descent.

¹⁵ This was about the time of the failure of the Anglo-American paratroop operation at Arnhem.

Sources and Endnotes

Sources: The Hired Hack

The main sources for this chapter are the archival files:

A367: C68800: J.H.C. Sleeman.

A472: W5053: John H. C. Sleeman - Arrest under National Security Act 1939-1940. Section 13 (2)

C123: 15182: Sleeman, John Harvey Crothers [Australian]

Publications:

Matters, Mrs Leonard W., *Australasians who count in London and who counts in Western Australia*, London, Jas. Truscott & Son, 1913.

Cheguin, Myles, *Japan and the Japanese - what Australians should Know!* New Century Press Pty Ltd, Sydney. [Mutch collection, Mitchell Library, Sydney]

Lockwood, Rupert, *War on the Waterfront*, Southwood Press, Marrickville NSW, 1987. (p. 100, re Sleeman's appeal to the AJA)

McMullin, Ross, *The Light on the Hill: the Australian Labor Party, 1891-1991*, Oxford: New York, Oxford University Press, 1991. (p. 135, re Frank Brennan; p. 146 re Evatt and Lang; p. 254 re Ward and Garden; p. 186 re Garden as 'Lang's hatchet man',)

Beckett's Budget, June 1927 – March 1931. [Copies in ANL, Canberra.]

Brisbane Courier, various dates, September 1922. [Brennan case]

Sydney Morning Herald, various dates, July-November 1932. [Swindell case]

Commonwealth Parliamentary Debates, II Geo VI, Vol. 190, Aliens Bill 1947, p. 1184.

National Archives Australia:

A1: 1932/2271: "Judge" Swindell. Undesirable.

A367: C18000/719: Objection No. 118. Adela Constantia Mary WALSH. Advisory Committee. [*dig.*]

A981: JAP 101 PART 3: Japan – relations with Australia. [*dig.*] [*Re Lamaro and the Japanese.*]

A5954: 568/2: Royal Commission relating to the "Brisbane Line" statements. [*dig.*]

C123: 1178: William Charles Boesser: Australian (German parents) [*re shadowing by police cadets*]

C443: J170: Japanese Chamber of Commerce, Sydney. [*Payments to Japanese agents. Membership lists of Japanese Society.*]

C447: 7: Extracted Documents and miscellaneous papers from Japanese Consular files. [*Payments to Australians, including Sleeman*]

BP242/1: Q24483: Ross, Dr Arthur John. Re 'Another Case for Japan'] [*dig.*]

Endnotes

[1] *The Australian Dictionary of Biography* says that John Sleeman was a publican; he might have been a publican at a later date.

[2] Sleeman claimed that he had enlisted at Boulder in November 1916.

[3] It would have taken a labourer about twenty years to earn that sum of money at that time.

[4] Crisp's statements are cited in Ross MCMullin's *Light on the Hill*. See Bibliography.

[5] Allan Melvin Hopkins, born 18 August 1919, joined the 10th Battalion Volunteer Defence Corps on part-time basis in August 1940, and transferred to the air force in May 1944. It is not certain whether this is the same Allan, nor is it known whether Sleeman managed to arrange this partial exemption.

[6] If Mutch had become Labor leader in 1925 and had gone on to become premier, the Governor of New South Wales would not have set a constitutional precedent by dismissing Lang in May 1932. Thus Governor-General Kerr would not have had this example when he was considering dismissing Prime Minister Whitlam in November 1975.

[7] It is in the nature of the Japanese script that Sleeman appears in Japanese documents as 'suriman'.

[8] Woodfield, a long-time resident in Japan with a Japanese wife, had undertaken some illegal commercial dealings for Japanese companies. The accusations against Prentice were probably unjustified, although he was regarded with some misgivings on account of his connections with Douglas Social Credit and Theosophy.

[9] *Australian Blue Book*: a reference book of information on society, commerce, politics, etc.

[10] Ross McMullin, in *The Light on the Hill*, calls Garden 'Lang's hatchet man'; he was probably involved in the Swindell scandal.

[11] Brigadier Simpson had known Dr Evatt since they had attended the Fort Street School together.

Sources: The Amorous Vichyite

The main sources for this chapter are the archival files:

A981: CONS 127 PART 1: Consul France at Sydney. [Activities of Consul-General (J. Tremoulet)]

A5954: 429/11: Internal Security: French Consul M. Tremoulet, Activities of. [*dig.*]

C320: F12: [NSW Security Service file - French Consul Tremoulet].

Sources and Endnotes

C320: F15 PART 1: NSW Security Service file – French Consul.

SP1714/1: N45622: Consul General for [Vichy] France – M Jean Tremoulet. [Security Service file]

Publications:

Winter, Barbara, *The Intrigue Master: Commander Long and Naval Intelligence in Australia, 1913-1945*, Boolarong, Moorooka Qld, 1995. (Chapter 9, New Caledonia).

Documents on Australian Foreign Policy, 1937-49, Vol. 4, July 1940-June 1941, Canberra, AGPS, 1980. (Documents 12, 79, 191)

"Australia and Vichy: the impact of divided France, 1940-1944", Lyn Gorman, Australian Journal of Politics and History, The; Summer, 1997. (For a continuation of the story beyond the time frame of this chapter.)

Sun (Sydney), 8 September 1941.

National Archives, Australia:

A472: W91: Seizure of enemy vessels – United Kingdom – Pierre Loti.

A981: CONS 121: Consuls – France at Fremantle.

A981: CONS 123: Consuls – France at Melbourne.

A981: CONS 124 PART 1: Consuls France at Melbourne and Sydney – Activities of Consul C. Lancial, Pt 1.

A981: CONS 124 PART 2: Consuls France at Melbourne & Sydney – Activities of Consul C. Lancial, Pt 2.

A981: CONS 126 PART 2: Consuls France at Sydney.

A6445: 4/1940: Shipping (a) Commissaire Ramel Cargo (b) Pierre Loti.

B6121: 99F/1: New Caledonia 1940 - Anti-British and anti-De Gaulle propaganda. [*Formerly MP1587/1.*]

BP361/1: 11/1/7 PART 1: Military Intelligence Correspondence. 1939-1941

National Archives of New Zealand: (Wellington, Aotearoa)

N Series 2: Item 30/68/3, Exchange of Intelligence, 1941-44

National Archives and Records Administration: (NARA), Washington, DC.

RG457: Entry 9003, German Navy Reports, B-Bericht 35/40, 6 Sept 1940, to 38/40, 27 Sept 1940.

Full Cabinet Submission by Sir Frederick Stewart, Minister for External Affairs: Agendum 486, 5 November 1940: ACTIVITIES OF FRENCH CONSUL-GENERAL, M. TRÉMOULET. (At the time of writing, this was available on the website of the Department of Foreign Affairs and Trade.)

http://en.wikipedia.org/wiki/Attack_on_Mers-el-Kébir, 3 July 1940.

Endnotes

[1] Many French people, particularly naval personnel, turned against Britain after the British attack on French warships at Mers el Kebir on 3 July 1940, but Trémoulet's hatred of Britain antedated this by years.

[2] Post war, Loubère became Vice-Consul in Melbourne, then Consul in Perth. He was very probably the Roger Loubère who wrote the book *Australie: cinquième continent*.

[3] Trémoulet: July 1937; Puaux: November 1937; Clémentel: November 1938; Lancial: November 1939.

[4] The internment order should have been signed by Percy Spender, Minister for the Army, but the records on Trémoulet are incomplete.

Sources: The Bigamous Abortionist

The main sources for this chapter are the archival files:

BP242/1: Q24483: Ross, Dr Arthur John – Queensland investigation case file. (*dig.*)

D1901: R38: ROSS Arthur John McLaren – Internee.

D1901: R39: ROSS Claude Vane – Internment. [*dig.*]

Publications:

McMullin, Ross, *The Light on the Hill: the Australian Labor Party, 1891-1991*, Melbourne, OUP, 1992 (pp. 128-29, re fraudulent enrolments and multiple voting)

Wake, Valdemar Robert, *No Ribbons or Medals: the story of "Hereward" an Australian counter espionage officer*, Mitcham SA, Jacobyte Books, 2004. See Index for references to Ross.

Macintyre, Stuart, *The Reds: the Communist Party of Australia from origins to illegality*, Allen & Unwin, St Leonards, 1998. (See Index re Hanlon and the 1938 election.)

Protestant Clarion, 3 February 1938. [Lyons' visit to Pope]

Protestant Clarion, 10 February 1938. [ALP electoral rorts]

Protestant Clarion, 7 and 14 April 1938. [Illegal pamphlets]

Clarion, 2 June 1938. [Hanlon not duly elected.]

Sources and Endnotes

Clarion, 22 December 1938. [Hanlon's appeal allowed.]

Clarion, 13 March 1941. ['Romans under cover']

Clarion, 5 June 1941. [Call to intern Mannix]

Protestant Clarion files are in the John Oxley Library, Brisbane

National Archives Australia:

A367: C59235: United Protestant Association, Queensland.

BP242/1: Q30589 PART 2: Japanese activities in Queensland. Part 2.

BP242/1: Q31930: Kashima, Toyokichi – Queensland investigation case file.

BP242/1: Q34603: STYLES, John Thomas – Queensland investigation case file. [*dig.*]

BP361/1: 11/1/7 PART 1: Military Intelligence Correspondence. [1939-1941]

C443: J86: J Chris Ross [Correspondence with the Japanese Consul General in Australia]

C443: J111: Major W J R Scott [Correspondence with the Japanese Consul General in Australia]

Endnotes

[1] Sunday Island, the largest in the Kermadec group, is now called Raoul Island.

[2] *Courier-Mail*, 14 November 1934.

[3] Cain was a serious embarrassment to the Vatican.

[4] There was a suspicion that the case of a girl who died from 'alleged malpractice' in June 1936 was connected with Ross.

[5] Valdemar Wake, in his book *No Ribbons or Medals*, makes several incorrect claims about Ross, including a rather silly one that he received £1,500 for *each* abortion. The going rate was about £20-£25.

[6] In a security sense, Woodfield was indeed a villain, but that is a different story.

[7] John Thomas Styles ran a coaching college and was also a journalist. He had a dubious history in the army reserve, and he had attracted attention by impersonating a Military Intelligence officer and by his involvement in a scheme to sell part of North Queensland to Fascist Italy. See Bibliography.

[8] While the work of the *Nisei* in America is well known, it has been virtually overlooked that there were some Japanese – though not many – in the Australian army.

Sources: The Vodka Priest

The main sources for this chapter are the archival files:

A659: 1939/1/16153: Maximoff, Michael Ivanovitch – Naturalisation [includes passport]

A659: 1940/1/289: Antonieff, V A – Naturalisation.

A989: 1943/320/1: Fascism: Russian Fascist Union.

A6122: 115: Russian Fascist Union. [*dig.*]

A6122: 187: Russian Fascist Union

BP242/1: Q17744: Valentin Antonieff – Queensland internee case file.

BP242/1: Q21869: Rodjestvensky, Ivan – Queensland internee case file.

BP242/1: Q30568: Russian Imperial Union.

BP242/1: Q32511: Russian Fascist Union.

D1901: A39: ANTONIEFF, Valentine Andrew – Internment.

D1901: S106: SHEVTZOFF Alexander Paul – Internee.

D1901: P690: PROOTKOWSKY Vassily Alexandrovich. [*sic*: Prootkovsky; *dig.*]

D1915: SA19249: Russian Facists. [*sic*]

Publications:

Stephan, John Jason, *The Russian Fascists: tragedy and farce in exile 1925-1945*, Hamish Hamilton, London 1978.

Protopopov, Michael Alex, 'The Russian Orthodox Presence in Australia: The History of a Church told from recently opened archives and previously unpublished sources', Ph. D. Thesis, 2005, Australian Catholic University, Fitzroy. Vic.

Smele, Jon, *Civil War in Siberia: The Anti-Bolshevik Government of Admiral Kolchak, 1918-1920*. Cambridge: Cambridge University Press, 1996.

For Anna Volkoff (Wolkoff) and Tyler Kent, see: http://en.wikipedia.org/wiki/.

Andrew, Christopher, *Defence of the Realm: The Authorized History of MI5*. Allen Lane (Penguin Group), 2009, p224-6.

Australian Dictionary of Biography, Vol. 7. [See adb.online for Antonieff.] For background of Cossacks in the White Army, see: http://militaryhistory.suite101.com/article.cfm/the_siberian_white_army_19181923

National Archives Australia:

A1: 1930/6864: Alexander GZELL – Naturalisation certificate.

A989: 1944/150/7/6: China - Rastislan Boris Fedoseyoff. Activities on behalf of Chinese Cause.

A1608: C19/1/3: War Section – Entry to Wharves & Ships. (Sabotage – Precautions Against). (National Security Reg. Amendment)

A4311: 102/4: Press and propaganda pro and anti Nazi [Copy of record seized from German Consulate Sydney at outbreak of World War 2].

A6335: 13: Nicholas Lagutin. [dig.] [There were two different persons of this name in NAA records.]

BP242/1: Q8093: Zuckschwerdt, George Alexander – Queensland internee case file.

BP242/1: Q9563: Peshkoff Vladimir – Queensland Internee case file.

BP242/1: Q16952 PART 1: Antonieff Alim Valentine – [son of Arch Priest Antonieff]

BP242/1: Q18176: George Pavlenko.

BP242/1: Q21537: Stepanoff, Aleksei Nikolaevich – Queensland investigation case file.

BP242/1: Q30589 PART 1: Japanese Activities in Queensland. Part 1. .

BP242/1: Q44289: Sommer, Waldemar – Queensland investigation case file.

C320: J227: [NSW Security Service file – Japanese fifth column activities]

C320: J240: [NSW Security Service file – Pre war activities of Japanese and training of interpreters]

D1901: P72: PESHKOFF Vladimir – Internee.

D1901: P73: POSHARSKY, Basil – Internee.

D1901: P74: POLE-ROGAN Nicholas – Internee.

D1901: S107: SMIKOFF Peter Manorovich. – Internee.

D1915: SA19060: A VON SKERST.

MP1049/5: 2026/19/48: Prisoner of War ex Ramses.

Endnotes

[1] For a transliteration of Russian names, see Appendix 1.

[2] Purchase of land by aliens was in some States and at various times forbidden by law.

[3] Other estimates place the number in Queensland as high as 3,000.

[4] Other monarchists supported the claims of Grand Duke Nikolai Nikolaevich.

[5] Posharsky had arrived in April 1926, aged 29. He had served in the Russian Imperial Army, and had been conscripted into the White Russian army in 1918, leaving it four years later as a Staff Captain. Stephan Andreeivich Logootin arrived in August 1923, aged 40.

[6] Given as 'Rasvedniks' in A6122: 115.

[7] Maximoff's daughter Nina later married Clement Byrne Christesen, founder in 1940 of the literary magazine *Meanjin*. She taught in various Brisbane private schools, and in 1946 founded the Russian Department at the University of Melbourne.

[8] See J. Smele, *Civil War in Siberia*.

[9] St Vladimir's Day is a movable feast, and it appears that it was on 28 July in 1935, but on the 12/25 July in 1937. Some dates in reports of occurrences regarding the various organisations are contradictory, and it is difficult to determine which are correct, no matter how authoritative they sound.

[10] The date is from Stephan, who is probably correct; other sources say he was born in Vladivostok.

[11] Actually Vera was Nina's much younger sister; she had married Leon Verjbitsky in January 1926.

[12] Stephan transliterates this correctly as 'Prutkovsky', but it is the same person, and his personal preference was 'Prootkovsky.

[13] Also given as Polianoff-Strogonoff or Poliakoff; born 15 April 1899.

[14] This third member was believed to be Sergei Slomkin in Sydney, but it does not seem to have been proven.

[15] The fourth large furniture factory and store in Brisbane was owned by Frederick William Tritton. It was suspected that the family was Russian because in 1939 their daughter, Lydia Ellen, married Alexander Kerensky, Prime Minister of the 1917 provisional post-revolutionary government, and she liked to pass herself off as a Russian aristocrat. Brisbane Nazis also denounced the Trittons as Jewish, when Norman Corbett Tritton, not her brother, was appointed private secretary to Prime Minister Robert Menzies. In fact, they were not Russian; nor were they Jewish, although Kerensky allegedly was.

[16] Gyorgy Uglichinin had by this time been naturalised and changed his name by Deed Poll to George George.

[17] 'Drigin' is surely a variant transliteration for Dr Constantin Driguine, for no 'Drigin' has been found in records.

[18] There seems to be an understandable confusion here between the publications of Rodzaevsky and those of Vonsiatsky.

[19] Gzell's son Vitaly spent five years in the army, being discharged as a major.

[20] The enmity between Russians and Jews was both centuries old, and a new, raw wound. Anti-Semitism in the White Russian community in Australia was not necessarily linked to support for Nazi Germany. Many of the leaders of the Revolution were Jewish, including Lenin, Trotsky and Kerensky, while the Soviet secret police had a high concentration of Jewish personnel. They were seen to have slaughtered the Tsar and his family, and to be bent on destroying the Orthodox Church. On the other hand, the Church had not been innocent in murderous pogroms against Jews. It was not Australia's business to sort out these old enmities, but to prevent the feuds from affecting Australia's security in wartime.

[21] Valentine's Day, not 14 February but 30 July by the Julian calendar, was 12 August by the Gregorian calendar, and 10 August was the nearest Sunday.

[22] 'Rastislav' is not a typically Russian name; it occurs more frequently in the Balkan states.

[23] It is doubtful whether he had any way of forwarding any information he obtained, although there were vague suspicions regarding Spanish consular personnel.

[24] Letter, 2 November 1943, Antonieff to his wife.

[25] Shabasheff's naturalisation was granted on 12 December 1928.

[26] Christopher Andrew, *Defence of the Realm*, pp. 224-26.

Sources: The Shanghai Gang

The main sources for this chapter are the archival files:

A472: W29367: J J Holland, A W Raymond, C H Cousins [sic s.b. Cousens] and others – Activities and association with Japanese re broadcasting. [*dig.*]

A1838: 1542/64: Security – Raymond, Alan W. – Alleged Japanese Collaborator [*dig.*]

A4144: 244/1946: Collaborators – Alan Raymond

A6126: 62: RAYMOND, Alan Willoughby (Volume 1) [*Contains transcripts of XMHA broadcasts.*] [*dig.*]

A6126: 63: RAYMOND, Alan Willoughby (Volume 2). [*dig.*]

A6126:1213: McDonald, Wynette Cecilia, [*Puttkamer's statement, 1 May 1946*].

SP1714/1: N38749: John Joseph Holland

Publications:

Winter, Barbara, *The Australia-First Movement*, Glass House Books, Carindale Qld, 2005.

The Most Dangerous Man in Australia?

Twomey, Christine, *Australia's Forgotten Prisoners: Civilian Interned by the Japanese in World War Two*, Cambridge University Press, UK, 2007.

Wasserstein, Bernard, *Secret War in Shanghai. An Untold Story of Espionage, Intrigue and Treason in World War II*, London, Profile Books, 1998. (Excellent for records of Shanghai Municipal Police, but he has wrong the date of Raymond's arrival in Shanghai, gives Wyn McDonald's name as 'Eyn', and has Holland's history prior to arrival in Shanghai wrong.)

Morling, Loreley A., *A Very Different Type, the true story of a recalcitrant journalist*, Loreley Morling, Swan View WA, 2000. (on J. J. Holland)

Commonwealth Parliamentary Debates, Vol. 171, pp. 527-28, 27 March 1942.

National Archives Australia:

A367: C65778: Russo Deter. Martyr Graham. Thomas A F; Pickering E H; Nakashiba Peter (also called Nash Peter) [*Should be Peter Russo*] [*dig.*]

A367: C69140: ALLEN Veronica Margaret (nee Connolly, also Omori)

A989: 1943/235/4/8: Defence Subversive activities – "The Break away from Britain League" concerning Allan W. Raymond.

A8911: 17: 'The Link' Organisation to promote Anglo-German Friendship – Mrs Melanie O'Loughlin.

D1915: SA20496: 'The Link'.

B6121: 176F: Japanese Espionage & Sabotage. [Formerly MP1587.]

BP242/1: Q23531: Woodfield, Henry William - Queensland investigation case file. [Oil supervisor, born Knutsford, England 29 June 1903, Japanese wife, family under surveillance]

K1171: OMORI M: OMORI Masunori (7113) [Japanese internee]. [*Incorrect; Omori left Australia before the outbreak of Pacific war.*]

K1171: CONNOLLY V M: CONNOLLY Veronica Margaret (aka Mrs W. Veronica Margaret Allen, Mrs O'Mori) (1375) [internee]

MP1588/11: WHOLE SERIES: COIC Appreciations. Sep 1940 – May 1942. [*re Wittouck*]

PP302/1: WA8: Japanese Activities.

NAA website: Passenger Lists: Fremantle 1927-1947.

New South Wales Supreme Court. Probate Records: 4th Series, No. 67479: Will of Henry Raymond:

Endnotes

[1] Material on Rodie, in the notorious Document "J", pp. 8-9, written by Lockwood for the Soviet Embassy, is full of emotional untruths. For example: Rodie was not involved in anything that happened on Ambon, because he was never there.

[2] As there could be a gap of several months between birth and registration, this is probably the correct registration.

[3] Birth registrations after 1914 had not been released at the time of writing, but Jean was apparently born about 1918. Both girls registered on the electoral rolls sometimes as Spice, sometimes as Raymond.

[4] Bowden was later murdered by the Japanese on Banka Island.

[5] Also written as *Fushimi Maru*.

[6] It is definitely the same person, but if she had admitted to being forty she would probably not have been accepted.

[7] The code was probably the one used by British warships in communications with British merchant ships.

[8] Mrs Everett became Raymond's secretary.

[9] This was the paper where Frank Cade worked when Raymond appealed to him for help.

[10] A decisive point might have been the decryption of a Japanese wireless transmission ordering that the killing of all prisoners of war should begin by late August.

[11] Lyons died in April 1939; Curtin did not become Prime Minister until October 1941.

[12] Puttkamer made this statement on 1 May 1946 in connection with discussions on the resumption of trade between Germany and Australia.

[13] Arguments as to whether Japan ever intended to invade Australia have become very bitter, and this is not the place to discuss the pros and cons.

[14] Bessie Nuria McDonald married Harry Percival Squires in mid 1940; his highest rank was Warrant Officer.

INDEX

A

Abwehr 32, 35, 153

Adelaide, HMAS 83, 128

Akiyama, Masatoshi (Consul-General) 70, 81, 84

Alliance Française 84

Anisimoff, Dmitry 106, 129

Antonieff, Alim 114, 119

Antonieff, Maria M. 120, 123

Antonieff, Archpriest Valentin A. Chapter 9

Antropoff, Alexander 120, 125

Appeals against internment 18, 19, 54-56, 100, 101, 112, 127, 150

Arco-Valley, Alexander N. (See Bohn, R.)

Asmis, Dr Rudolf 2-9, 10, 12, 15-17, 25, 27, 28, 40, 42, 50, 51, 53

Ausland-Institut 51, 52

Auslands-Organisation (AO) 33, 35

Australia-First Movement 74, 136-138, 140, 143, 144

Australian Journalists Association (AJA) 73, 133

B

Barnwell, W. H. 10

Barossa News 53, 55

Beasley, Jack 66, 67

Becker, Dr J. Heinrich 4, 8, 15, 20, 21, 28, 50-53, 55, 56

Beckett, William J. 65, 76, 77

Beckett's Budget 63, 65, 66, 68

Beckmann, Paul 53, 54

Black Dragon Society 98, 108, 136

Blacket, Captain W. R. 144

Bohlmann, Ilma 52

Bohn, Richard Rudolf von Chapter 4.

Bovell, Lillian 6-8, 10

Bowden, V. G. 137, 139, 167

Bradley, W. J. (KC) 75

Brenac, André 85, 86, 88

Brennan, Frank 65

Brennan, Dr T. C. (KC) 56, 57

Brewster-Jones, Hooper Josse 48, 156

Brewster-Jones, Robert 54

Brisbane Line 77, 144

Brücke, Die 3, 15, 26, 51, 53, 126

Brundahl, Lars G. (Brundall, Bründahl) Chapter 2

Brundahl, Bessie W (née Rogers) 15, 16, 20

Brundall, Lars (Lawrence) V. 13, 22

Bulletin (Sydney) 137, 141

Bund des Deutschtums 3, 15, 50, 53

Burggraf, Karl M. 3, 9

Burkard, Louis I. Chapter 1

Büsing, Hans (Consul-General) 12, 14

C

Cade, Frank 136, 137

Caiger, Captain George 101

Callide Valley 103, 105, 107, 110, 113, 114, 125

Calwell, Arthur 21, 22, 58, 63, 77, 141, 156

Cameron, Archie 58

Canberra Times 60

Catholic Action 94, 95

Censorship 6-8, 25, 57, 58, 77, 80, 83, 84, 86, 87, 97, 101, 110, 117, 119, 120, 121, 124, 141

Century 76

Cheguin, Myles (Sleeman) 69

Chinese Eastern Railway 106. 110

Clark, Detective W. J. 120, 123

Clayton, Walter S. 10

Clémentel, Pierre 87

Coleman, Percy 67

Commonwealth Investigation Branch (CIB) viii, 14, 25, 35, 36, 39, 40, 41, 51, 54, 55, 80, 82, 89, 91, 93, 95, 114, 115, 118-120, 122, 127, 139

Commonwealth Security Service (CSS) viii, 9, 10, 44, 71, 74, 75, 77, 84, 99, 128, 129, 137, 144

Index

Connolly, Edward Bernard 65
Connolly, Veronica Margaret 136
Cook, Kenneth Easton 70
Country Party 3, 64
Courier-Mail (Brisbane) 93, 115
Courrier Australien 80, 86
Cousens, Major Charles 133
Crafti, Eduard 114, 120, 122, 123
Crisp, L. F. 66, 67
Curtin, Prime Minister John 58, 74, 142

D

Daily News (Sydney) 17
Daily Telegraph (Sydney) 10, 98
Darré, Walter 16, 27
Dawes, Sir Edwyn Sandys 25
Denis, Lt-Col Maurice 81-83
Derevsky, Lt-Col (monk-priest) 116
Deutsche Arbeitsfront (DAF) 4, 28, 30, 31, 34
Deutsche Welle 140
Document "J" (Petrov case) 76, 148, 149
Doi, Kenzo 123
Dorn, Günther G. T. Chapter 3
Drehnen, Otto von 3, 5, 7,
Driguine, Dr Constantine 115, 164
Dumont d'Urville 80, 82
Dychem (I.G. Farben in Australia) 32-34

E

Elink-Schuurmann, Tom (Dutch Consul-General) 81
Emelianoff, Evgenia 120, 123
Emelianoff, Roman 118
Englart, Edward Conrad 120
Erhard, Hermann 3
Erickson (Eriksen), Alexander (See Bohn, R.)
Etappendienst 24, 25, 27-29
Evatt, Dr H. V. 9, 58, 59, 67, 68, 72-77, 86

F

Fashist 110-112, 116, 131
Fedoseyeff, Rastislav Boris 123
Fewtrell, Major-General A. C. 74
Finzel, Lt R. E. (later Temp. Major) 116, 119, 123, 124
Fitchett, Ian 9, 10, 149
Foote, H. L. 119
Forde, F. M. 'Frank' 58, 59, 73, 74, 100
Fördendes Mitglied (SS) 27
Forgan-Smith, Premier William 95, 96
Fortbildungsverein 53, 55
Fraser, Reginald Arnold 48, 53
Frauenschaft 27, 51
Free French 80, 82-86, 88
Freyberg, Colonel Baron Egloff von 4, 39, 40
Friends of the Hitler Movement (Tanunda) 53, 55
Friends of the Third Reich (Brisbane) 118

G

Garden, Jock 71, 74, 76
Gaulle, General Charles de 80-84, 86, 88
Gellé, Dr Louis de 84
General Electric (AEG) 32-34
General Stuart Heintzelmann 20, 35
George, George (See Uglichinin.)
German-Australian Centennial Committee 51
German-Australian Chamber of Commerce 3-5, 7, 15, 16, 27, 32
German Club (Adelaide) 50, 51
German Club (Brisbane) 110, 116, 121
Gestapo viii, 15, 28, 33, 52
Gielow. Pastor Kurt 126
Goebbels, Josef 29, 95, 124
Goers, Charles 53
Göring, Hermann 16, 38, 42
Gullet, Sir Henry 7
Gzell, Alexander A. 106, 112, 116, 120, 164

H

Haas, Walter de 24
Hafendienst (Harbour Service) 28
Hahndorf 51, 52
Hanlon, Edward M. (Ned) 94-96, 100
Harbin (Manchuria) 109, 110, 115, 117-122, 124, 125, 127-129, 131
Hardie, Major John Leslie 47, 156
Hardt & Co. 16, 17, 24, 27
Hardt, Gustav 27
Hardt, Herbert E. Chapter 3
Harmstorf, Ian 47, 62, 156
Haslinger, Dr Franz J. 32
Healy, Jim 120
Hedinger, Hans (Swiss Consul-General) 8, 10, 17, 42, 43
Heiler, Willi 28
Hellenthal, Dr Walter (Consul) 16, 51, 52
Henschel, Alfred (SS officer) 22
Herbert, Xavier 4
Hermannsburg Mission 39
Himmler. Heinrich 16, 27, 95
Hirschfeld, Dr Eugen 25
Hitler Youth 20, 37
Holland, John J. Chapter 10
Holt, Harold 22
Homburg, Emma L. L. (née Herring) 46, 49, 51, 53
Homburg, Friedrich Wilhelm Adolf 45, 62
Homburg, Fritz 46, 48, 49, 53-56, 60-62,
Homburg, Gerta (m. H. J. Brewster-Jones) 46, 48, 54
Homburg, John 46, 48, 49
Homburg, Hermann Robert Chapter 5
Homburg, Marsi 46, 49, 51-54, 57, 58
Homburg, Renolf 46, 49, 50, 52, 55, 59, 60, 156
Homburg, Reta (m. H. Krawinkel) 46, 49, 52
Homburg, Robert (jnr) 46-49, 53
Homburg, Thusnelda (m. Fraser) 46, 48
Hopkins, Thomas J. 68. 70
Hughes, Alfred T. ("Ben") 10
Hughes, William Morris 70, 85

I

Ichikawa, Taijiro 70
Indo-China 81, 83, 84, 86, 98, 138
Industrial Workers of the World 104
Iron Islet (Qld) 93, 94, 101

J

Janssen, Josef 25, 29
Japanese Chamber of Commerce (Sydney) 68
Jenner, Dorothy 81, 82
Johnston, W. (British Consul, Noumea) 7
Jones, Lt-Cmdr Ira J. Pryce 122, 123

K

Kalgoorlie 64, 65
Kelly, Mary I. (Keenza) 33, 34
Kerensky, Alexander 163, 164
Kinkead, J. J. B. 75
Klemzig 51
Knowles, Sir George 144
Köhler, Captain R. 13, 15, 21
Kolchak, Admiral V. 107, 108, 112, 113, 121
Korzhenevsky, Col. Vsevolod V. 108
Khrapovitsky. Metropolitan Anthony 113
Krawinkel, Heinrich 29, 49-52, 54, 56, 57, 59, 60
Krawinkel, Karl 49
Krawinkel, Marie 52, 59, 60
Kreuz und Adler 38
Krupp 1, 4-6, 10, 39
Kuroki, Tokitaro (Consul, Noumea) 81, 82

L

Labor Daily 66
Labor League 66, 70, 75, 76
Labor Party (ALP) 58, 65, 66, 68, 71, 74, 95, 100
Ladendorff, Walter 15, 16
Lagutin, Nicholas F. 104
Lancial, Charles E. D. 8, 82, 85, 87, 88
Lang, J. T. (Jack) 63, 66-68, 70, 72, 76, 77
Latham, Sir John 144

Index

Laughlin, Austin 30, 35
Lazarus, Ethel 13, 18
Leipzig International Trade Fair 12, 14, 16
Leske, Pastor Everard 47
Lindquist, H. Olof 139, 140, 142, 143, 146
Linger, Carl 51
Liverpool (Camp) 2, 26, 41, 74, 75, 87, 126
Lloyd, Colonel E. E. L. 14
Lockwood, Rupert 76, 133, 149, 166
Logootin, Stephan 106,107, 112, 115, 132
Lohmann @ Co. 1, 24
Lohmann, Alfred 1, 152
Lolua, Victor 124
Long, Cmdr Rupert B. M. 80
Louat, Dr F. R. 75
Loubère, Roger L. 84, 160
Loveday (Camp) 42, 125, 126, 128
Luckner, Count Felix von 29. 41
Lyons, Prime Minister Joseph 94, 142

M

Magrin, Edgar Earle 80
Makin, Norman 80
Martin, Justice F. R. B. 56, 57
Mathy, Captain Eugen 7, 26, 27, 29
Maximoff, Capt. Michael I. 106, 107, 110, 112, 116, 119, 120, 132, 164
McBride, Senator Philip 54
McCauley, Harold 67
McDonald, Winifred A. (Wynette, Gwen) Chapter 10
McEwen, John 80
McGuire, Dominic Paul 97
McIlwraith, Rev. William D. 97
MacKay, William J. 75
McKernan, Michael 24
Mendelsohn, Estelle L. 13, 22
Menzies, Prime Minister Robert G. 72, 80, 82
Mertgen, Captain Emil 25, 26
Michel, Captain 81, 82

Miller, General Evgeny K. 108, 127
Military Intelligence (MI) 12, 20, 21, 29, 30, 41, 54, 60, 68, 70, 74, 86, 89, 92, 96, 97, 99, 111, 117, 119, 138, 147
Mitsui 69, 93
Mutch, Thomas D. 68, 158

N

Nash Put 109, 123, 131
Natsiya 109, 117, 118, 124, 131
Naval Intelligence Division (NID) 32, 80, 83, 97, 119-123, 125, 127,
Nazi Party (NSDAP) viii, 5, 10, 16, 20, 21, 23, 24, 27, 28, 32-34, 38, 41, 49, 50, 53, 56, 116, 118, 127
Nerother League 30, 153
Netherlands East Indies 30, 31, 33, 98, 138, 139
New Caledonia 4-6, 28, 79-83, 86-88
New Guinea 4, 31, 40, 41, 100
New Zealand 3,12-14, 16, 18, 21, 22, 27, 29, 81, 83, 88, 91, 133, 142
Nickel 1, 4, 5, 8, 82
Nord Deutscher Lloyd (NDL) 1, 2, 4, 25, 26, 152
Norton, Ezra 86
Noumea (See New Caledonia.)
Novoye Slovo 117, 123

O

O'Loughlin, Melanie 136
Orenburg Cossacks 108, 116
Otabe, Kenichi 70, 71, 82
Ouglitchinin, Sergei (See also Uglichinin.) 108, 126
Overlack, Peter 24

P

Page, Sir Earle 3
Papen, Franz von 38
Pao, Dr (Chinese Consul-General) 41
Pavlenko, Grigory P. (George) 124, 126
Pearce, Sir George 48
Pearl, Cyril 9, 10, 149

Pélicier, Georges (Governor) 82, 83

Pétain, Marshal H. Philippe 8, 82

Peshkoff, Lt-Col. Vladimir P. 108, 110, 116, 121, 123-125, 132

Peukert, Hans 41, 42

Plate, Oscar 24, 25, 27

Pole-Rogan, Nicholas G. 112, 119, 122, 131

Polianoff-Strogonoff (See Pole-Rogan.)

Popoff, Col. Ivan I. 108, 112, 132

Posharsky, Vassily (Basil) 106, 121, 123, 125, 164

Prentice, Lt-Col. J. M. 74, 75

Price, Lt Charles A. 61

Prisk, Maud (née Herring) 49, 55

Prootkovsky, Vassily A. 111, 113, 122, 126, 127, 131

Protestant Clarion 94-98, 100

Protopopov, Michael 114, 126-128, 130

Puaux, Vice-Consul Frank 86-88

Publicist 137, 138, 140

Puttkamer, Baron Jesco von 143

Q

Queensländer Herald 50

Quièvrecourt, Cmdr Toussaint de 80, 82, 83

R

Ranger, Ernest C. 94, 97

Raymond, Alan W. Chapter 10

'Raymond', Irene 134, 135, 137

Red Flag Riots (Brisbane) 104

Renz, Hans 28

Robbins, G. Howard 93-95

Rodie, Lt Arthur F. (Bill) 133, 166

Rodjestvensky., Lt-Col. Ivan P. 110, 112, 115-118, 120-129, 132

Rodukoff, Paul 116, 132

Rodzaevsky, Konstantin V. 109, 110, 117, 123, 129, 131

Romanoff, Grand Duke Kyril V. 106, 127

Romanoff, Grand Duke Nikolai N. 116

Romanoff, Grand Duke Vladimir K. 127

Ross, A. Lalytha 90, 98, 99

Ross, Dr Arthur John M. Chapter 8

Ross, Cecily (m. Harrison) 90, 98, 99

Ross, Christopher 89, 90, 92-94, 96-99, 101

Ross, Claude V. 90, 91, 96-101

Ross, Dorothy J. (née Sharp) 91, 93

Ross, George 91, 96, 101

Returned Servicemen's League (RSL) 21, 22

Russian Fascist Union (RFU) Chapter 10

Russian General Military Union (ROVS) 108, 110, 115, 124, 127, 132

Russian Imperial Union (RIU) 106, 115, 116, 132

Russian Orthodox Church Chapter 10

Russky Avangard 110, 141

S

St Nicholas Church 106, 108, 113-115, 124, 128, 129

Saint Seraphim of Sarov parish 129

Sane Democracy League 107

Sato, Kennosuke 133

Sautot, Henri (Governor) 82, 83

Seger, Dr Oscar (Consul) 17, 22, 28, 52, 68

Seita, Prof. Ryonosuke 98, 99, 102

Shabasheff, Alexander F. (priest) 105, 106, 108, 112-114, 127

Shanghai 13, 18, 22, 23, 98, 101, 109-114, 116, 118-121, 124, 128, 129, 131. Chapter 10

Shanghai Times 134, 138, 141

Sharwood, William H. 56, 57

Shaverin, Feodot (monk-priest) 113, 128

Shedden, Sir Frederick 80

Shevtzoff, Alexander P. 113, 114, 116, 125, 132

Shevtzoff, Tamara (née Antonieff) 114, 125, 126

Shlemin, Archimandrite Methody 113, 126, 129

Simpson, Brigadier William B. 35, 77

Singapore 31, 50, 81, 86, 98, 117, 133, 135-138, 141, 142, 145

Skerst, Arnold von 14, 32, 127

Sleeman, John H. C. Chapter 6

Sleeman, Sarah 64, 72

Index

Smerdon, G. M. 93, 95
Smikoff, Lt Peter 108, 112, 121, 123, 128
Social Credit Party 94, 96, 97, 136, 158
Spanish Foreign Legion 36, 37
Special Branch (Police) 54, 70
Spender, Percy 54, 57, 72
Stauffenberg family 36, 37, 43
Staveren, Th. E. van 33, 34
Stekloff, Konstantin A. 110, 112, 121, 122, 131
Stepanoff, Aleksei N. 110
Stewart, Sir Frederick 84, 85
Street, Kenneth W. (Justice) 2
Sun News Pictorial (Sydney) 136, 141
Sunday Telegraph (Sydney) 9, 12, 22
Suzuki, 'Henry' Kanjiro 99-102, 123-125
Swindell, Judge Frederick S. 67
Swiss Consul-General (Hedinger) 16, 28

T

Tanunda 20, 46, 49, 53, 55, 60, 61
Telegraph (Brisbane) 119
Telephone intercepts 68, 70, 72, 86, 100
Thangool 105, 107, 108, 112, 122, 125
Tokimasa, David Hidemichi 71
Tolstoff, *Ataman* Vladimir S. 106, 107, 111, 116, 129, 132
Tourchinsky, Father Adrian G. 112, 114
Toyama, Mitsuru 98, 109, 136
Trémoulet, Jean Gaston G. M. Chapter 7
Trial Bay 2, 3, 26
Tuband, Amélie 82
Tyrrell, Captain B. 111

U

Uglichinin, Gyorgy I. (aka George George) 105, 108, 114, 116, 117, 120, 164 (See also Ouglitchinin.)
United Protestant Association 94, 95
Ural Cossacks 106-108, 116, 129

V

Vichy French 9, Chapter 7
Vitoshinsky, Vladimir M. 106, 107, 111, 112, 115, 116, 132
Vitte, Alexander K. 109, 110, 116, 118
Volkoff, George S. 115, 126
Volkoff, Anna 128
Vonsiatsky, Anastase A. 110-112, 121, 126, 129, 131

W

Wake, Inspector Robert B. 93, 99
Walsh, Adela Pankhurst 106
Ward, Edward J. (Eddie) 66, 67, 69, 71, 72, 74, 76-78, 144
Waterside Workers Federation (WWF) 120, 121
Watt, A. R. J. (KC) 72, 73 \
Wawn, Florence 20-22
Webb, George S. 95, 96
Weber, Waldemar 34
White China 67, 72
White Russian Army 106-108, 112, 121, 129
Witte, O. Hugo (Consul) 118
Woelke, Otto 28
Woodfield, Harry 74, 98, 158
Woolloongabba 105, 108-110, 113, 114, 117, 120, 121, 129

X, Y, Z

XRD orders 57, 119

Yoneda, Kenichiro 41, 42

Zeitungsdienst Graf Reischach 31-33
Zuckschwerdt, Yuri A. (George) 121

www.ingramcontent.com/pod-product-compliance
Lightning Source LLC
Chambersburg PA
CBHW031145160426
43193CB00008B/261